THE IMPROVISER'S BASS METHOD

by
Chuck Sher

FOR ELECTRIC &
ACOUSTIC BASS

ISBN 0-9614701-0-0

About The Author

Chuck Sher has been playing bass since 1967. He has been on the road several times with Jon Hendricks (of Lambert, Hendricks, and Ross) and has played in Hendricks' "Evolution of the Blues." He has also worked with many San Francisco musicians over the years including Eddie Sears (pianist with Woody Herman and Tony Williams), Jules Broussard, and recording artists Vince Wallace, Ed Kelly, Jessica Williams, Smiley Winters, and Pee Wee Ellis. He has taught privately and at several Bay Area music schools and has studied briefly with Gary Peacock, Steve Swallow, and Eddie Gomez.

Acknowledgements

In creating this book, I have been greatly helped by the following people who contributed information, exercises, transcriptions, ideas, finances, etc. My sincere thanks to you folks: Bob Bauer, Lennie Lasher, Jeff Neighbor, Bobby Vega, Bob Magnusson, Steve Swallow, Chuck Metcalf, Mark Kennedy, Lisa Goulder, Ed Sullivan, Dick Conte and the KJAZ Library, Jimmy Nadel, Mark Levine, Paul Breslin, Chris Amberger, Charlis and Jerry Dunham, Esther and Maury Sher, and my wife Abby.

Cover Design by Stanley Whitehead of Artwright Studios, San Francisco.

Dedication

This book is dedicated to Barry Commoner and the Citizens' Party. Barry Commoner is a world-renowned environmentalist, author, energy expert, and political activist. The Citizens' Party is a newly-formed, truely democratic alternative to the military-big business-political status quo which is leading us towards unparalleled global disaster. Do yourself and the rest of us on the planet a favor and check them out, while there is still time.

Foreword — HOW TO USE THIS BOOK

<u>EVERYONE:</u>

All the exercises and ideas in this book are designed to improvise on. The longer you spend varying each exercise, the more useful it will become to you, so try to develop each one, whenever possible, in the following ways:

1. Extend the exercise both higher and lower on the bass than the written musical example, so that each idea can be played all over your instrument, ascending and descending.

2. Play each exercise in several keys until transposing it becomes comfortable.

3. Keep the same notes as the musical example (more or less), but change the rhythms used to play them. Try repeating or leaving out notes, as well. By doing this, these exercises will become relevant to different styles of bass playing.

4. Use little pieces of the exercise as the basic theme for improvising some music of your own - either in one key or on the changes of a tune. Try playing along with records and referring back to pieces of the exercise as often as possible. In this way, each exercise will generate licks that you can use immediately.

5. Forget the written musical example and make up lines of your own based on the idea being discussed.

<u>LESS ADVANCED PLAYERS</u>

This book is organized so that each section of each chapter takes one subject and goes from elementary to advanced exercises on it. Less experienced players should use the following procedure instead of reading straight through the book:

1. Go through chapters 1 and 2 as written. If some of the written musical examples (here or anywhere) are too hard, skip them until later, but <u>practice the exercise anyway</u>, using lines of your own.

2. Do only the first exercise or two in each section of chapters 3 through 9. These will give you an overview of the rudiments of bass playing. Look briefly at chapter 12, too.

3. After these have been digested, go back and do another exercise or two in each section of chapters 3-9. Repeat this process until you finish each chapter.

4. Find a qualified bass teacher to help you assimilate the information in this book, since it is presented here in concentrated form. It might also be helpful to use this book in conjunction with more elementary books, in order to give you more practice reading easier musical examples. Acoustic bassists should go through one or more of the traditional bass methods, such as Simandl's, paying special attention to the fingerings.

HAVE FUN

CONTENTS

Chapter 1 – THE PHYSICAL ASPECTS OF PLAYING

THE BASS

The bass itself consists of its body (1), the fingerboard (2), the nut (3), the bridge (4), the tuning mechanism (5), and the four strings which are tuned E A D G from the lowest sounding to the highest.

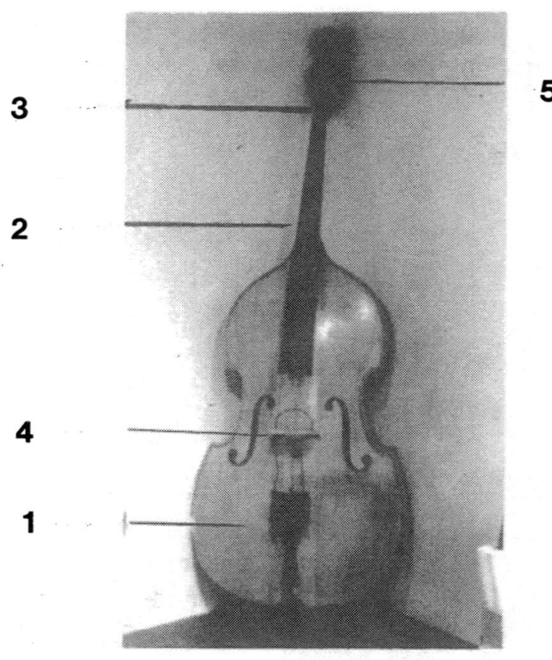

THE STANCE (Acoustic Bass)

The body of the player should be behind the bass enough to bow the E string comfortably. The left armpit should not touch the body of the bass. The left elbow should be up and forward so that the whole arm rotates as you play different strings.

THE LEFT HAND

The left hand's basic posture is a relaxed kind of claw in which the fingers are spread apart from each other and arched so that the fleshy part of the fingertips press the strings down. This arch is much more pronounced on the acoustic bass than on the electric bass. On acoustic bass, this arch is the continuation of an unbroken arch of energy from the spine to the arm, to the palm (where a baseball glove kind of pocket is created), and finally to the fingers. In this way, the strength of all of these muscles contribute to holding the strings down. For beginning players it will take time for this claw to feel natural. As you practice, however, just periodically remind yourself to approximate this position of the hand.

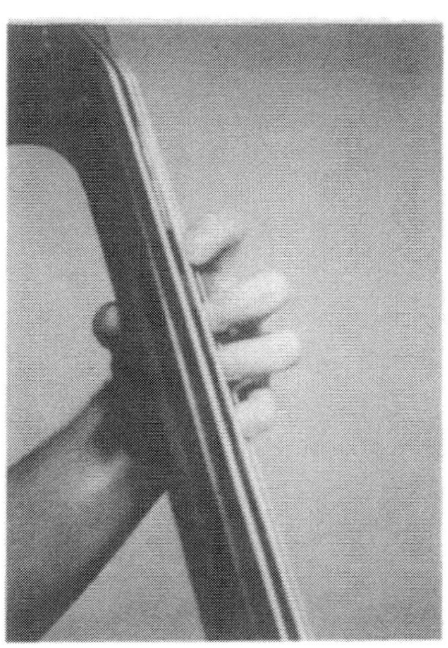

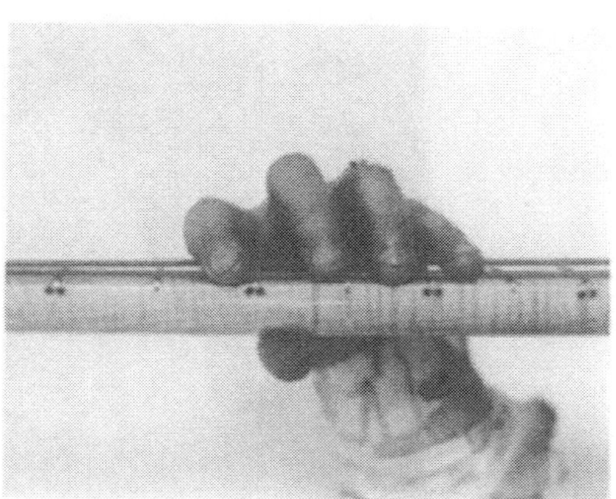

On acoustic bass, the thumb joint should remain unbroken. Most electric players bend the thumb backwards. The thumb should be across from the 2nd finger when playing acoustic bass, and across from the 1st finger when playing electric bass. This position should be maintained as the left hand glides from position to position.

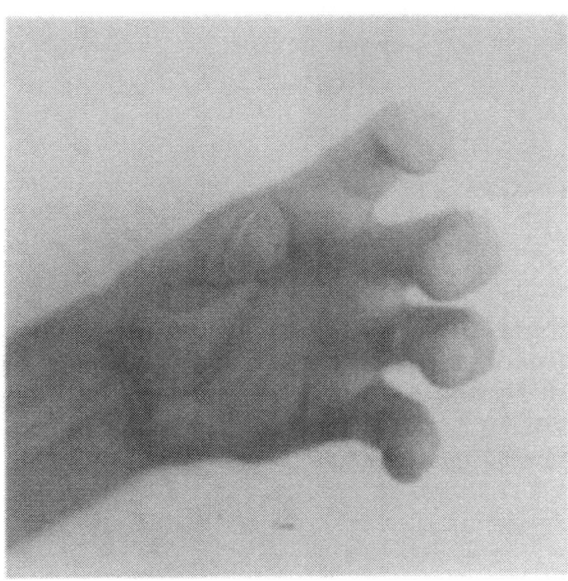

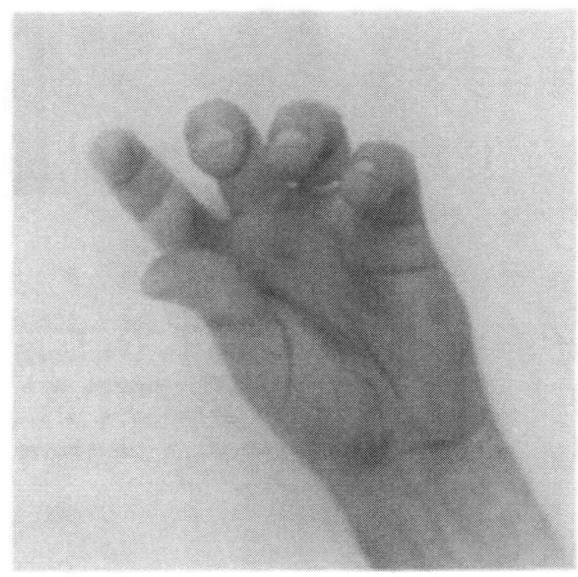

On acoustic bass, after E or Eb is reached on the G string, the thumb starts
to come around to the side of the neck as you go up the string. Finally, at
approximately the 12th "fret" up from the nut, the thumb comes on top of the
fingerboard and its right side at the joint is used to hold the strings down,
in addition to the 1st, 2nd, and 3rd fingers. This is called the thumb position.
Once in the thumb position, it is useful to extend it lower than the 12th fret,
so that unnecessary shifts between the thumb position and the lower positions
are avoided.

The thumb position should be learned along with the lower positions.
It isn't any harder than the others.

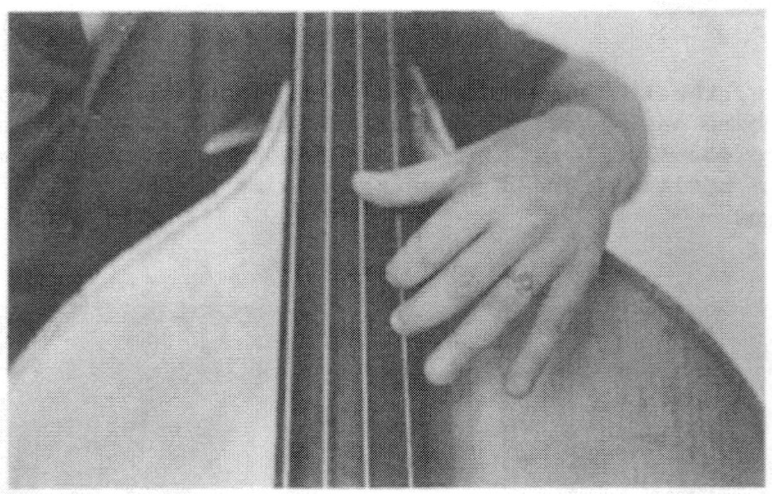

In the lower positions, the fingers that are not in use should be kept relaxed and as close to the strings as possible. The pinky should remain above the
string so that the fingers are perpendicular to the strings, not angled off. In
general, try to eliminate all excess movement in the left hand - it's function
is only to serve as a platform to support finger movements.

THE RIGHT HAND

The right hand in pizzicato playing on the acoustic bass can be used in one of two ways. The first way alternates the tip of the 1st and 3rd or the 1st and 2nd fingers. The hand is held perpendicular to the strings. The 2nd way has the hand at a 45° angle to the strings and the side of the 1st and 2nd fingers are used. Electric bassists use the perpendicular approach or else use a pick. In any case the direction of force used is half towards you and half down into the fingerboard.

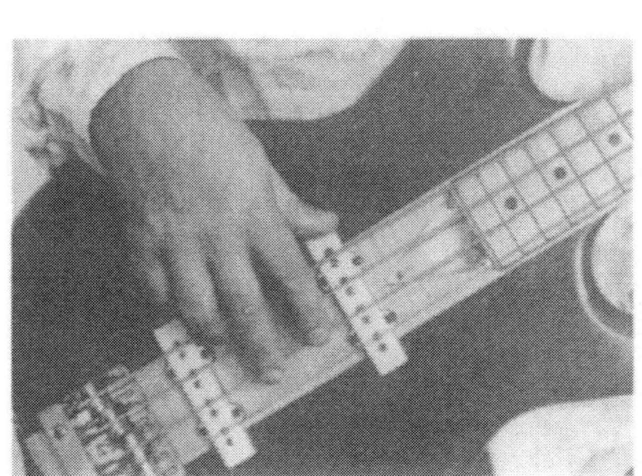
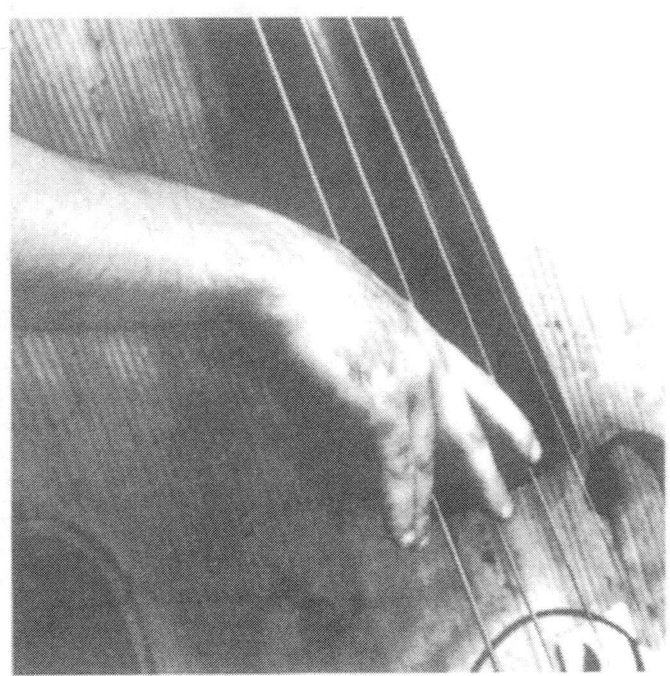

On acoustic bass, the thumb will rest on the side of the fingerboard, near the bottom. Electric basses often have thumb rests, or the E string is used for that purpose. Moving the thumb closer to the bridge gives you more power, while moving it further away gives you more speed and sensitivity. On electric bass, when plucking the strings with the thumb, it should be placed right at the bottom of the fingerboard. Try hitting a string both on the downstroke and the upstroke of the thumb, in addition to using the fingers to give you more rhythmic versatility. On acoustic bass, when using the bow, make sure that it remains perpendicular to the strings at all times and that the right elbow does not bend very much, the right shoulder and wrist being the main sources of motion.

Chapter 2 — BASIC THEORY

PLAYING THE MAJOR SCALE

When two notes are played on a musical instrument, the difference in pitch (higher or lower) is called an _interval_. In Western music, the smallest interval is the _half step_, i.e. up or down one fret on a guitar, or each succeeding note (black and white) on a piano. If you go up 12 half steps, you will find a note that sounds the same as the starting note but higher. These two notes are an _octave_ apart and have the same letter name (A,B,C,etc.). The string that the higher note is played on will be vibrating at exactly twice the rate of the lower string. The 12 notes between a starting note and its counterpart up an octave make up the _chromatic scale_. Out of these 12 notes, 7 are used to create the _major scale_. Here is a fingerboard chart of one octave of the C major scale on the bass:

Exercise 1 - Play these notes slowly, both up and down the scale.

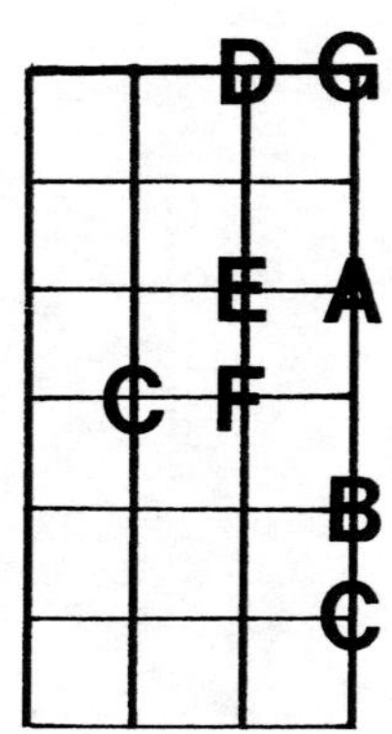

Exercise 2 - Play the scale and sing along with it as you play.

Exercise 3

Here is the C major scale again, only without using the open strings this time. The fingerings given here are from lower to higher notes.

Acoustic Bass Fingerings

C - 1st finger
D - 4th finger
E - 1st finger
F - 1st finger
G - 4th finger
A - 1st finger
B - 2nd finger
C - 4th finger

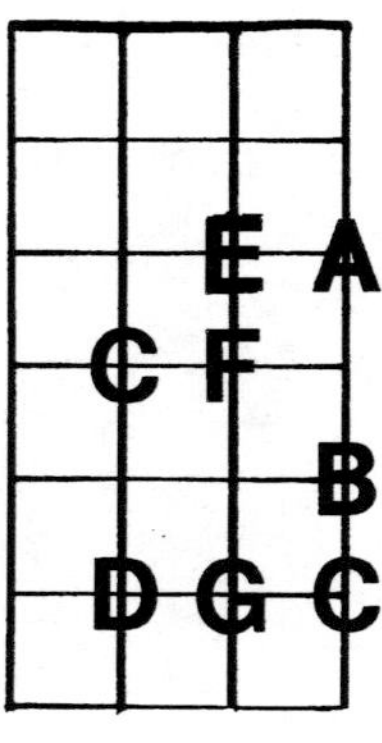

Electric Bass Fingerings

C - 2nd finger
D - 4th finger
E - 1st finger
F - 2nd finger
G - 4th finger
A - 1st finger
B - 3rd finger
C - 4th finger

(CONT.)

Try the following ways to play the scale:

a) Play the scale up and down until it is comfortable.

b) Try playing each note a couple of times before going on to the next note.

c) Sing a short rhythm to yourself, even as simple as the first 3 notes of "Jingle Bells." Find the main pulses or <u>downbeats</u> inherent in the rhythm, e.g.

Jingle Bells, Jingle Bells, etc.
↑   ↑   ↑   ↑

These downbeats should occur at regular intervals in time so that a steady beat is created. Once the rhythm is clear to you, play it using only the note C, then play it on D, then on E, etc. all the way up and down the scale. Make sure that you change notes on a downbeat only, not inbetween notes.

d) Take the rhythm and play it using this scheme:

| rhythm on C | on any other scale note | on C | on any other scale note | etc. |

e) Do d) but play the rhythm, or variations of it, using two or three different notes instead of just one before coming back to C. Experiment with different licks using the 2 or 3 notes but spend the same amount of time on C as on all the other notes combined. Make sure that you come back to C on the downbeat, i.e.

| rhythm on C | on other notes | on C | on other notes | etc. |

Once this is comfortable, lengthen the phrase used on C so that there will be more time to play the other scale notes. Expand this until you are using any or all of the scale notes to lead you back to C.

f) Do e) but alternate coming back to C and F instead of always coming back to C. Be sure that C and F always occur on a downbeat, i.e.

‖: rhythm on C | on other notes | on F | on other notes :‖

(The double lines with two dots means to repeat the sequence inside them.) After that feels right, substitute other scale notes for F in the above scheme, one at a time.

g) Do f) using longer sequences of main notes, e.g.

‖: C | other notes | F | other notes | G | other notes | C | other notes :‖

Do this using other sequences of main notes like, C F C G, C D E D, C A D G, or C F E D. Playing bass on tunes often involves nothing more than this procedure of hitting the root of each chord as it occurs and then playing around with the basic scale, leading you to the root of the next chord.

(CONT.)

h) Do g) but after hitting the main note once or twice, spend the rest of the
   time getting to the next main note in different ways, e.g.

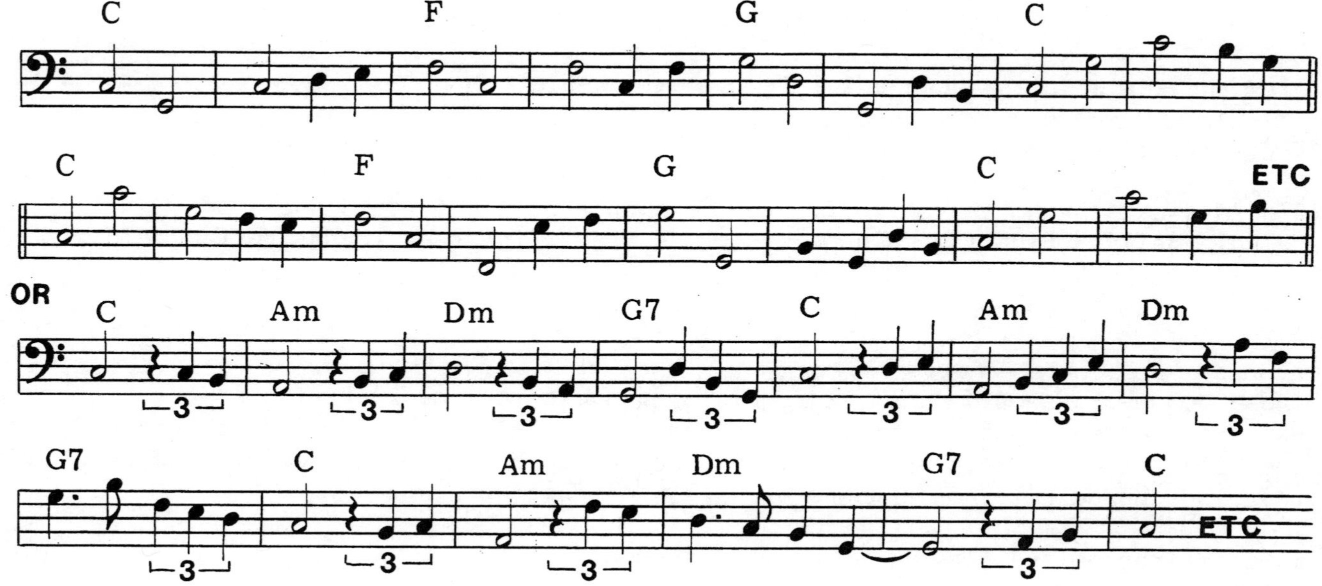

i) Do g) but don't use a prearranged sequence of chords, just land on any note
   in the scale for your main notes, coming back to C when you want to end the "tune".

The next three variations are optional:

j) Sing a rhythm to yourself. Experiment with playing that rhythm or variations
   on it using only C and 2 or 3 other scale notes. You will find a number of
   possibilities by repeating notes, by changing the order of notes (don't always
   start on C), etc. Expand this until you are using any or all of the scale notes.

k) Play the C major scale up and down, then try singing a little tune or bass line
   to yourself using C major scale notes. Once it is clear to you, find the first
   note on the bass and then find the other notes one at a time, until you have
   the whole line down. Then try variations on it using other scale notes, different rhythms, etc.

l) Here are fingerboard charts for the A minor and G7 (Mixolydian) scales. Notice
   that they have the same notes as the C major scale. The only difference is what
   the starting note (the <u>tonic</u>) of the scale is.

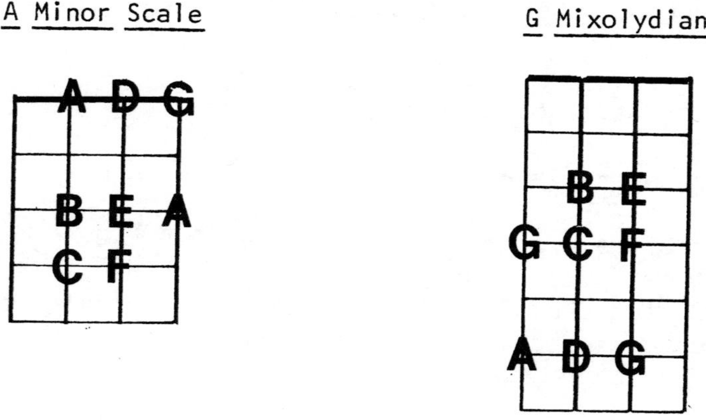

Do Exercise 3 using these scales instead of C major by having A or G as the
tonic note to return to instead of C.

TUNING THE BASS

In order to make sure that your bass is in tune, first tune your open A string to a piano or pitch pipe. Many people find it easier to locate this A if they loosen the string a little, hit the piano note, and then tighten the string right up to match that pitch.

Next, tune your other strings to your open A string in the following way: Find the D on the A string by playing the first 4 notes of the A major scale. The open D string should sound the same as the fourth note of the scale.

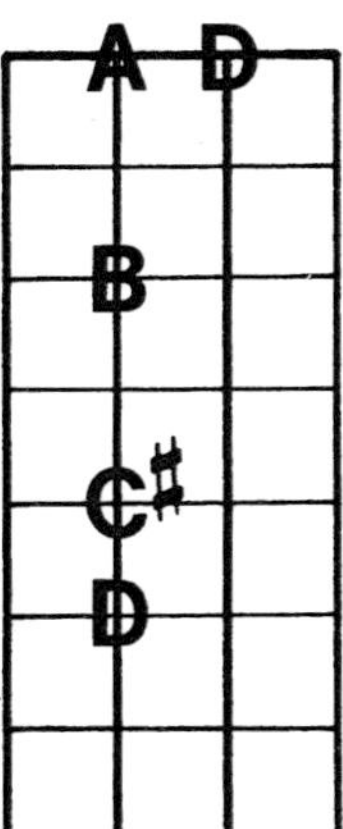

By doing this for each pair of strings, they will become tuned to each other.

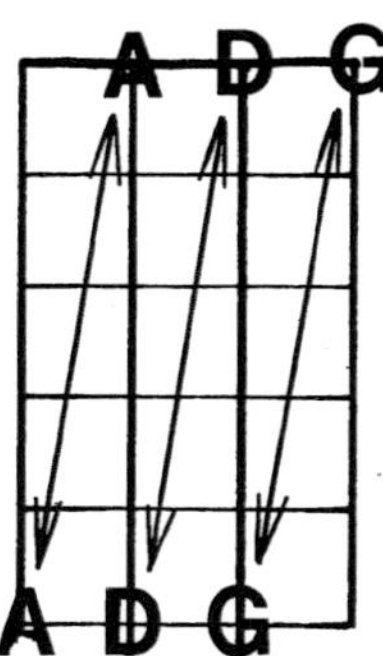

An even more accurate method of tuning is to compare the harmonics above the note D on the G string and above G on the D string. They should sound the same and this relationship will apply to each pair of adjacent strings.

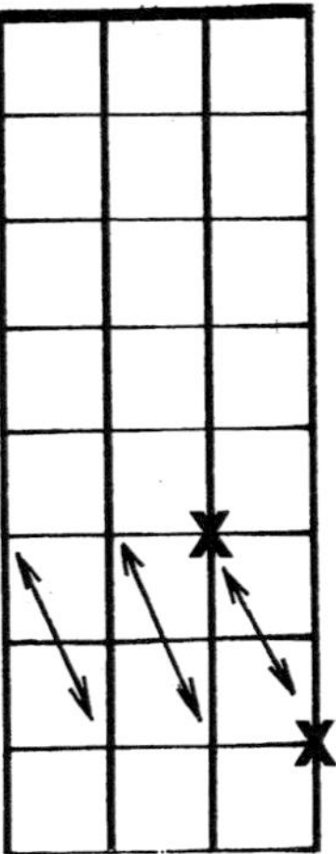

READING MUSIC

a) Notes

Here are the names of the notes as they are written on the staff and as these same notes appear on the bass:

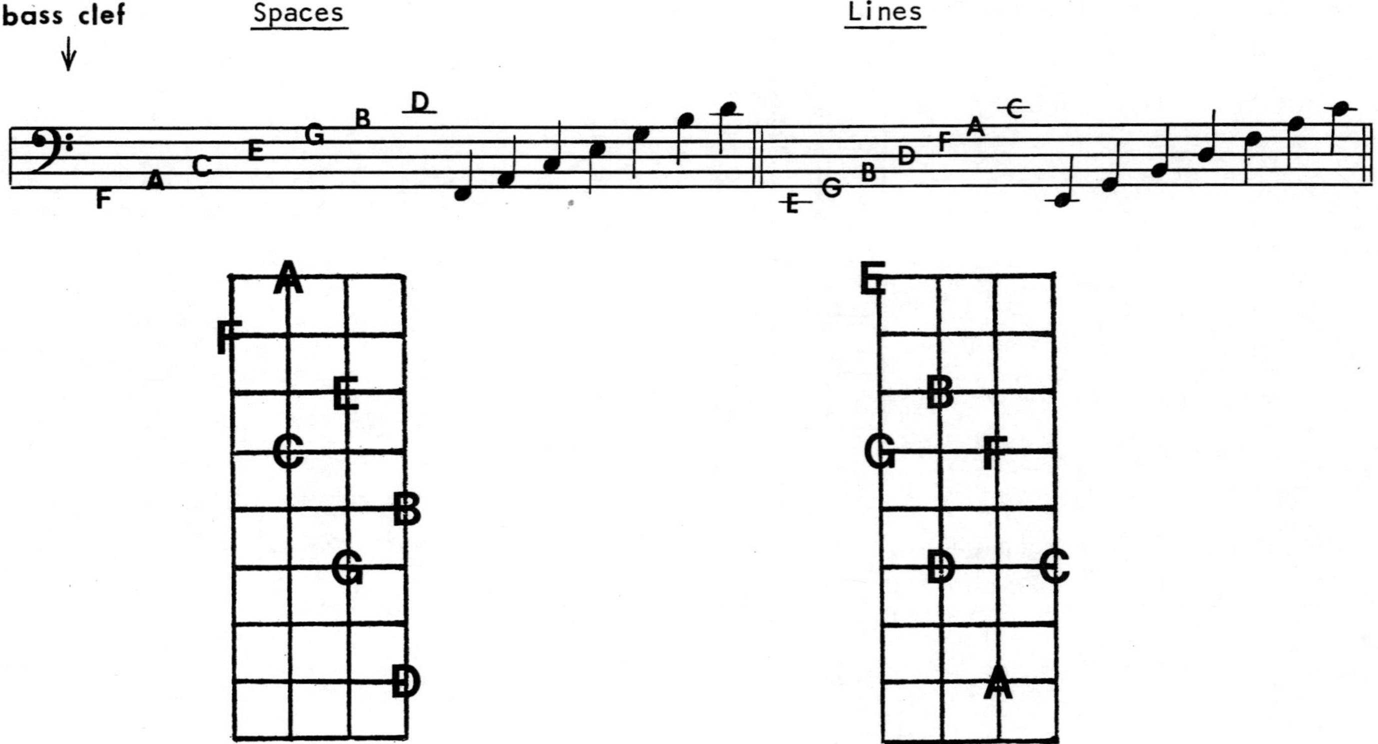

The distance between E and F and between B and C is a half step, but between the other notes in the C major scale there are two half steps. This is called a whole step. Each of the notes inbetween two notes a whole step apart in the key of C has two names. The note inbetween A and B, for example, can be looked at as A raised (sharped) a half step, or as B lowered (flatted) a half step. Thus the note between A and B can be called A sharp (A#) or B flat (Bb).

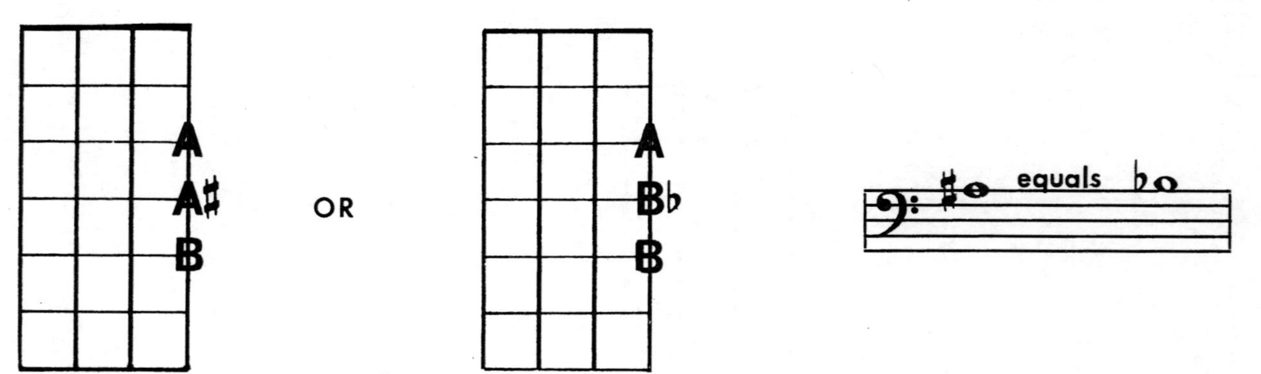

The sharps and flats are called accidentals. To cancel an accidental previously used, a natural sign (♮) is used. Accidentals, including the natural sign, only apply to the bar they are written in (See next page).

b) Rhythm

    The basic unit of rhythm is the beat. These beats are regularly recurring pulses, equally spaced apart in time. Listen to some music and feel where these basic pulses occur.
    The beats are grouped together into measures or bars, seperated on the staff by vertical lines known as bar lines.

Here are the notes and rests commonly used:

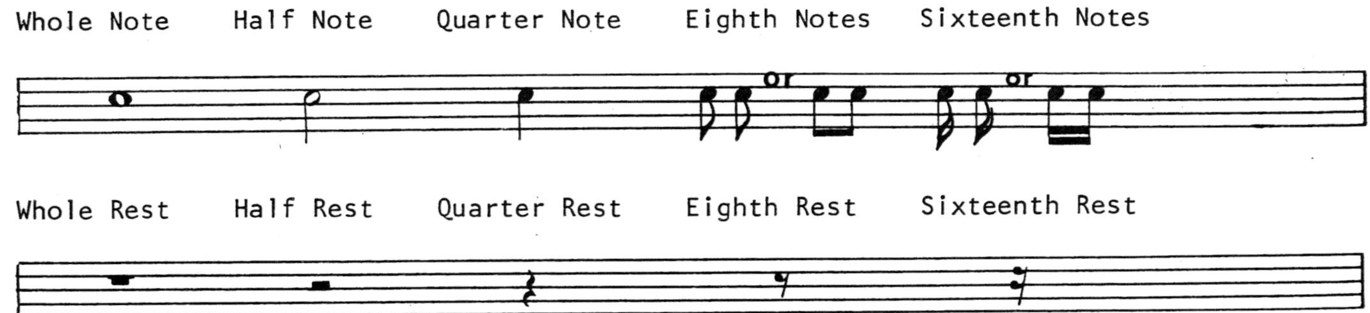

One whole note has the duration of two half notes.
One half note has the duration of two quarter notes.
One quarter note has the duration of two eighth notes
One eighth note has the duration of two sixteenth notes.
The rests have the same duration as their corresponding notes (♩ = 𝄽 etc), except that a whole rest takes up the entire bar, no matter how many beats it contains.

Triplets are composed of 3 beats of exactly the same duration occuring during time of 2 beats. Thus ♪♪♪ divides a quarter note into 3 equal parts, and ♪♪♪ divides a half note into three equal parts.

Tied notes are played as one note, e.g.

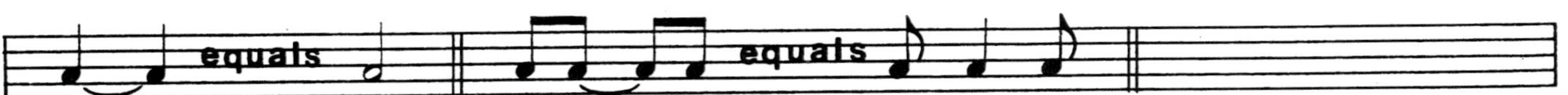

A dot after a note or rest increases it's value by half, e.g.

c) <u>Time Signatures</u>

At the beginning of a composition, you will often find a <u>time signature</u>. It will look like this (or some other combination of numbers):

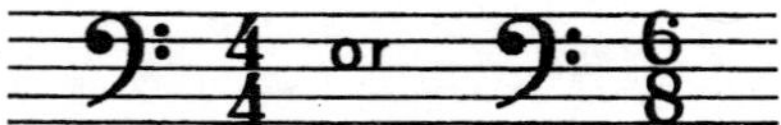

The top number tells you the number of beats per measure, while the bottom one tells you what kind of note (half note, quarter note, eighth note,etc.) will receive one beat. Thus 4/4 time will have four quarter notes per bar, 6/8 will have six eighth notes per bar, etc.

Here are several bars of 4/4 and how they are counted using different kinds of notes.

4/4 is sometimes called common time. If this same measure is felt to have two main pulses instead of four (i.e. a bar of 2/2), it is called cut time. They are abbreviated like this:

<u>Double time</u> means that the bars go by at twice the rate of speed as normal. <u>Double time feeling</u>, however, means that the bars go by at the original rate but the beat is now felt to be twice as fast. Thus a bar of 4/4 in a double time feeling is actually a bar of 8/8.

Exercise 4

Listen to some music and see if you can hear the beginning of each bar. The vast majority of tunes will have four beats per measure. Count along with the music (1 2 3 4, 1 2 3 4, etc.) Try tapping your foot on each beat. Try tapping it on 1 and 3 only. Try tapping it on 2 and 4 only.

d) <u>Key Signatures</u>

<u>Exercise 5</u>

Draw a fingerboard chart of the D major scale. It will have the same intervals between the notes as in the key of C major (half steps between 3 & 4 and between 7 & 8), but it will start on D instead of C. Here is the D major scale written on staff paper, with suggested fingerings for both acoustic and electric bass underneath each note. 1 = 1st finger, 2 = 2nd finger, 3 = 3rd finger, 4 = pinky, 0 = open string.

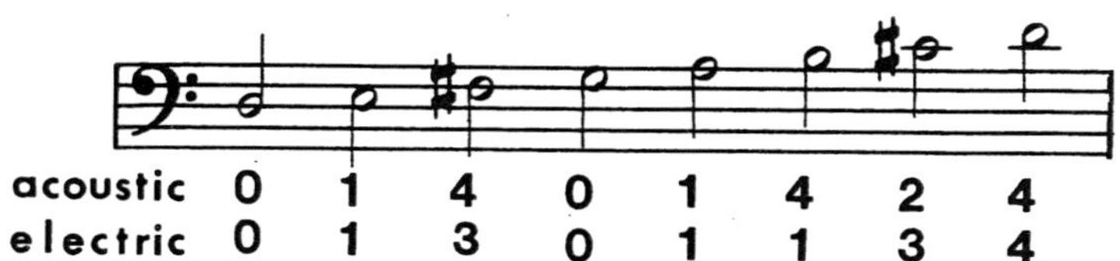

If a tune or an exercise is in the key of D major, there will be two notes that have accidentals (C# and F#). These are put at the beginning of the staff instead of being written in front of the note each time it occurs. They apply whenever that note is played in any octave. This is called the <u>key signature</u>. Thus the key of D major is written like this:

Here are the key signatures of all 12 major keys:

Notice that a flat is added every time the tonic of the key goes up a fourth, or that a sharp is added every time the tonic goes up a fifth. You should memorize the order in which this occurs (i.e. first Bb, then Eb is added to Bb, then Ab is added, etc.)

Here is a fingerboard chart for the C natural minor scale:

Acoustic Bass Fingerings

C - 1st finger
D - 2nd finger (shift to it)
Eb - 4th finger
F - 1st finger (shift back)
G - 2nd finger (shift to it)
Ab - 4th finger
Bb - 1st finger (shift back)
C - 4th finger

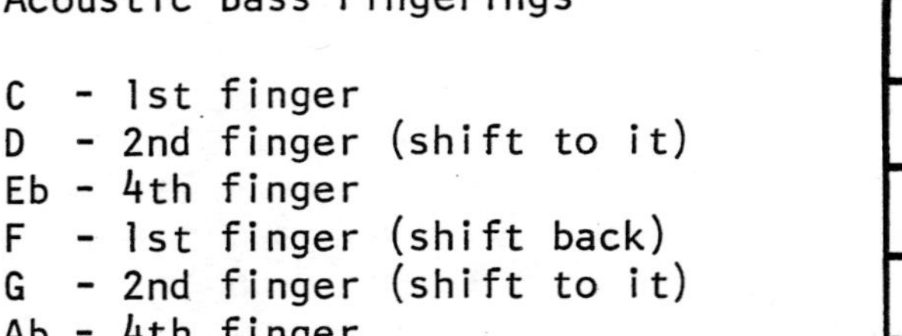

Electric Bass Fingerings

C - 1st finger
D - 3rd finger
Eb - 4th finger
F - 1st finger
G - 3rd finger
Ab - 4th finger
Bb - 1st finger
C - 3rd finger

Here are the C major and C minor scales written a staff paper. Each note of the scale is also given a number, called its scale degree, often written in Roman numerals.

C major scale

Scale degrees ⟶   1   2   3   4   5   6   7   8=1

C minor scale

Scale degrees ⟶   1   2   3   4   5   6   7   8=1

Notice that in a minor scale, the half steps are between 2 and 3 and also between 5 and 6.

Exercise 6

Play the C major and minor scales and compare the sound, both for the whole scale and smaller pieces of it, e.g.

(CONT.)

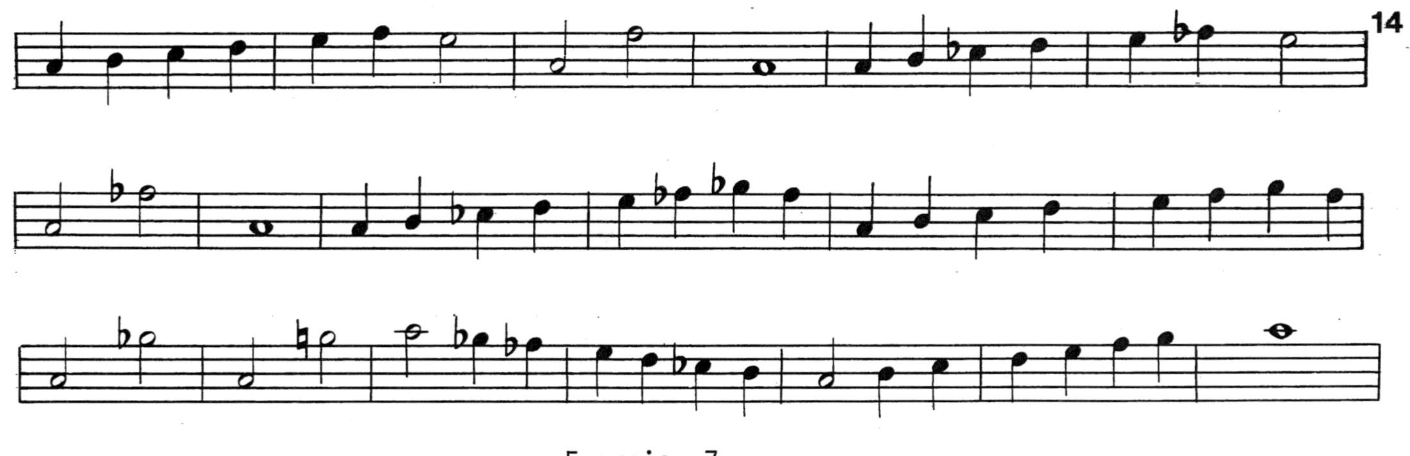

Exercise 7

Here is one octave of each of the 12 major scales. Play them all at least once as written, then hum a rhythm to yourself and use it or variations on it to play the scale, as in Exercise 3.

By playing the major scale starting on the 6th note, a minor scale is formed that has the same notes (and therefore the same key signature) as the original major scale. It is called the relative minor of the major scale. The fingering patterns you learned for C major and C minor using no open strings are the basic ones for all major and minor scales, but you should also try playing them using the open strings whenever possible.

C MAJOR A MINOR

F MAJOR D MINOR

Bb MAJOR G MINOR

Eb MAJOR C MINOR

Ab MAJOR F MINOR

Db MAJOR Bb MINOR

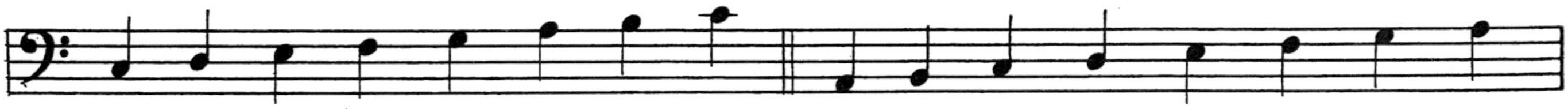

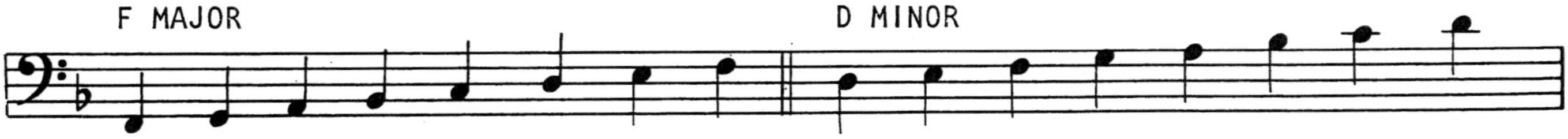

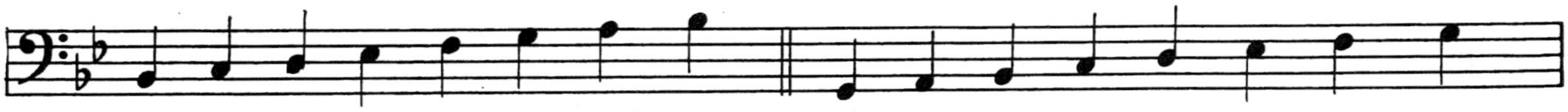

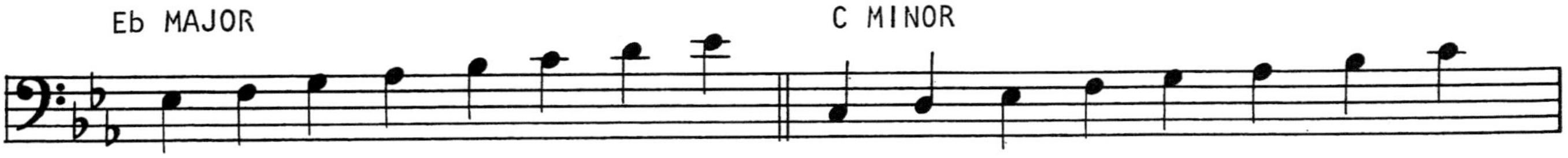

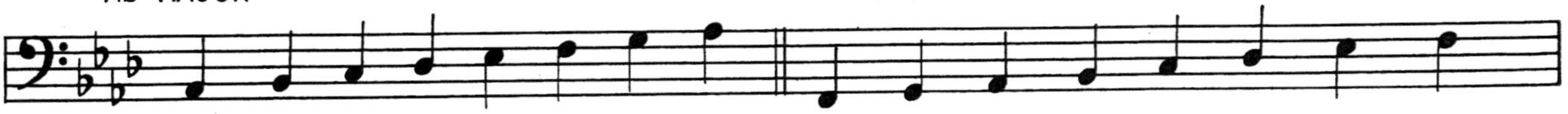

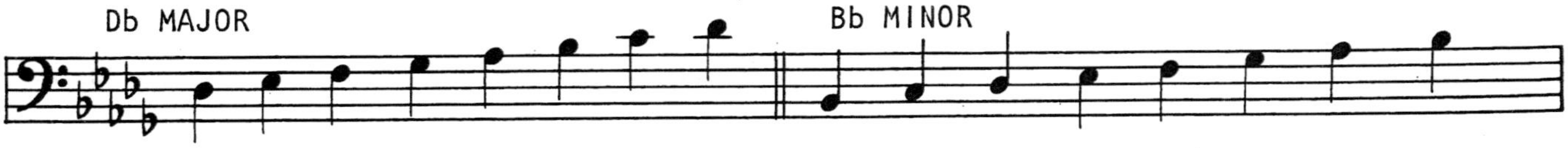

(CONT.)

Gb MAJOR | Eb MINOR

B MAJOR | G# MINOR

E MAJOR | C# MINOR

A MAJOR | F# MINOR

D MAJOR | B MINOR

G MAJOR | E MINOR

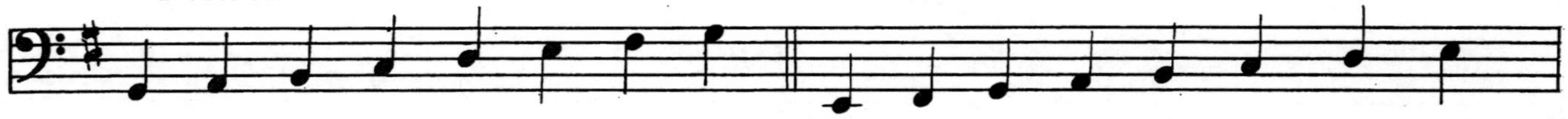

Exercise 8

By taking every other note of these scales, the corresponding chords are created. Here are the major and minor triads composed of the 1st (or root), 3rd, and 5th scale degrees of the major or minor scales. In addition, try playing the root an octave above the one written here.

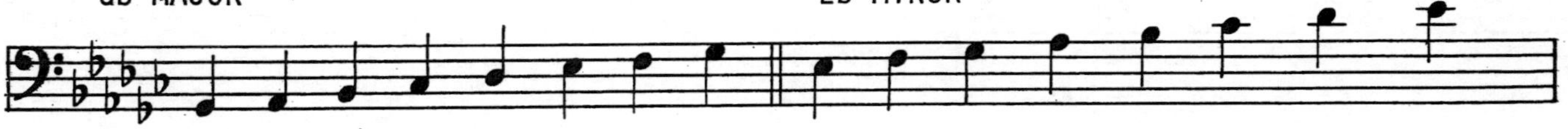

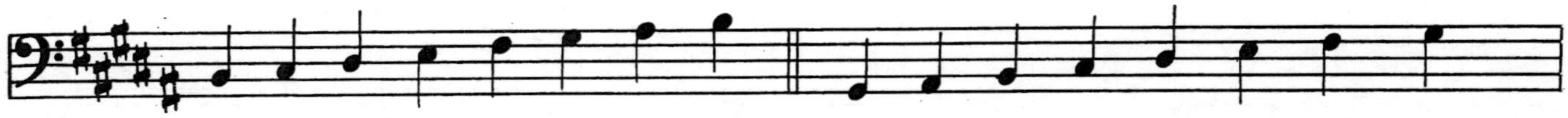

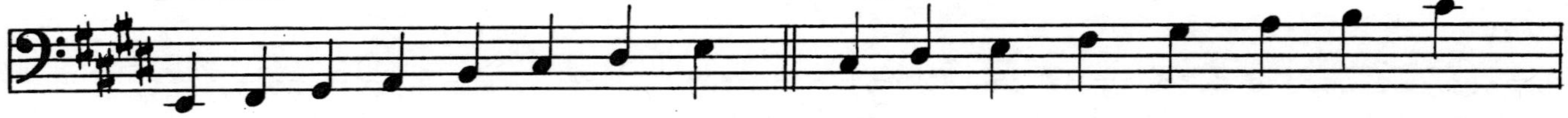

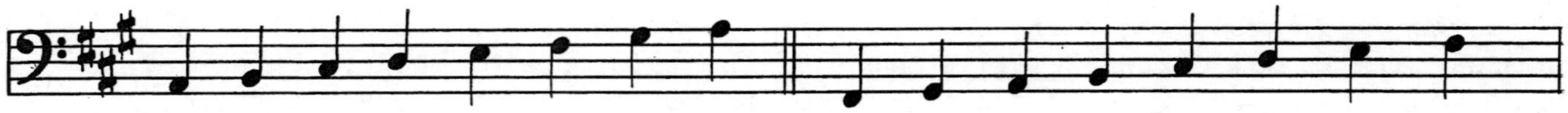

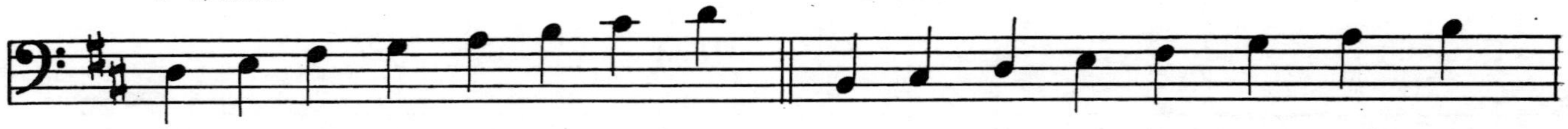

Play them as written first, then hum a rhythm to yourself and play the chord using that rhythm or the groove the rhythm creates. The fingerings for F# major and F# minor can be used for all the ones after that too. Notice that the chords from A upwards can be played starting on more than one string. When chords are played one note at a time like this, they are called arpeggios.

E Major | E Minor | F Major | F Minor

F# Major | F# Minor | G Major | G Minor

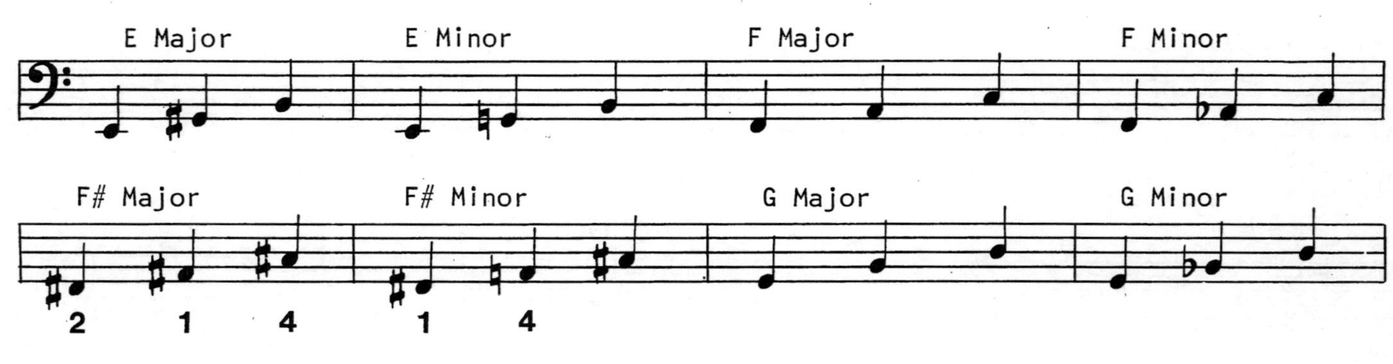

(CONT.)

Exercise 9

By adding the 7th note of the scale to these triads, we get the major and minor seventh chords. Follow the same instructions as in Exercise 8.

Exercise 10

Pick a chord and add some chord notes both above and below what is given in Exercise 9. Then try adding another note from the parent scale to it. Hear how each scale note colors the sound of the chord without altering the basic tonality, e.g.

Exercise 11

a) Take 2 seventh chords and alternate playing them, one or two bars apiece. Try repeating some notes and leaving out others. Also notice the use of chromatic connecting tones in this next example.

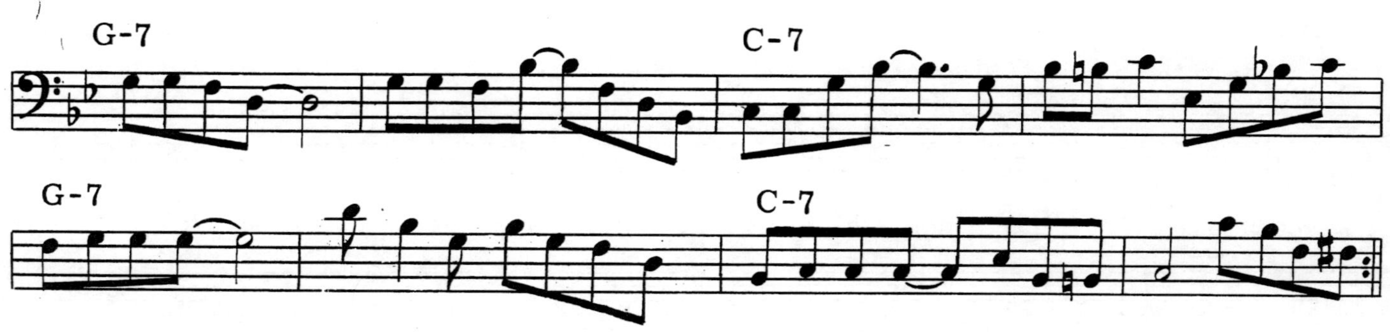

b) Alternate playing two 7th chords, but add a note from the scale to connect two chord notes or to end an arpeggio with. This combination of scales and chords can create more interesting lines than either one alone, e.g.

BASIC HORIZONTAL POSITIONS

Exercise 12

Play the following notes ascending and descending:

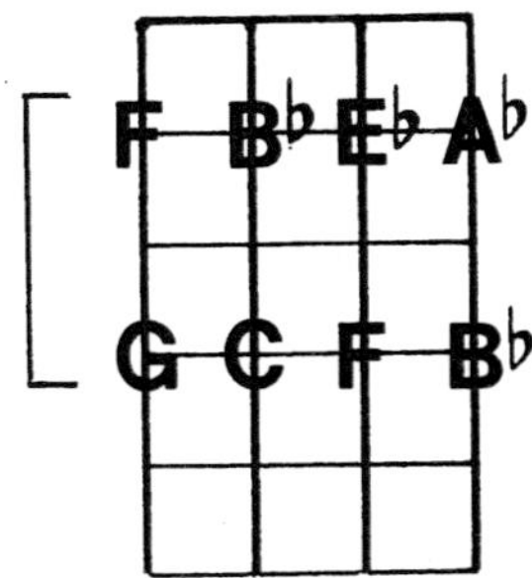

This two fret position should be played without shifting the hand up or down
the fingerboard at all. Acoustic bass fingering is 1 and 4 on each string. Electric players may use that or 1 and 3 if they can.

Exercise 13   (Electric bass only)

Play the following three fret position, using the 1st and 4th fingers only.

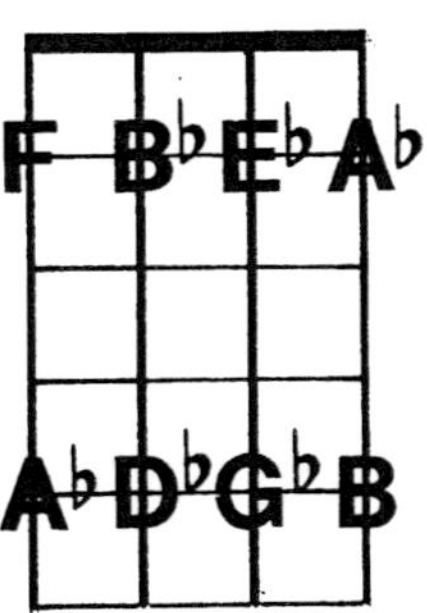

Depending on the size of your fingerboard and the size of your hand, these
three fret positions may not be useful on the first couple of frets, but after
that you should be able to stretch your hand to include three frets without
straining. Within these three fret positions, each finger is responsible for
the notes lying on one fret. Thus in the above diagram, the first finger will
play the F, Bb, Eb, and Ab; the 2nd finger will play the notes a half step up
from there, etc. This one finger per fret fingering system is the most efficient
way to play electric bass and should be used whenever possible.
The following exercises in this section are written to illustrate different
ways to practice the two fret positions, but electric bassists should also do
each one using these three fret positions as well.

Exercise 14

Practice two fret positions starting on each note of the E string. Hum a rhythm to yourself, and use it or variations on it while playing the notes in each position.

Exercise 15

Spend some time in one two fret position. Try to hear one note as the main note or tonic, and keep returning to it to resolve your phrases, e.g. here are some licks having C as the tonic of the position encompassing C to D on the G string. Try using these to end your phrases with, after you have played in the position for awhile.

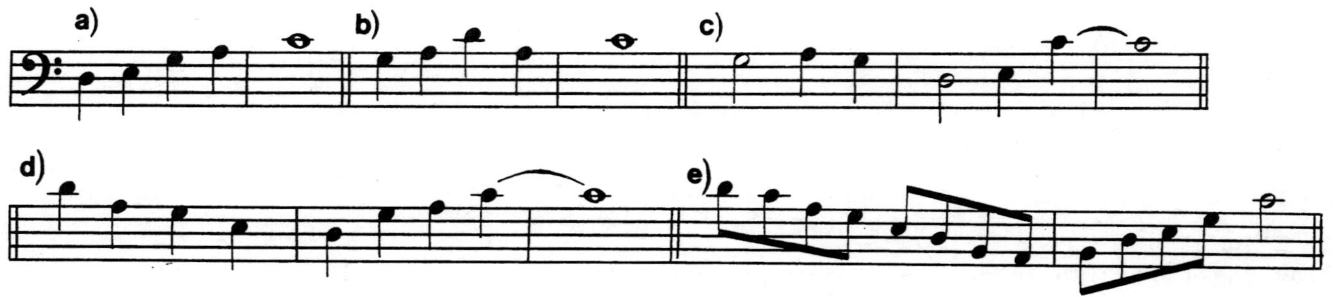

Here is an example of how A could be the tonic of the same position:

(CONT.)

Here is a chart of A minor and C major positions, using both 2 and 3 fret
ones. Any major or minor tonality can be played by transfering these positions
to other starting notes.

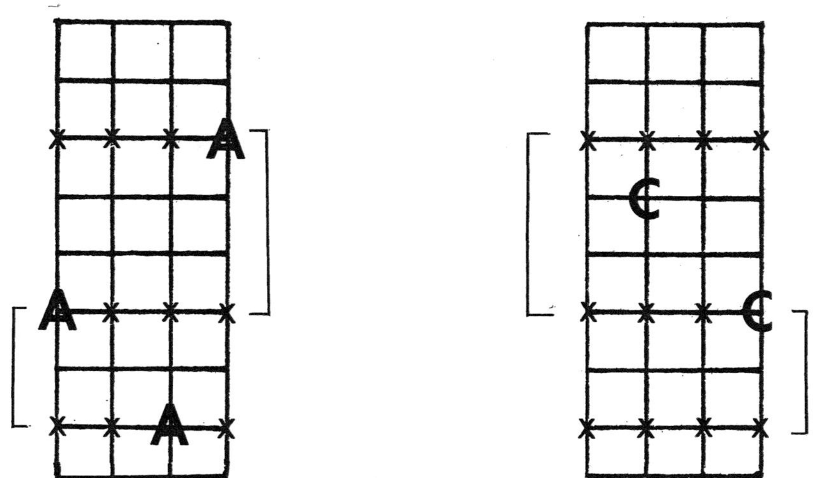

Exercise 16

Add the chromatic notes in the middle of the position, e.g.

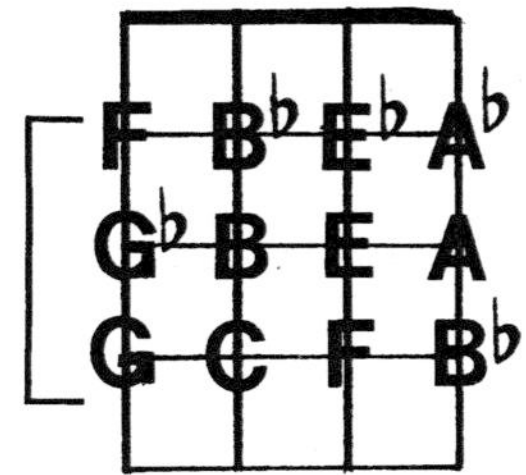

Experiment with different combinations of these notes. This is especially
good for bluesy-type lines, e.g.

Exercise 17

Practice alternating between two adjacent positions. Here, for example, are two positions a whole step apart. Change positions according to the brackets.

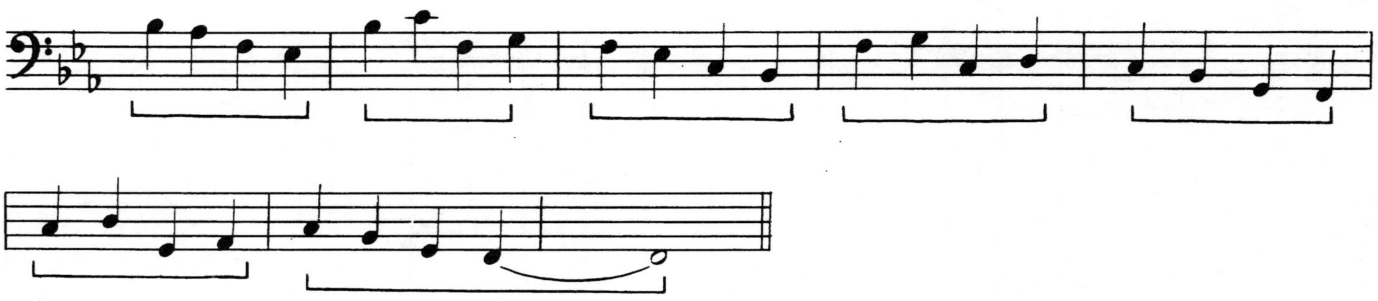

Try the following exercise (which uses progressively larger jumps between positions) without looking at your left hand. The 1st two notes in each bar are on the G string, the last two are on the D string.

By improvising at length on exercises like these, you will develop a strong sense of these positions and how they are related to each other. This will serve as a foundation for everything else you play, since each note you play should be thought of as being a part of one position or another.

Exercise 18

By putting in all the notes between the notes of the C major scale, we get
the chromatic scale starting on C. Fill in the rest of the notes on the following charts, so that you know the names of every note on your instrument.

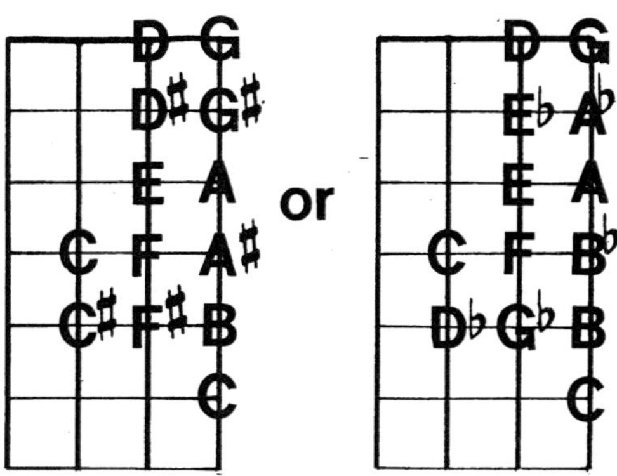

Exercise 19

a) Play the chromatic scale starting on C, both ascending and descending.

b) Keeping C as your tonic note, improvise some music using the chromatic scale.

Exercise 20

Here is the chromatic scale again, but returning to C after each note. The recurring C is called a pedal tone and in this exercise is always played on the A string. Each pair of notes is an example of one of the 12 kinds of intervals within an octave. The names of the intervals in this exercise also apply if the 2nd note is below the first one, since intervals only measure distance between notes. Thus, C down to Bb is a whole step as well as C up to D. Memorize the name of each interval and what it sounds like.

Note: a ½ step is also called a minor 2nd, whole step = major 2nd, flat 5th = raised 4th.

Exercise 21

a) Try extending Exercise 20 both above and below its limits, e.g.

b) Try starting pieces of Exercise 20 on different notes. This is called transposing.

OR

Here is a chart of the names of the intervals in the second octave above a tonic.
The 5th and both 7ths are usually called the same in any octave:

Interval Distance from Tonic	Octave	-9th	9th	-10th	10th	11th	+11th	(5th)	-13th	13th
Example in C	C	Db	D	Eb	E	F	F#	(G)	Ab	A

By going down a fifth or up a fourth each time, the following sequence, known as the cycle of fifths, is created.

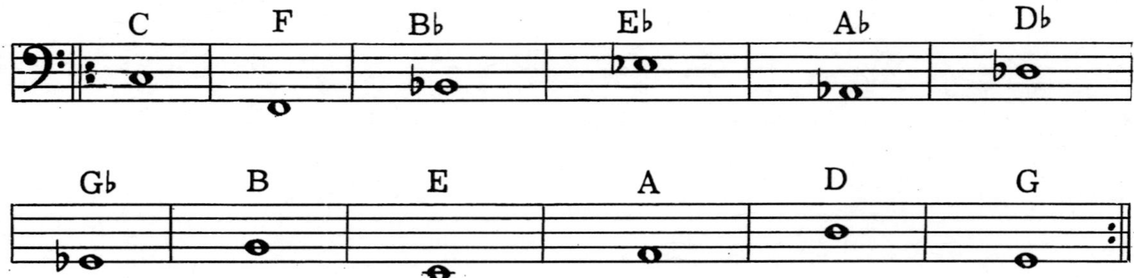

Notice that C is up a fourth from G and so the whole cycle starts over again.

Exercise 22

Hum a rhythm to yourself and use it or variations on it on each note of the cycle.

Exercise 23

Experiment with going up a fourth instead of down a fifth (or visa versa),e.g.

Exercise 24

Play each note and a fifth above it. Thinking of the two notes as one unit will make it easier to keep your place.

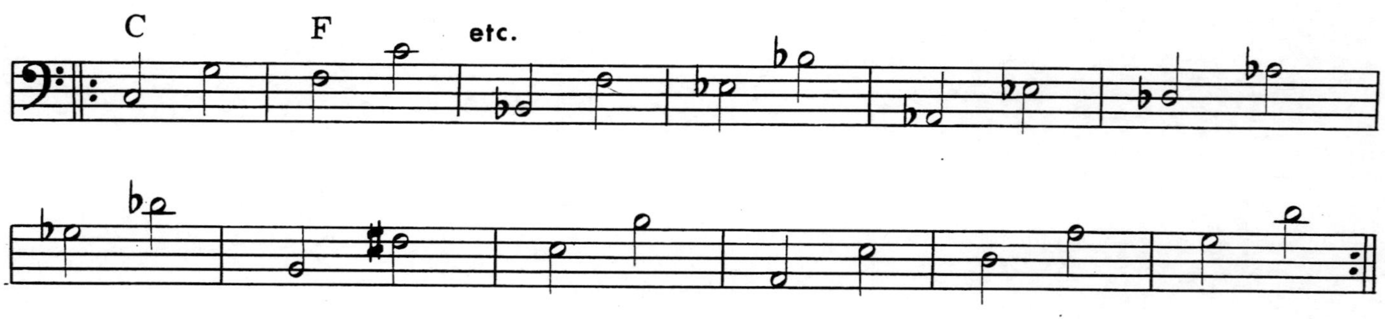

Exercise 25

Add both a fifth and an octave above each note, e.g.

Exercise 26

Sing a Latin-type rhythm to yourself. Use it on the notes in Exercise 25, e.g.

Notice the chromatic connection between the fifth of one chord and the root
of the next one, e.g. F to Bb or Bb to Eb in the above example.

Exercise 27

a) Play a major triad on each note of the cycle of fifths, e.g.

(CONT.)

b) Play a minor triad on each note of the cycle, e.g.

Do this for the major and minor 7th chords, too.

Exercise 28

By adding a note a minor 7th above the root of a major triad, a dominant 7th chord is created. Here are dominant 7th chords starting on each note of the cycle.

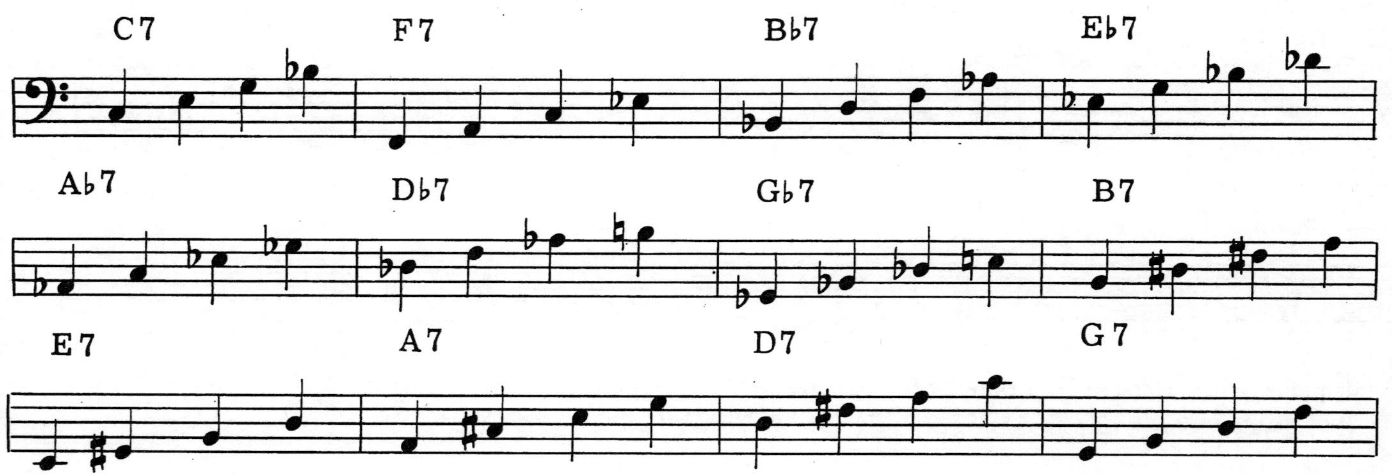

Exercise 29

Take four chords on the cycle and repeat them over and over (this is called a vamp). Play a phrase on the 1st chord and then transpose it or a variation on it to the other chords, e.g.

Exercise 30

Play the major and minor scales through the cycle of fifths, i.e. C major,
F major, Bb major, etc., or A minor, D minor, G minor, etc. Notice that only
one note changes each time.

Exercise 31

Notice that each pair of notes on the cycle of fifths can be looked at as
the fifth and 1st (tonic) notes of a major or minor scale, e.g. C is the 5th
note of the F scale; F is the 5th note of the Bb scale, etc. The chord built
on the 5th degree of the scale is usually a dominant 7th chord and strongly
resolves to the chord built on the tonic. Thus G7 leads to C, C7 leads to F, etc.
This V7 to I progression is the basis of much of Western music, so practice
each pair of chords on the cycle as a V7 to I progression until you can hear
the tension $\longrightarrow$ resolution, e.g.

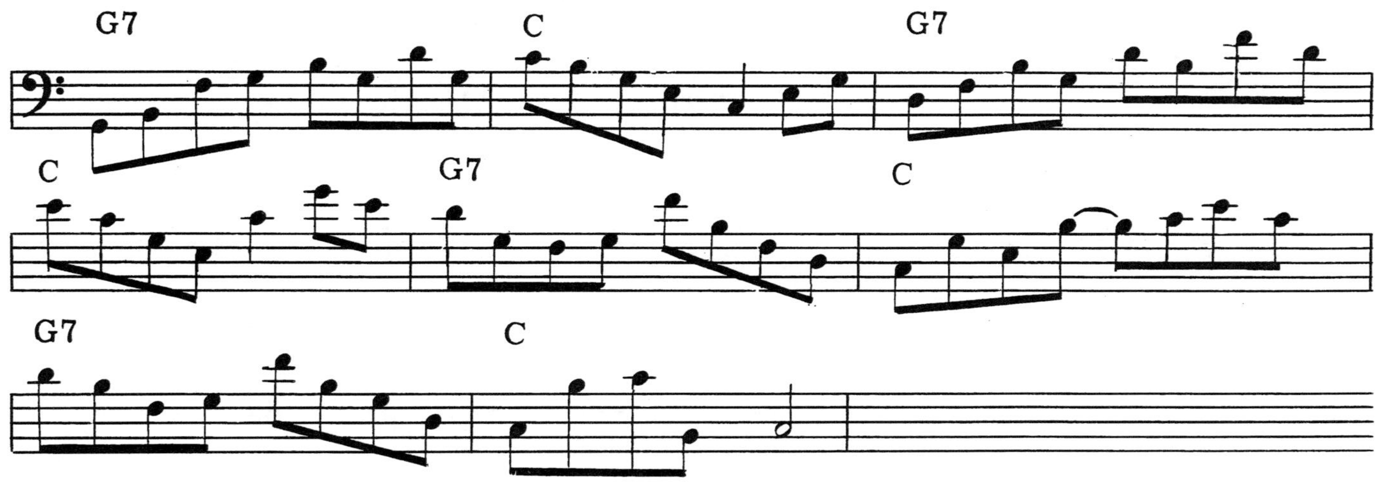

Exercise 32

After G7 to C feels comfortable, try adding other notes to the G7 chord,
one at a time. Every note except F# can become an extention of the G7 sound,
e.g. G7 plus E.

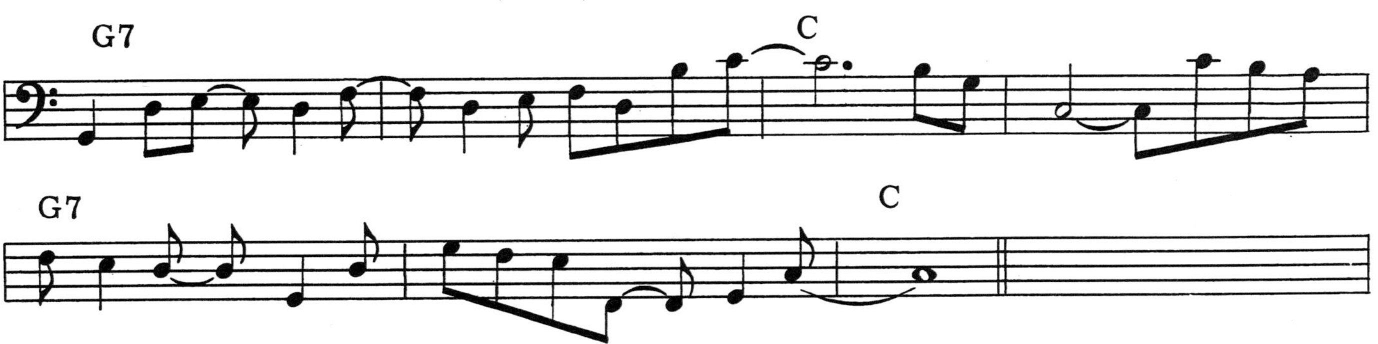

Exercise 33

Most tunes use the cycle of fifths to create strong chord resolutions. Pick a tune you know and see if you can locate pieces of the cycle of fifths in it. Here, for example, is a bass line on the changes of "Autumn Leaves", a tune which uses the cycle of fifths throughout.

Chapter 3 — SCALE STUDIES

HORIZONTAL SCALE POSITIONS

(Less advanced players: Go all the way through this 1st section before going on.)

Exercise 1

Play the notes in the following positions both up and down the scale. Once each one is comfortable, improvise some music using those notes.

a) Here are the notes of the C major scale that can be played in the lowest position without moving the hand up or down the fingerboard.

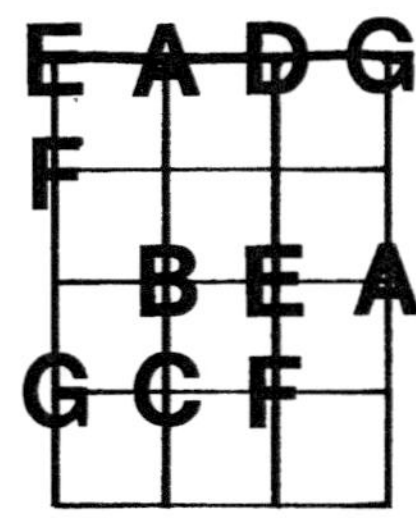

b) Going up the fingerboard, we find another position containing successive C major scale notes that can be played without shifting on electric bass or with only ½ step shifts on acoustic bass.

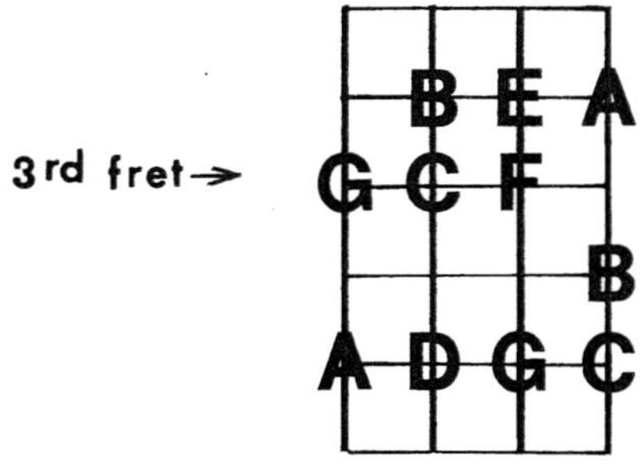

c) Going from A on the E string to D on the G string gives us this position.

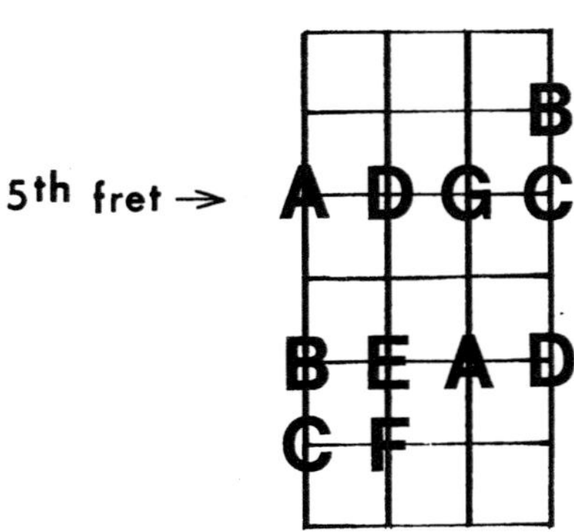

d) Starting on B on the E string gives up this position.

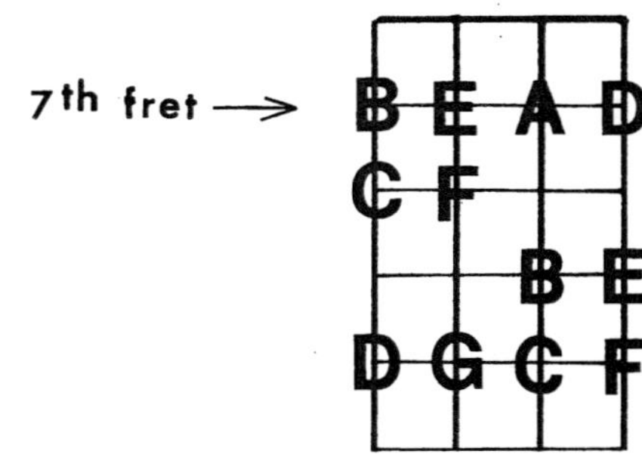

e) Finally, starting on D on the E string, we get this position.

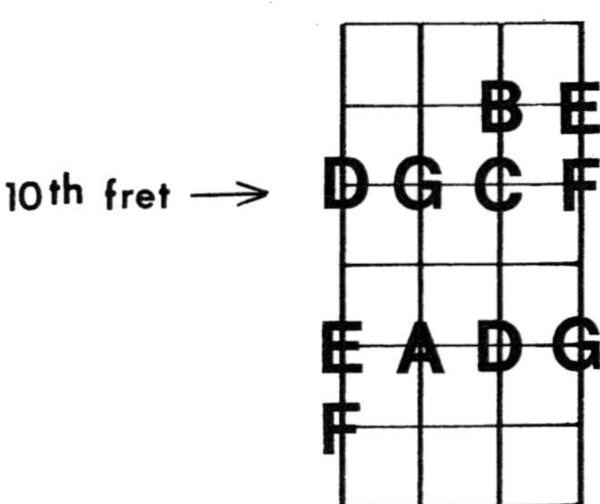

Exercise 2

Play a scale in one position using a steady stream of notes, but changing directions often. Be sure not to skip any scale degrees when you change direction. E.g. Here is the C major (or A minor) scale in 1st (or lowest) position.

Try changing the rhythm to create a more interesting line on this exercise, e.g.

Exercise 3

Here is a fingerboard chart for the entire C major or A minor scale, using all the scale notes on all four strings, plus fingerings for each position.

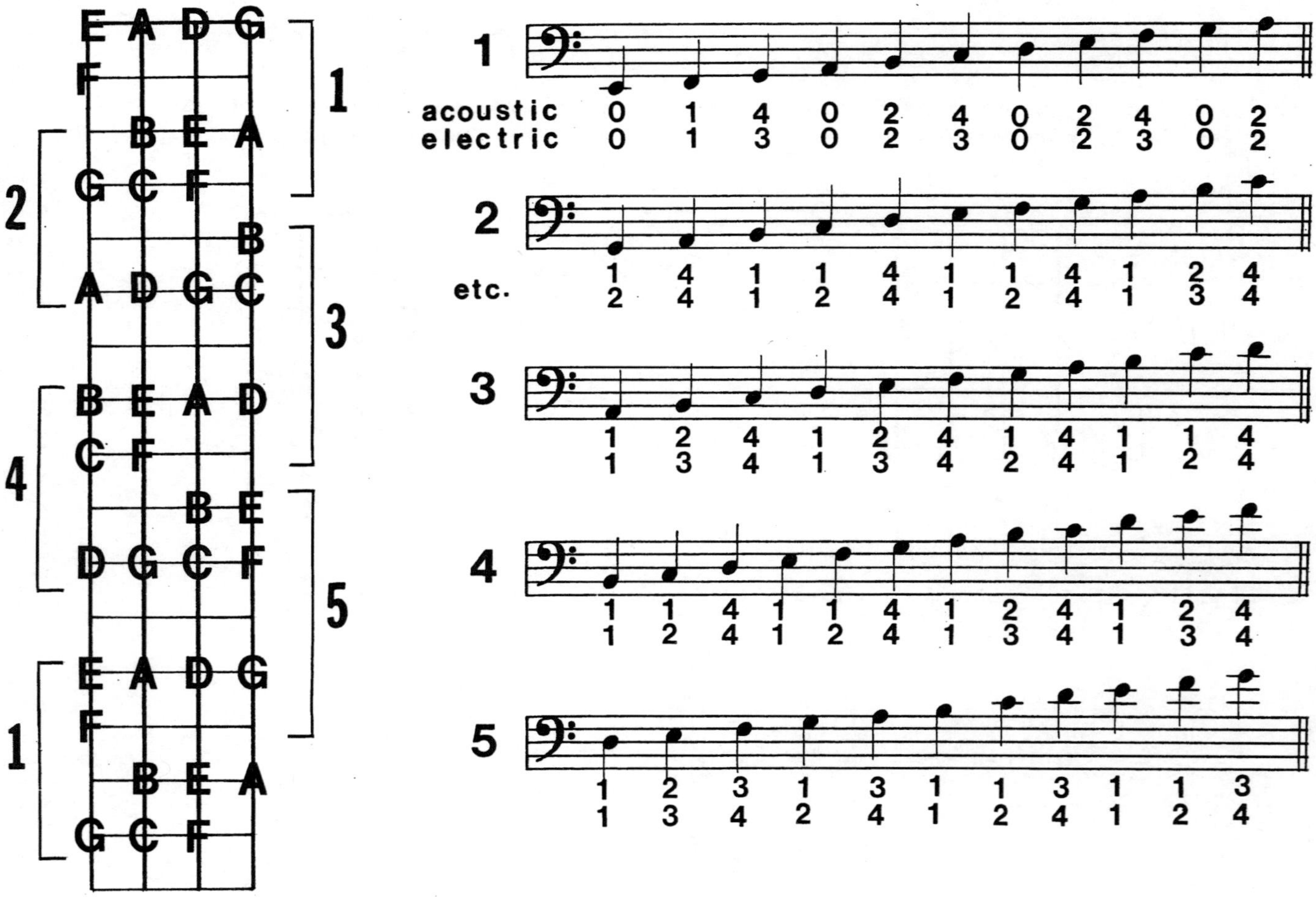

Note: By the time the 11th "fret" is reached on acoustic bass, the 3rd finger can be used instead of the 4th.

Exercise 4

After the 5th position, the 1st position occurs again, only up an octave this time. Thus there are only five positions to learn and these will be the same for any major or minor scale. The only difference will be which one occurs at the top of the fingerboard.

Pick a key besides C and verify this for yourself. Try thinking of the lowest note in each position in order to find where the positions are in the new key, e.g. the 3rd of the scale is the lowest note in the #1 position, the 5th of the scale is the lowest note in the #2 position, etc.

The keys of D,E,G, and A major will have slightly different configurations at the top of the fingerboard because the open strings allow two whole steps to be played without shifting. After that , the normal positions will occur. Here, for example, are the Bb and E major scales and their positions:

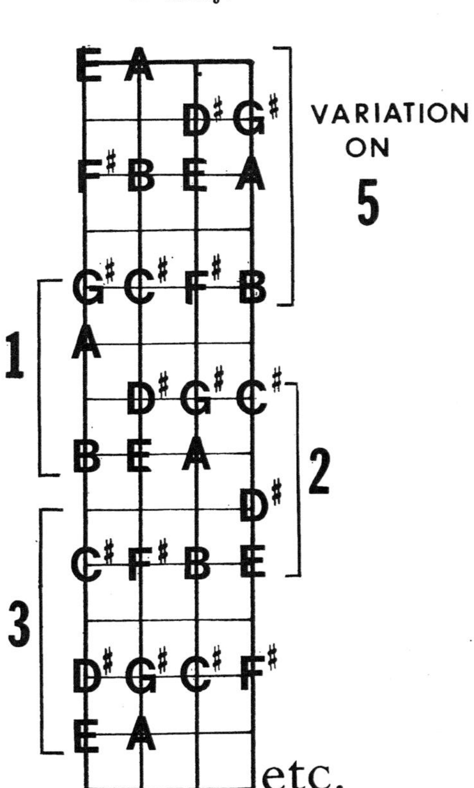

After each position is comfortable by itself, try playing them one after another so that the relationship between them is clear. Then practice connecting the positions by going up one and down the next, etc.

Exercise 5

Next try changing positions every two bars. Once this is easy, try playing in a different position every bar. Since you probably won't have time to play all the notes in each position, try concentrating on two strings at a time, especially the upper two strings.

Exercise 6

a) Play the lowest position for the C major scale (#1); then play this same position starting up a half step (on F) so that it fits the Db major scale; then the D major scale, etc. chromatically up to at least the A major scale. Do this for each of the 5 positions until transposing them is easy for you to do.

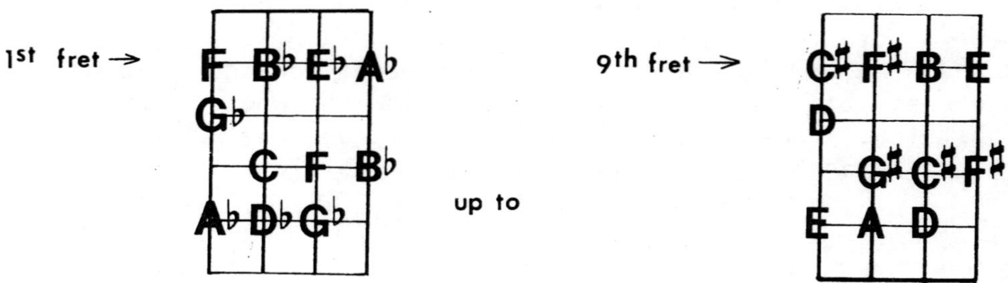

b) Try ending your phrases on the tonic of each of these scales, even though it isn't the lowest note, e.g. D major, 1st position.

c) Try playing the tonic for a bar and then other notes in the position for a bar or two or three.

d) Use one position at a time as the basis for playing around in a key, e.g. D major, #2 position.

THE DIATONIC MODES

Exercise 7

The diatonic or church modes are created by playing one octave of the major scale starting on each of the scale degrees. Here are the modes of the C major scale. Each mode can be played in 3 different positions which are indicated underneath the mode - find and practice each way to play them.

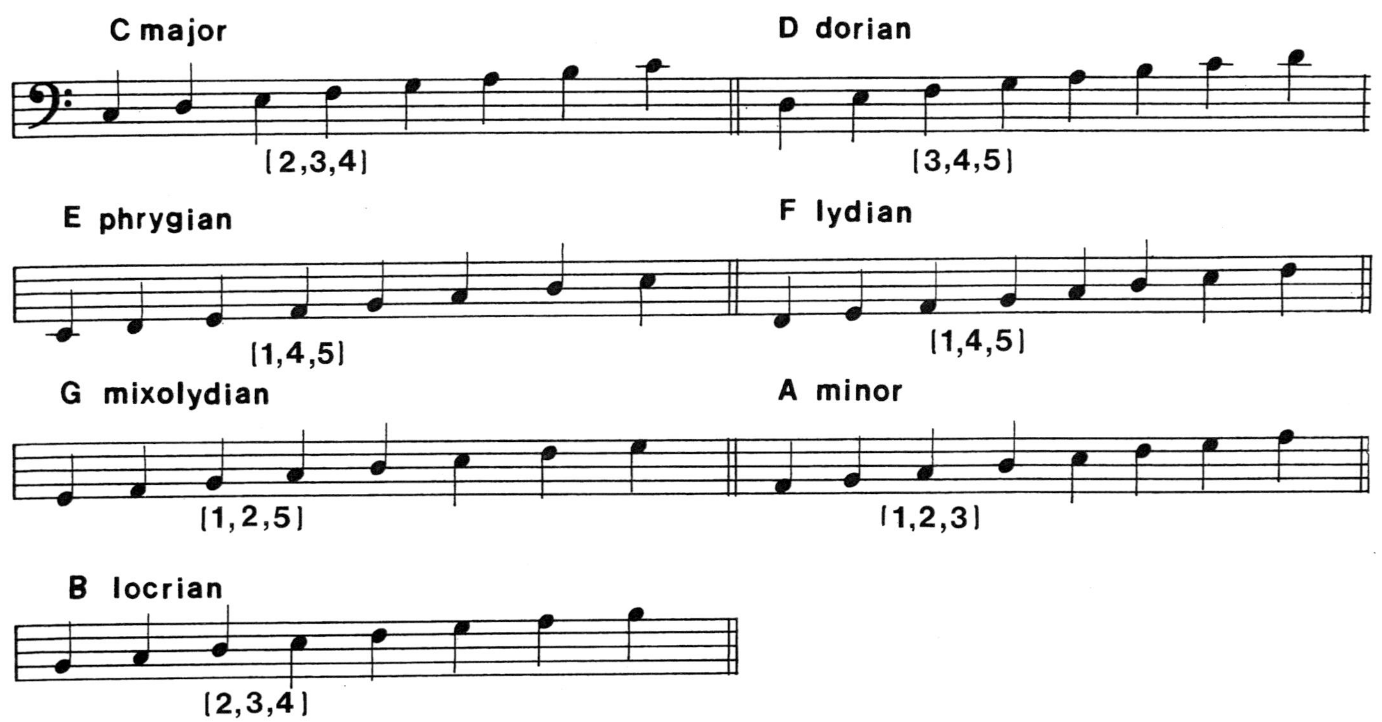

Exercise 8

Take one position at a time and find all the modes in it, e.g. the 1st position contains the Phrygian, Lydian, Mixolydian, and Minor modes.

Exercise 9

These modes are often used as tonic scales in their own right. Here are examples of bass lines based on several of the modes of the F major scale.

a) G Dorian (equals G minor scale but with a major 6th)

b) A Phrygian (equals A minor scale but with a flat 2nd)

c) Bb Lydian (equals Bb major but with a raised 4th)

d) C Mixolydian (equals C major scale but with a flat 7th)

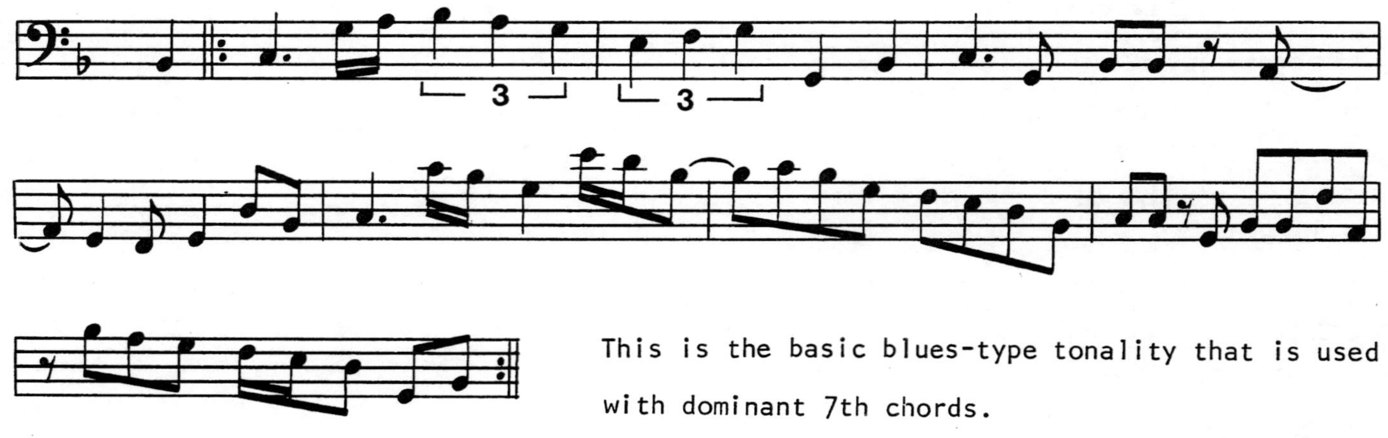

This is the basic blues-type tonality that is used with dominant 7th chords.

Exercise 10

By playing every other note of these modes, we get the scale chords of a key (see Chapter 4 - Scale Chords). Here is a simple chord progression using the scale chords built on the 1st, 4th, and 5th degrees of the C major scale. The notes that are used to connect the roots of the chords can be thought of as all belonging to the C major scale, but if you think of them as belonging to seperate modes on each chord, their relationship to the chord will be clearer.

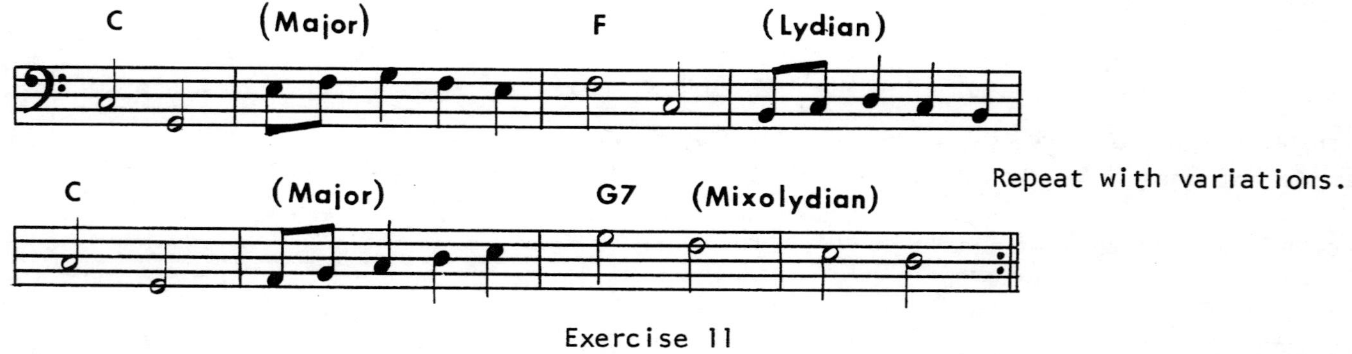

Exercise 11

Take a mode and transpose it to another starting note. Here, for example, are the C and Bb mixolydian modes. Each 2 bar phrase can be played in one horizontal position.

VERTICAL SCALES - SHIFTING

Here are some general guidelines for vertical fingering situations:

1. When you are going up or down a scale on one string and cannot play the next notes without leaving the position you are in, shift the whole hand, including the thumb, so that the 1st finger plays the next note when ascending or the 4th finger when descending. Do not keep going up the string with the 4th finger or down the string with the 1st finger.

2. If a particular ascending passage has only one note above a completed position, play the two lowest notes on the string with the 1st finger so that the highest note is played with the 4th (or 3rd) finger. When descending, play the two highest notes with the 4th (or 3rd) finger. On acoustic bass, this will only happen when there are an odd number of notes (not including the open string) to be played on one string. By shifting at the beginning of the phrase, you will create an even number of notes from there on, which can be played in groups of two.*

3. In general, shift as soon as possible so that you get to the final position on any given string as soon as possible. The final position will generally end with the 1st finger when descending and the 4th or 3rd when ascending.

Exercise 12

Here are various 3 and 4 note pieces of the C major scale played only on the G string, with suggested fingerings underneath (acoustic on the top, electric on the bottom.)

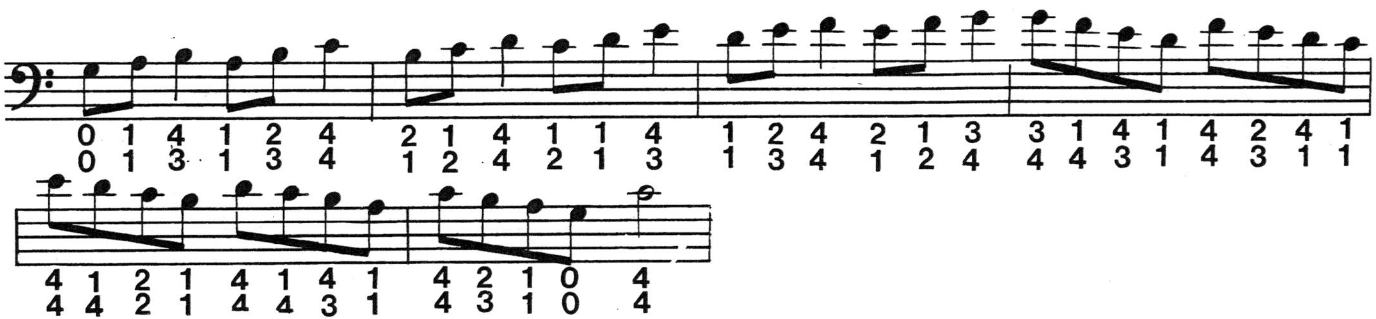

* The main exception on acoustic bass is 3 note phrases that go up a whole step and then up a half step. They are generally fingered 1 2 4. Conversely, when descending a whole step and then a half step, try 4 2 1. On electric bass, four note phrases should be played so that three of them fit into one position, whenever possible, which will sometimes contradict this 2nd guideline.

Exercise 13

Here are different length phrases in C major on 2 of the 4 strings. Try this same idea on the lower strings, too.

a) G String

b) D String

Exercise 14

Once the last two exercises are comfortable, try making some music using mostly one string. Start with going up and down in one key at a time, then try doing it on the changes of a tune. The following example is to be played on the D string unless otherwise indicated underneath the note.

(CONT.)

Try longer pieces, too.

Exercise 15

Use an open string as a pedal tone to act as a tonal center for pieces of
a scale, e.g. a G dorian funk line all on the G string.

Exercise 16

By combining the horizontal and vertical ways of playing the C major scale,
you can get from low G to D on the G string in several ways (acoustic fingerings
are shown on top, electric ones on the bottom):

A)

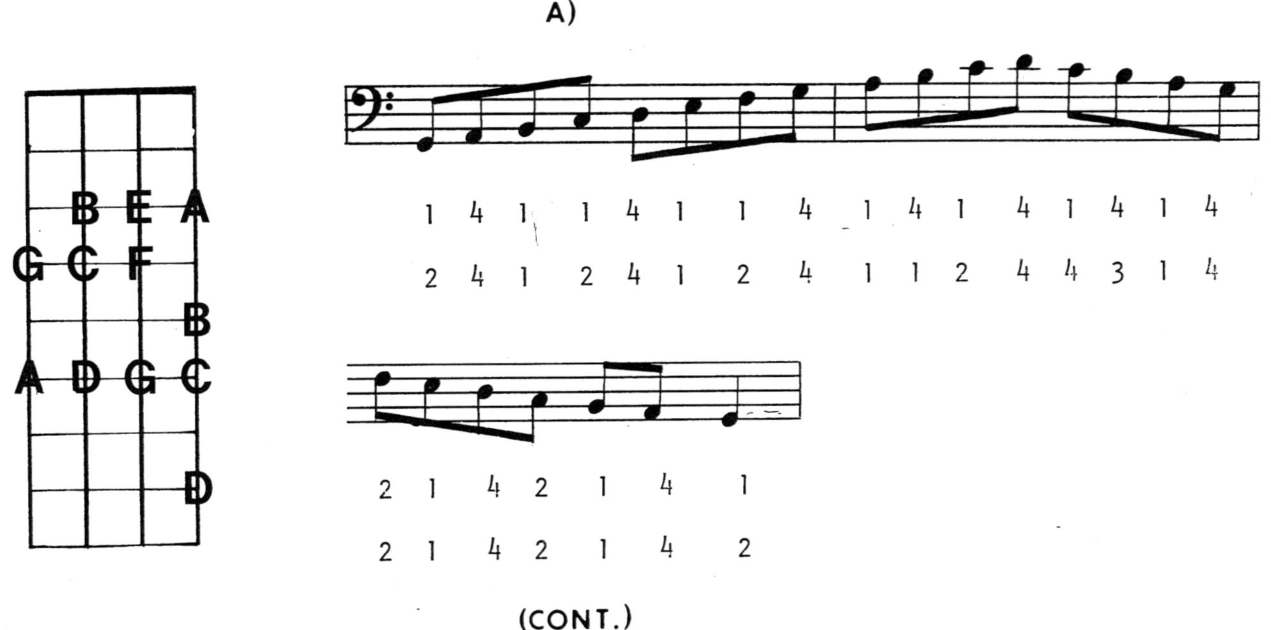

(CONT.)

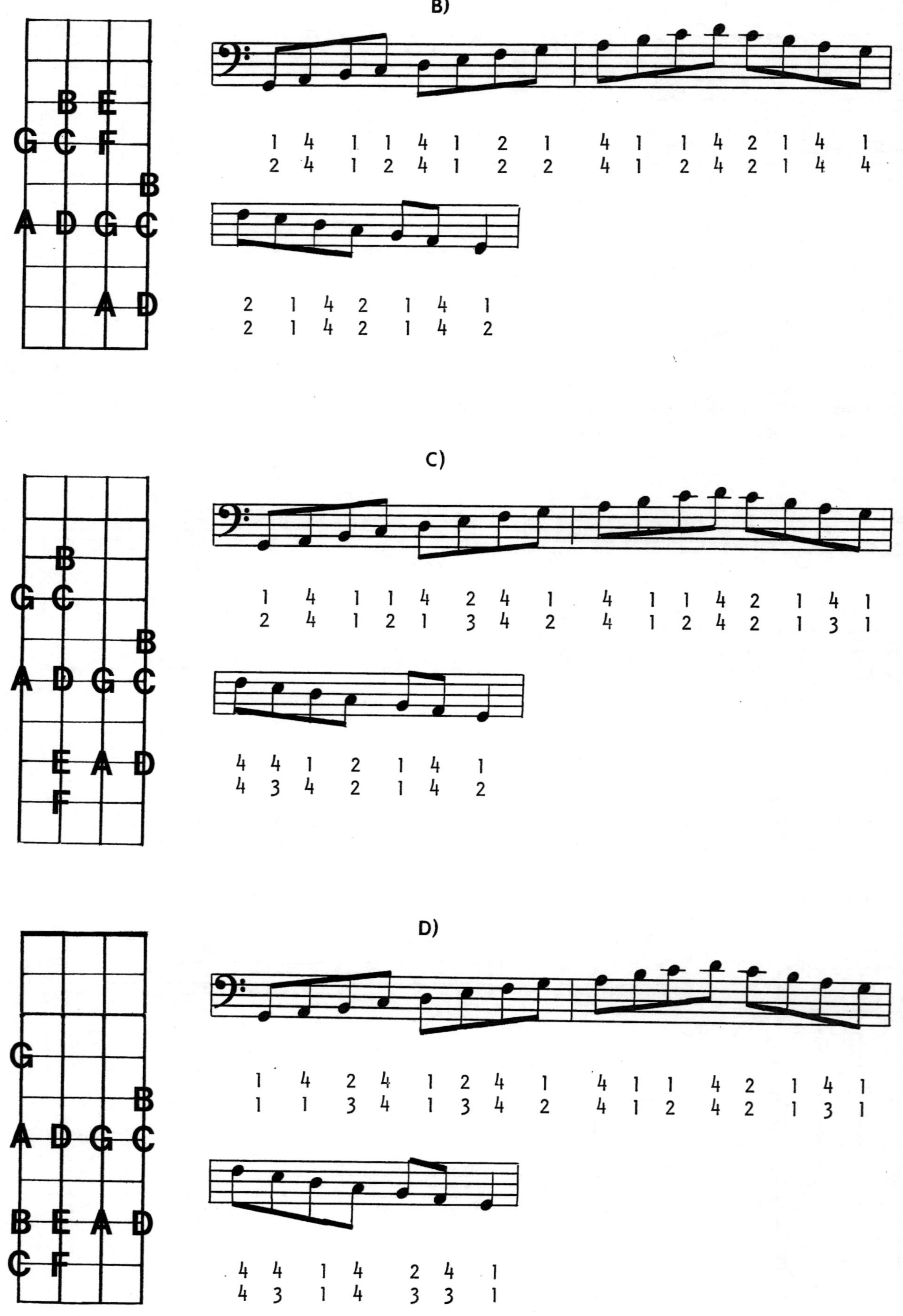
B)
C)
D)

Exercise 17

Use vertical motion (on any string) to combine adjacent horizontal positions into one larger unit, e.g.

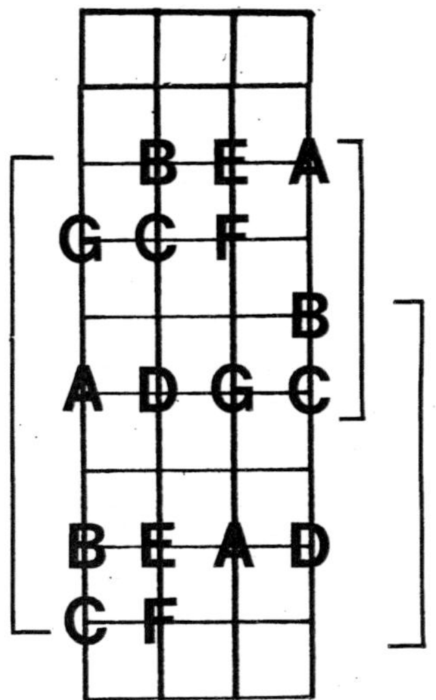

Exercise 18

Besides the horizontal and vertical aspects of this larger position, try connecting the strings to create a diagonal motion, e.g.

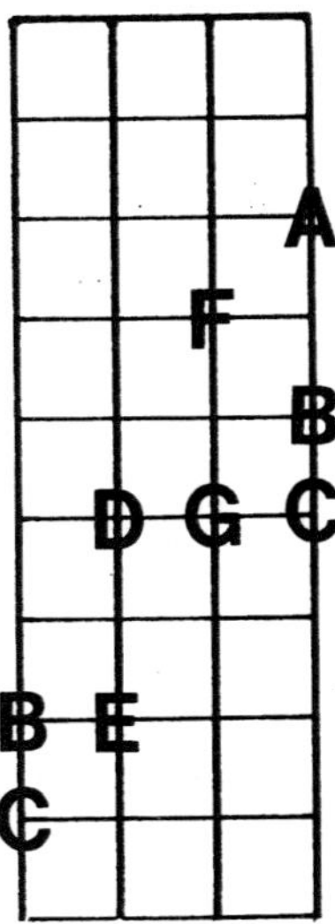

By extending the ideas in these last 3 exercises all over the fingerboard, total facility in a key can be developed.

SCALE FRAGMENTS

Exercise 19

Play pieces of the scale off of each scale degree using the same number of notes for each. Use ascending and descending fragments, e.g. C major.

a) 3 note fragments

b) 4 note fragments

In the exercises in this section, try just thinking of the scale degree you started the fragment on (the circled notes in the above example) and let the rest of the phrase follow automatically. In this way, it will be easier to keep your place in the exercise.

Exercise 20

Play 3 or 4 note fragments but start the fragments on any series of scale
degrees, e.g.

Exercise 21

Try playing different length scale fragments off of one note. Use ascending
or descending fragments, e.g.

Exercise 22

Play scale fragments, any length, ascending, descending, or both, starting on any scale degree, e.g.

Exercise 23

Play scale fragments using both horizontal and vertical ways to play the scale. Try using the strings indicated under the notes in the following phrase.

Exercise 24

Play scale fragments in different keys, e.g.

Exercise 25

a) Play scale fragments using the roots of the chords of a tune as starting
notes, e.g. "Autumn Leaves." In this example, you can use the G natural
minor scale throughout, except for the D7 bar which can take either the
G harmonic or melodic minor scales.

Try using ascending fragments, too.

b) Try this tune using other chord members besides the root as starting notes, e.g.

Most bass lines will, at different points, use both roots and other chord
members on beat 1, so try making up a bass line combining both a) and b).

c) Try the tune using the main melody notes as starting notes for scale fragments. In this next example, every other bar starts with the same note as
the melody the 2nd time through.

SCALAR PATTERNS

Here are some 3 and 4 note patterns in the key of C that are neither chords nor pieces of the scale:

More patterns can be created by the following means:

a) Take each pattern and change the order of notes, e.g.

b) Take each pattern and use repeated notes to lengthen it, e.g.

Try these two ideas on scale fragments, too.

Exercise 26

Take a scalar pattern and play it off of each note in the scale. Use only scale notes to fill out the patterns. Play it ascending and descending, e.g.

(CONT.)

Exercise 27

Play a scalar pattern off of any series of notes in the scale, e.g.

This example uses variations of one pattern.

Exercise 28

Play scalar patterns off of each note in the scale, but instead of changing the intervals in the pattern to conform to the scale, keep the pattern exactly the same each time, e.g.

TWO OCTAVE SCALES

Exercise 29

Shown below are several alternate ways to play two octaves of the major and minor scales on both acoustic and electric bass. The numbers refer to the degrees of the scale. Pick a key (the charts will work for any one) and play it up and down using one of the charts until it is comfortable, then use it as the skeleton for improvising on the scale.

a) MAJOR SCALE (Acoustic Bass)

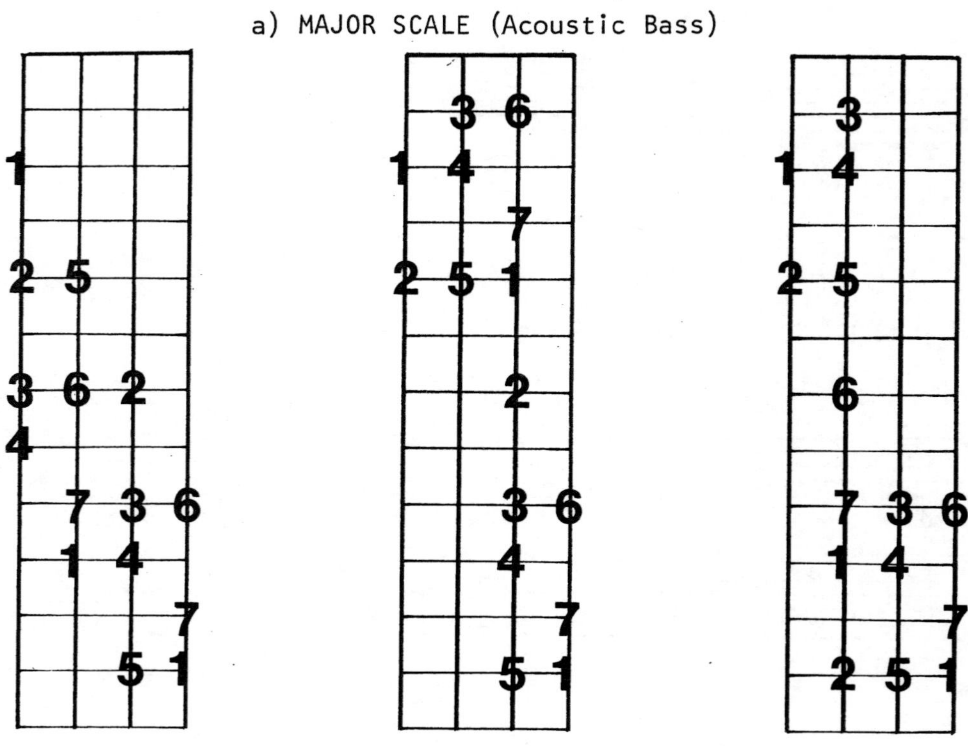

b) MAJOR SCALE (Electric Bass)

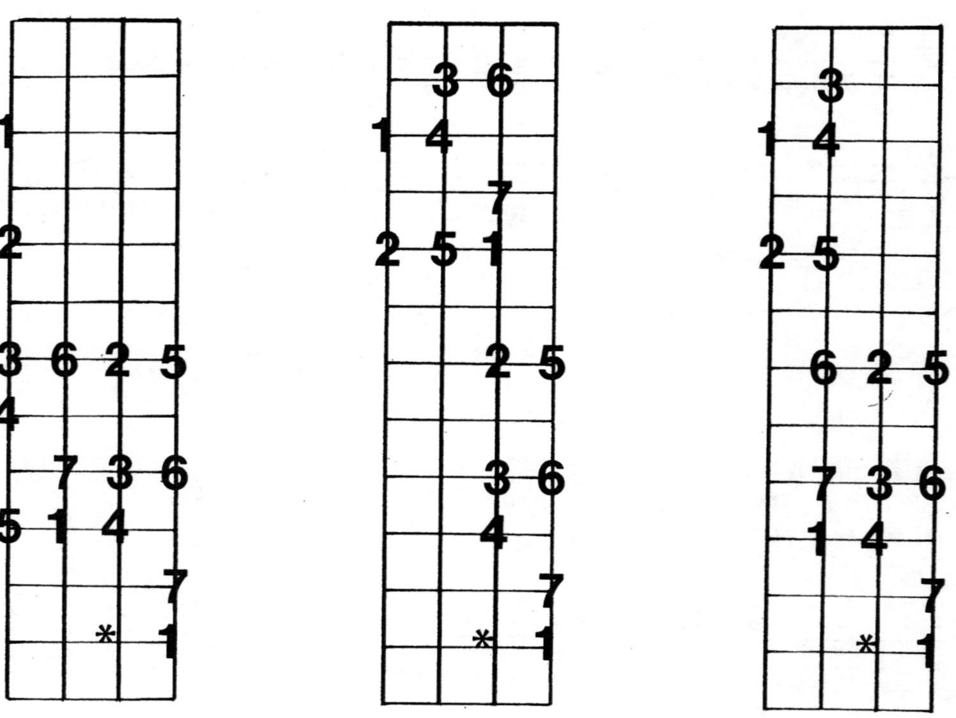

* Play the 5th on the D string when descending

c) MAJOR SCALE (Acoustic or Electric)   d) MINOR SCALE (Acoustic Bass)

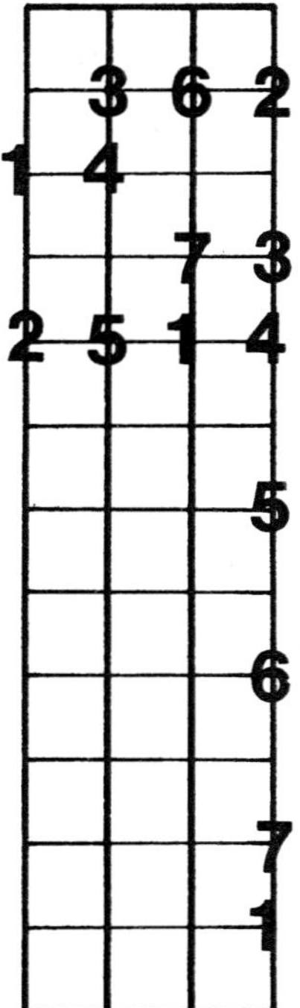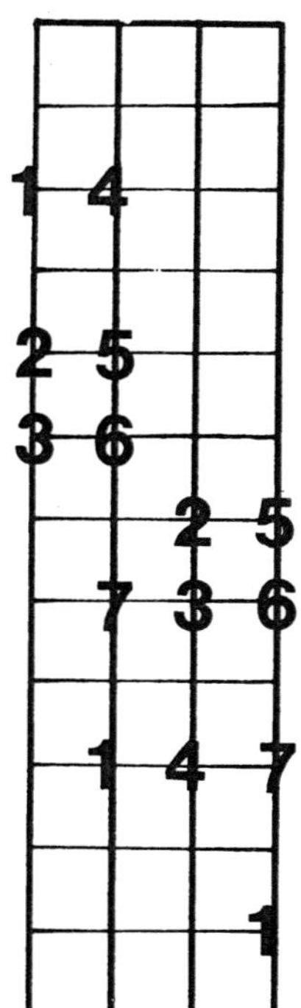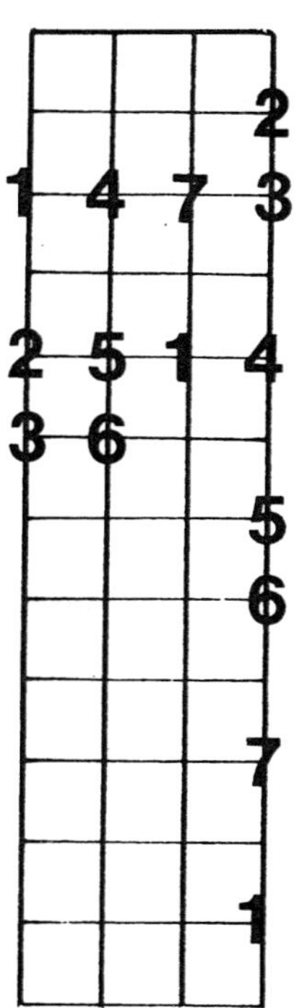

e) MINOR SCALE (Acoustic or Electric)   f) MINOR SCALE (Electric Bass)

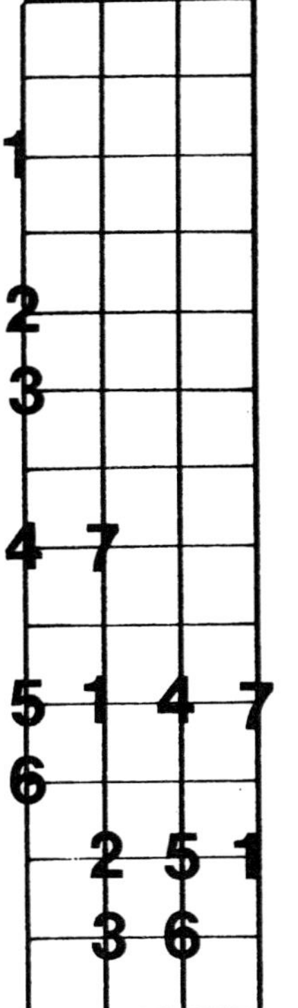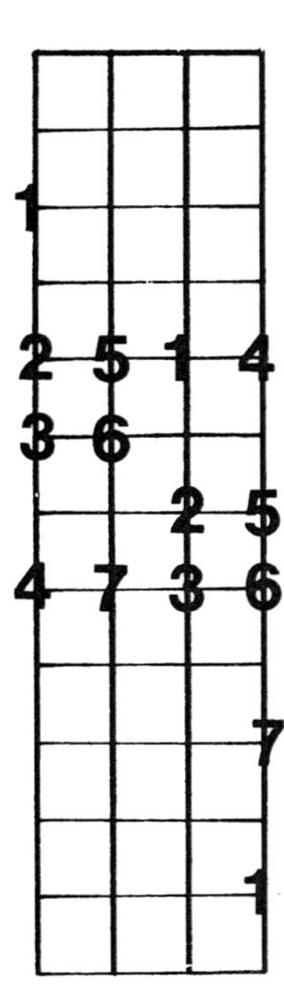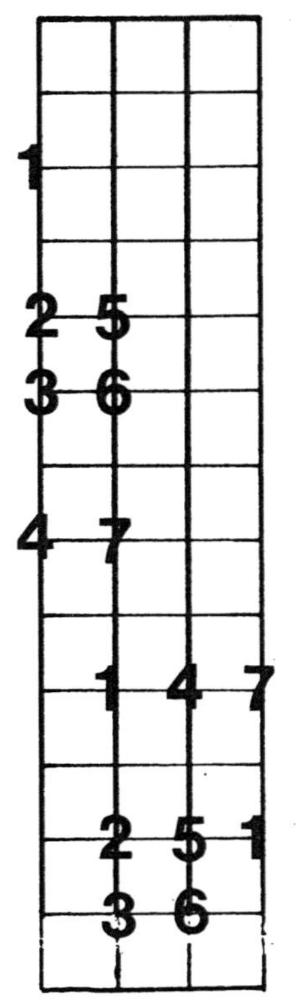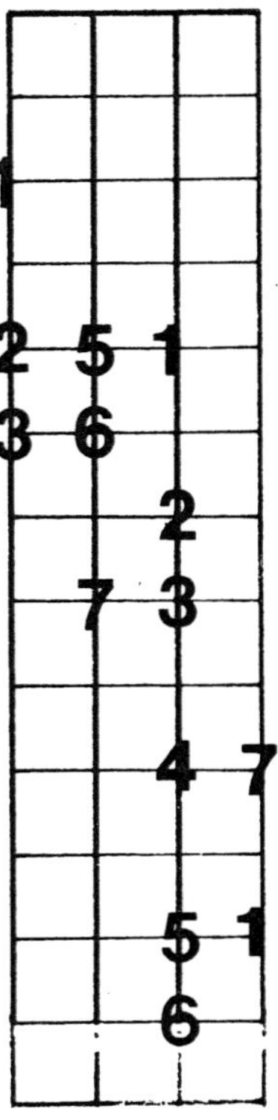

Exercise 30

By flatting the 7th of these major charts or by flatting the 2nd of the minor ones, they will create two octave patterns starting on the 5th of another major or minor scale. These will be useful for the keys of Bb up to E. Here is an example of one major scale (derived from the 1st example in Exercise 29 a), and one minor scale (derived from the 1st example in Exercise 29 f).

a) MAJOR SCALE (Acoustic Bass)

f) MINOR SCALE (Electric Bass)

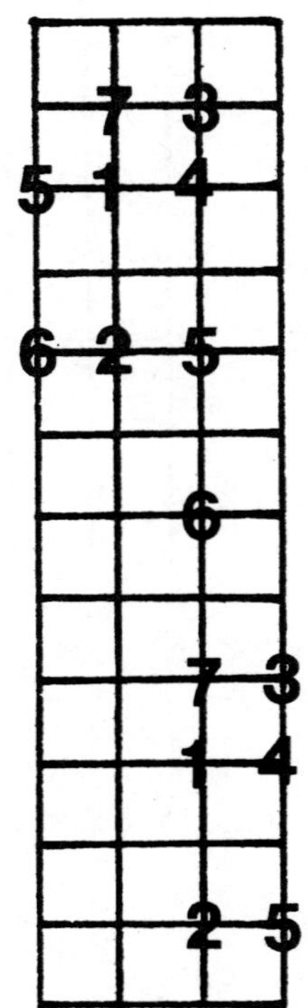

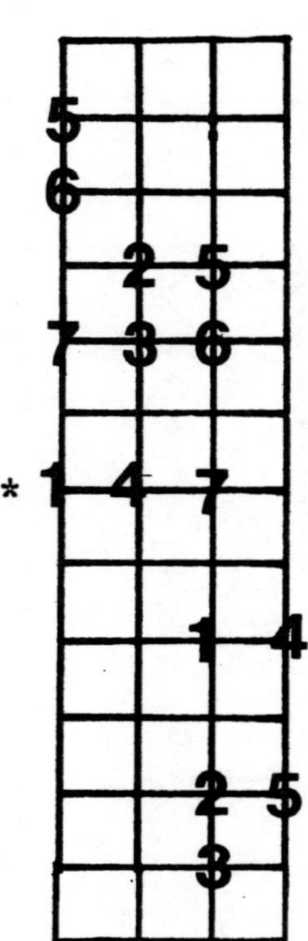

* Play the root on the A string when ascending

NON-DIATONIC SCALES

Exercise 31

Here are some common scales you should learn. Play each one up and down the scale and then make some music using only scale notes.

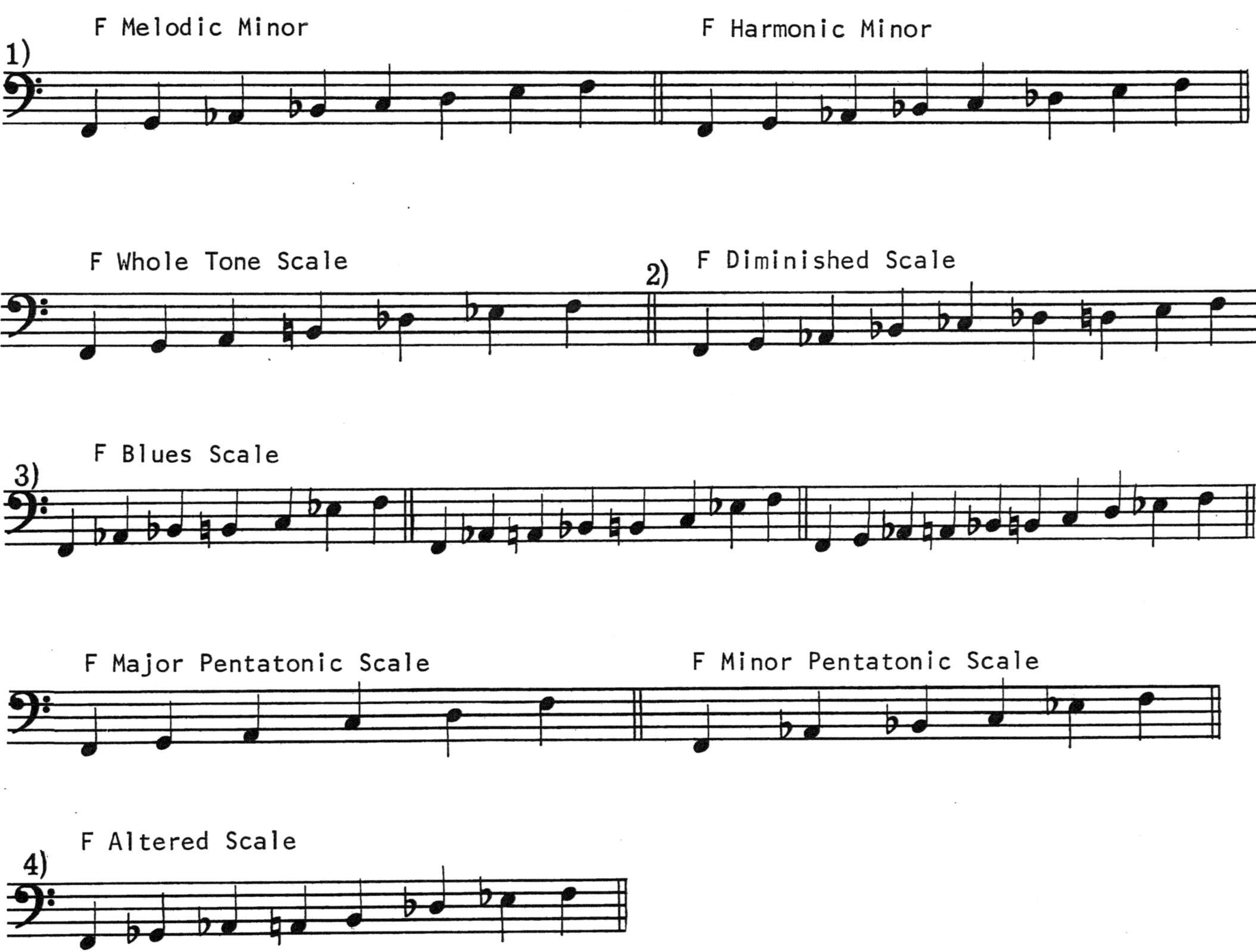

1. Classical theory uses the natural minor scale as the descending version of the melodic minor. In this book, however, melodic minor will mean the scale shown above, both ascending and descending.
2. Notice that the diminished scale alternates whole steps and half steps. If you start with the ½ step 1st, another kind of diminished scale is formed.
3. Several different versions are shown. Play the shortest one first.
4. Also called the diminished/whole tone, Pomeranian, or Super Locrian scale.

Exercise 32

Here are four different types of patterns to use on the whole tone scale. Extend each one all over the bass. There are only 2 different whole tone scales; verify this for yourself.

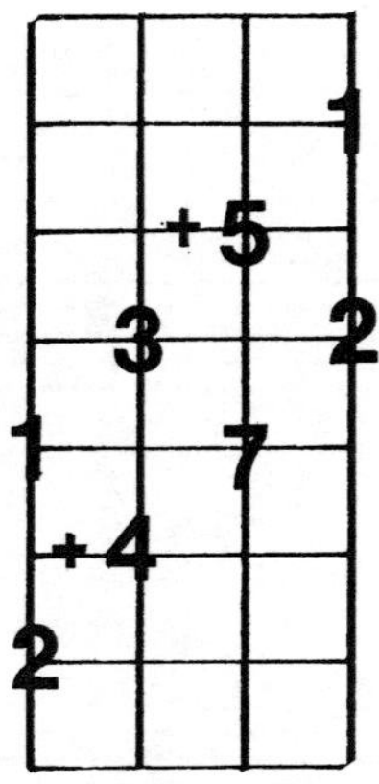
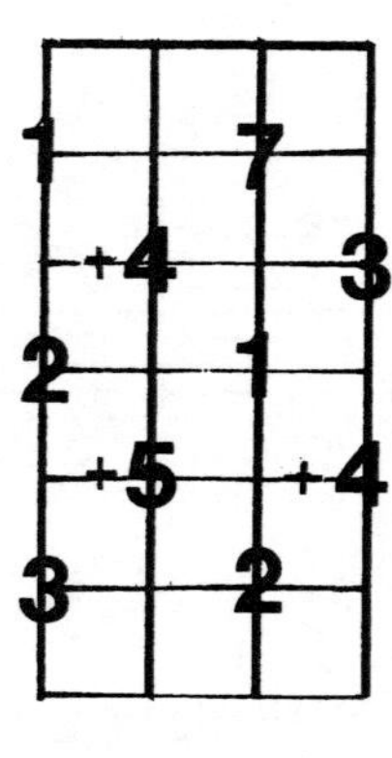
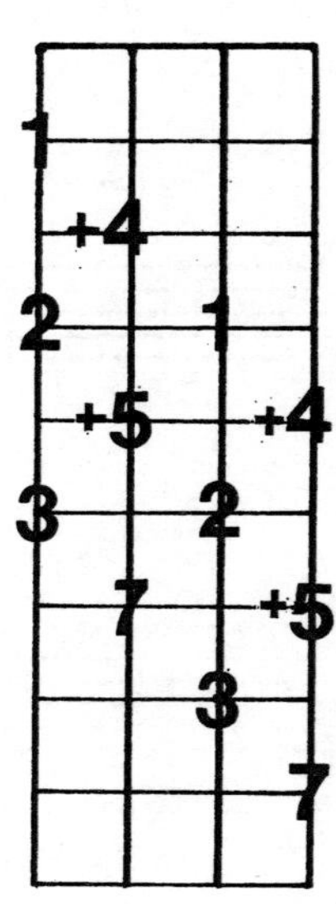
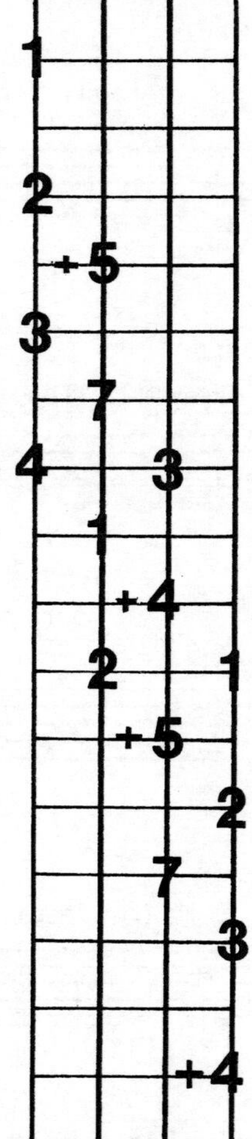

Exercise 33

Here is a fingerboard chart for the melodic minor scale.

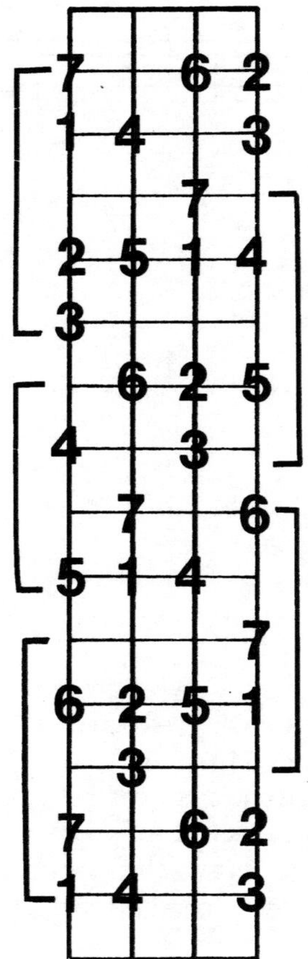

Exercise 34

Here is a fingerboard chart for the diminished scale. Notice that it can be
viewed as whole steps seperated by half steps or visa versa. It can also be seen
as a melodic minor scale with both + and - fifths. Another way to think of this
scale is to see it as being made up of the 1st 4 notes of the minor scale, starting a tritone (b5th) apart, or even minor thirds apart. There are only three
different diminished scales - the others have the same notes as one of those 3,
e.g. C diminished scale equals the Eb, Gb, and A diminished scales. This same
principle applies to diminished chords as well.

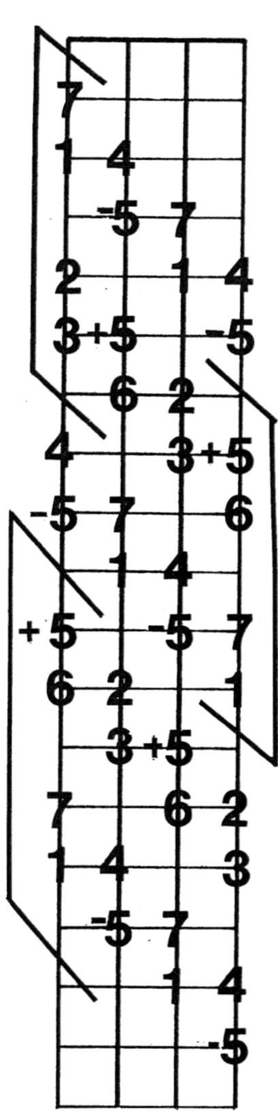

Exercise 35

Here are some unusual scales. Have fun.

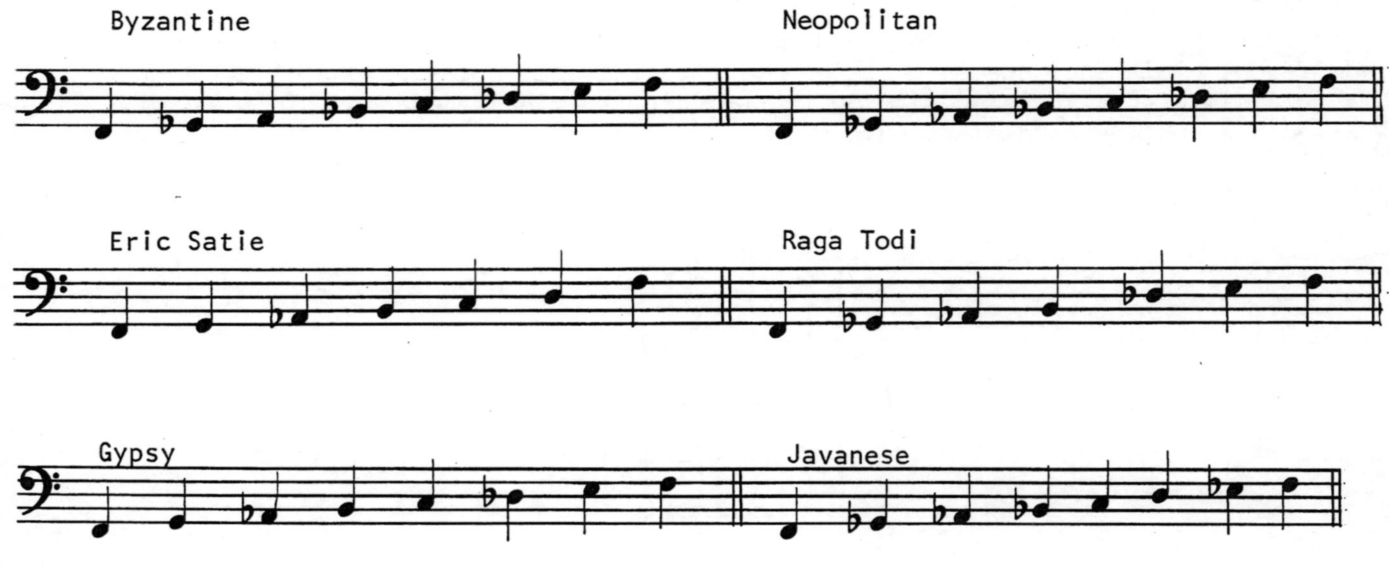

Exercise 36

Other scales can be produced by starting the scales in this section on different notes, just like the church modes were derived from the major scale. Here is the E harmonic minor scale, for example, starting on each note besides E.

ADVANCED SCALE EXERCISES

Note: Some of these exercises are variations of intervals off of scales.
See Chapter 6.

Exercise 37

Play the exercises in this chapter changing scales a) after every phrase or
b) in the middle of a phrase, e.g. C major to Eb major.

Exercise 38

Play scalar exercises using a scale other than major or minor, e.g.

a) Scalar patterns off of the chromatic scale, e.g.

b) Seconds off of the diminished scale, e.g.

c) Scale fragments off of the minor pentatonic scale, e.g.

d) Thirds off of the Byzantine scale, e.g.

Exercise 39

Use the scales derived from the chords of a tune (see Chapter 9) to practice your scalar rudiments. For example, here are different permutations of the 1235 scalar pattern on John Coltrane's tune, "Moment's Notice."

Exercise 40

Practice these exercises using different rhythms, e.g. fifths on C minor.

Exercise 41

Use repeated notes to vary an exercise, e.g. thirds in C major.

Exercise 42

Use the chromatic scale to embellish diatonic scale playing, e.g. C minor.

Exercise 43

Use various scalar rudiments to create a bass line on a tune, e.g. "Minority".

Exercise 44

Here are the main harmonics on the G string. They can be played starting from the 12th fret going up towards the bridge or back towards the nut. Play the corresponding ones on the other strings as well.

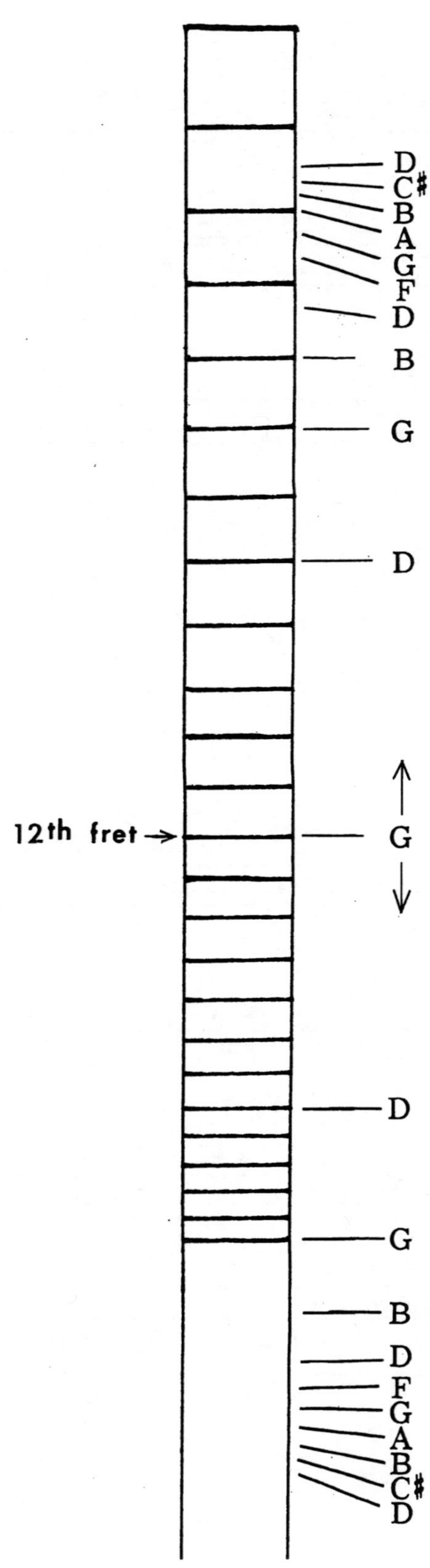

Exercise 45

If we take the harmonics on the G string and reduce them down to a scale, we get the following one:

G Mixolydian (#4)

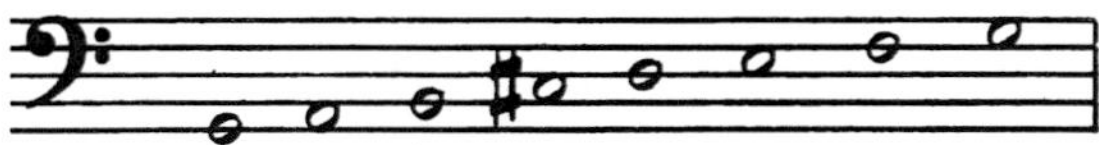

Here are some other scales with the same notes as G Mixolydian (#4), that are created by starting the scale on other notes besides G. All these scales will fit the fingerboard chart for the melodic minor scale shown earlier.

D Melodic Minor   C# Altered Scale

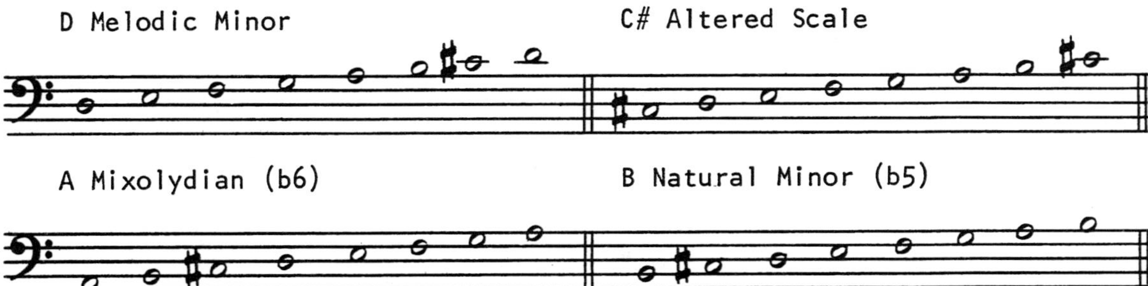

A Mixolydian (b6)   B Natural Minor (b5)

Notice that an altered scale can be thought of as the melodic minor scale whose tonic is a half step up from the tonic of the altered scale. So on a C# altered 7th chord, try thinking of the corresponding scale as D melodic minor.

Exercise 46

Here is the D major scale played using only harmonics (except for the low F#). The high C is actually between a C and a C#. The numbers refer to the order of notes of the first octave of an ascending D major scale.

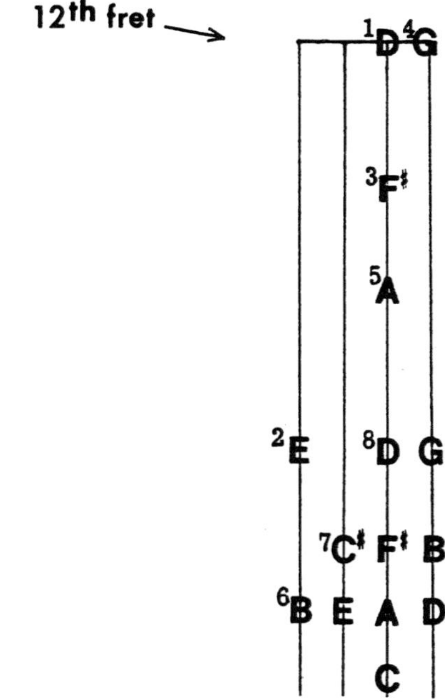

Chapter 4 — CHORD STUDIES

CREATING CHORDS

Chords are generally created by playing every other note of a scale, e.g.

When a tune uses one of these chords, the corresponding scale is generally used (see the beginning of chapter 10, too). When more than one scale is possible, the surrounding chords will determine what scale to use (see the beginning of Chapter 9 for a complete discussion of this).

Next is a chart of most of the chords used in improvised music and their most common extentions and alterations.

Chord Name	Symbol	Spelling	Common Extentions and Alterations
C Major (triad)	C maj. C		C6 C (add 9) C 6/9 C (add 11)
C Major 7th	C maj.7 C Δ		C maj.9 C Δ (#11) C Δ (b5) C Δ (+5)
C Minor (triad)	C min. C-		C-6 C-9 C- 6/9
C Minor 7th	C min. 7 C-7 Cm7		C-7,9 C-7,11
C Minor (Maj.7)	C≜		C Δ ,9
C Dominant 7th	C7		C7(-9) C9 C7(+9) C7(b5) C7(+5) C 13
C Suspended 7th	C sus.		
C Augmented	C +		C Δ (+5) C+7
C Half-Diminished	CØ C-7(b5)		CØ9
C Diminished	C�o		C�o (Δ)
Polychords	(Example) A / C		

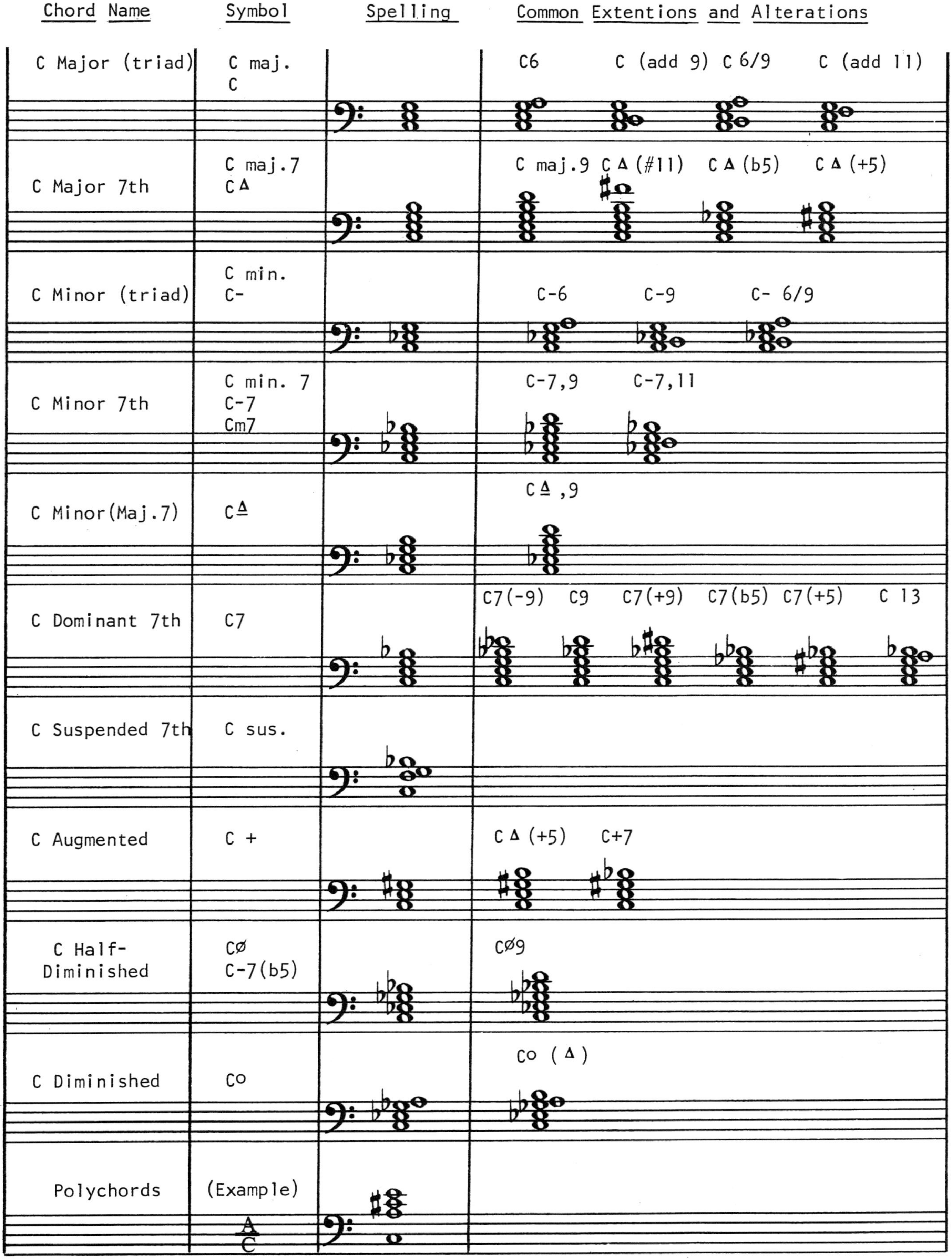

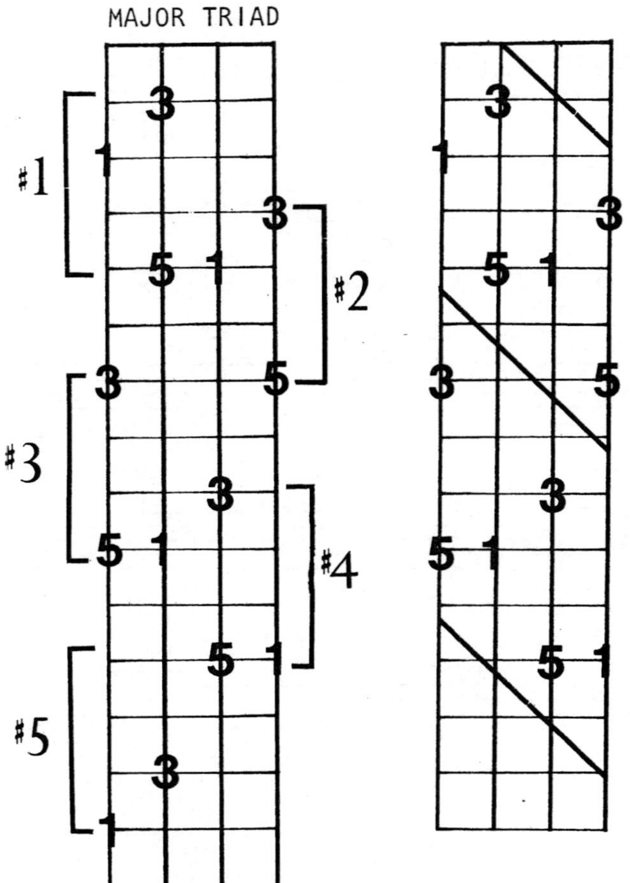

Here are fingerboard charts that show both horizontal and diagonal positions of the major triad. The numbers on the strings refer to the scale degrees of the notes making up the chord. These positions will be the same for any major triad, the only difference being which one occurs at the top of the fingerboard. The horizontal fingerboard charts for major, minor and dominant chords are derived from the corresponding scale diagrams. Verify this for yourself.

Note: To get an overview of all the notes of a chord on the fingerboard, find the two diagonal positions, then add the lower one up an octave. This will divide the fingerboard into low, middle, and high registers - very useful.

Exercise 1

Pick a chord and find which position occurs at the top of the fingerboard and the other positions will follow in sequence. The lowest position on some chords will be a variation of one of the positions (due to the open strings being used) but after that the regular positions will occur, e.g. A Major triad.

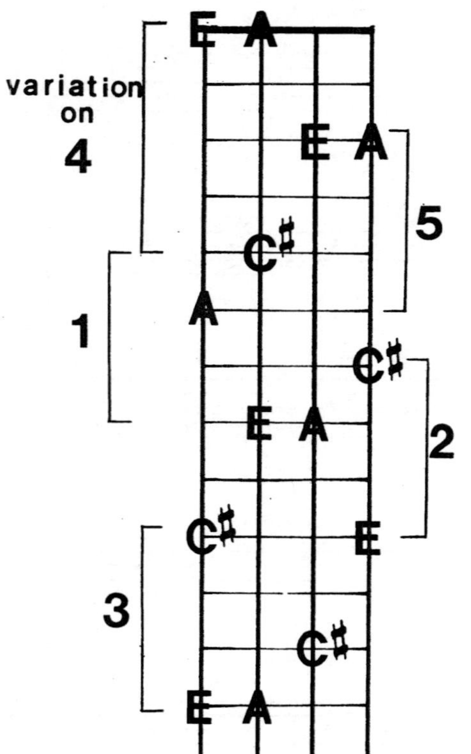

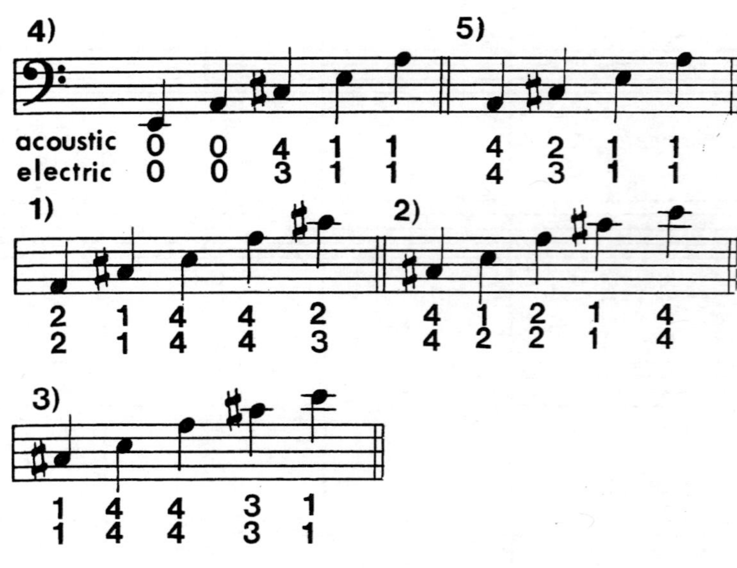

Here are some more chord types:

MAJOR 7TH   MAJOR 6/9

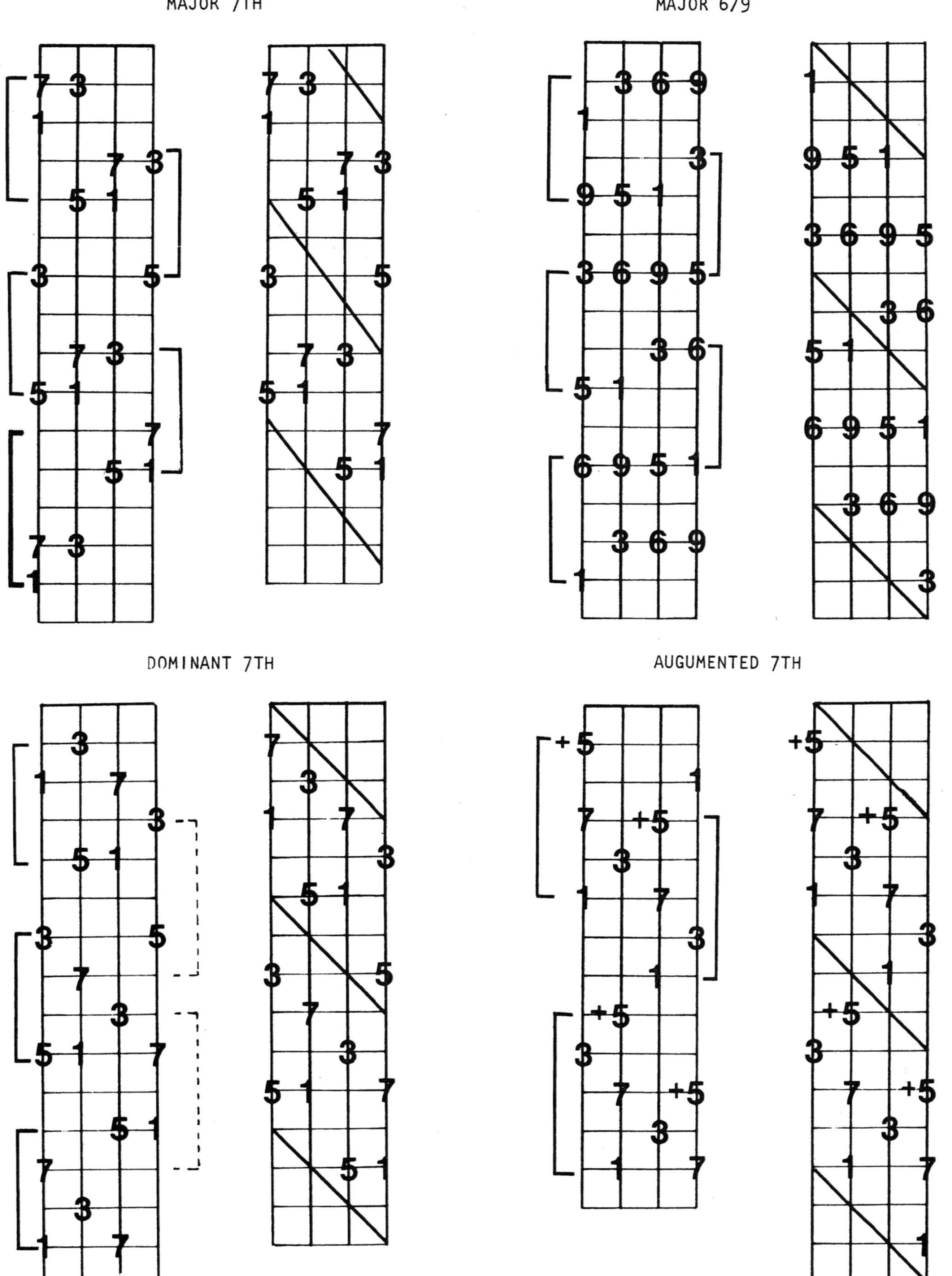

DOMINANT 7TH   AUGUMENTED 7TH

SUSPENDED 7TH

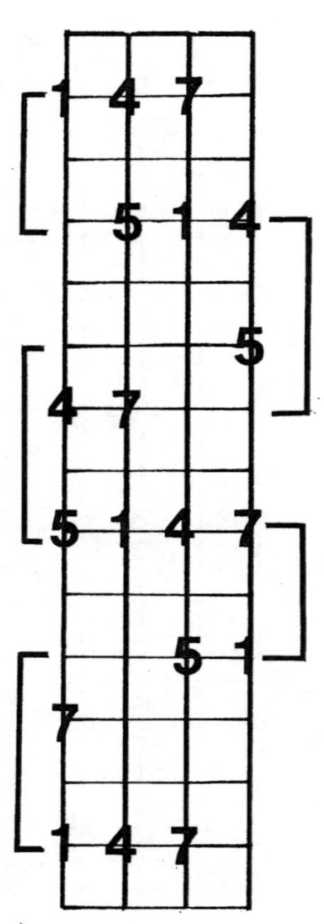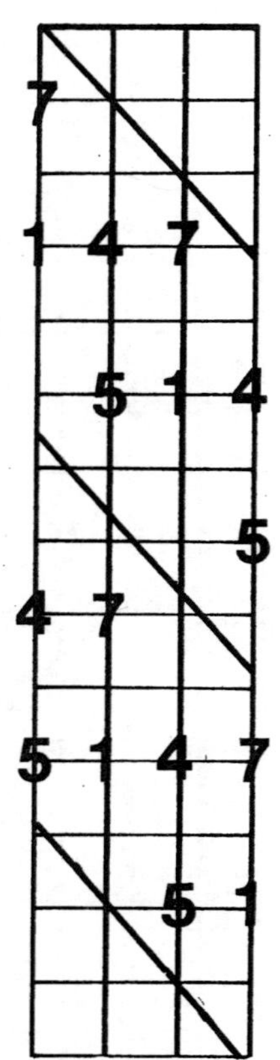

MINOR TRIAD

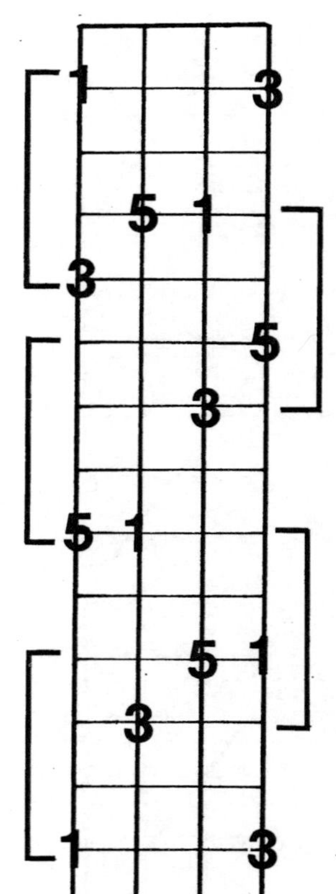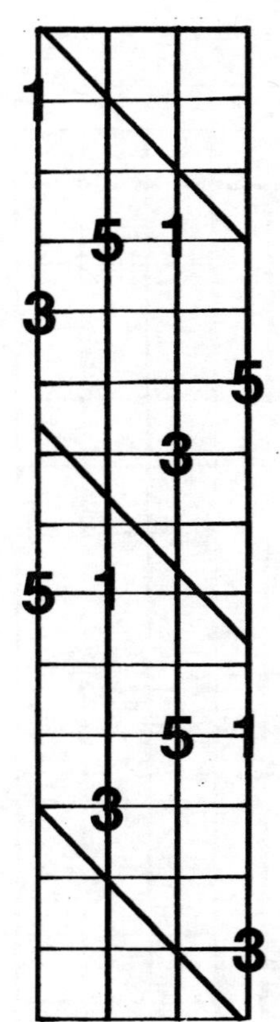

MINOR 7TH

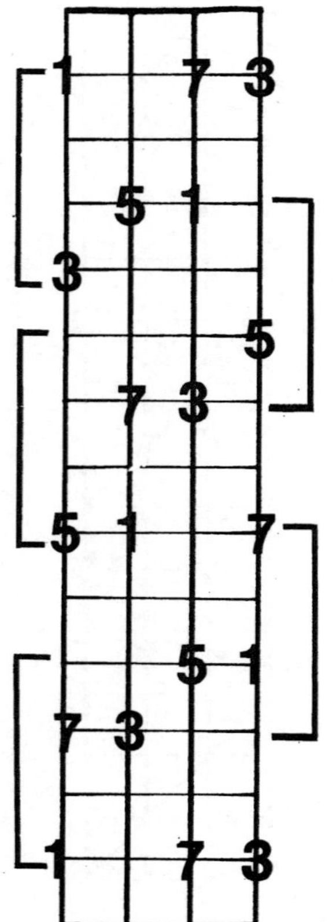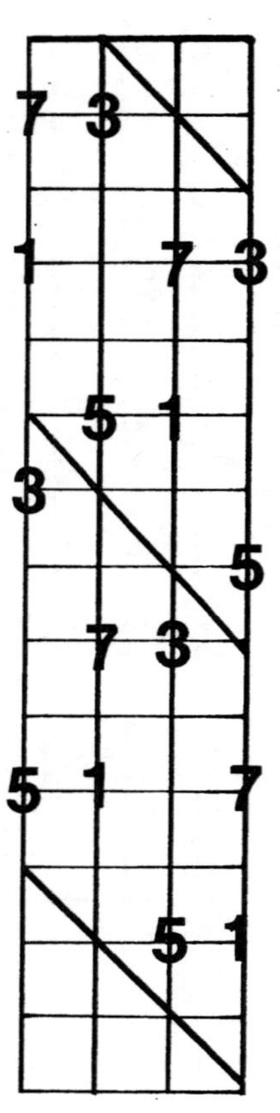

HALF-DIMINISHED

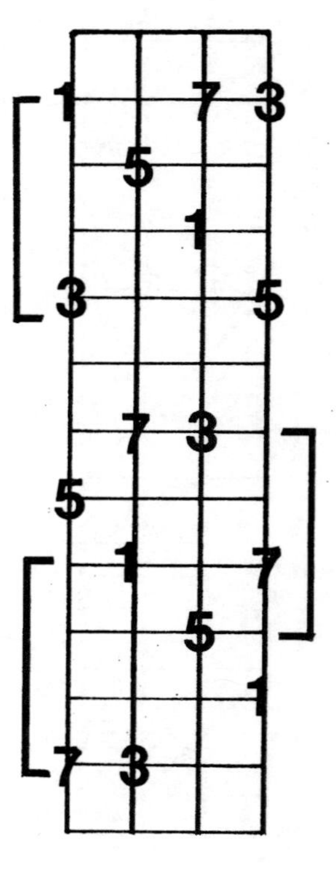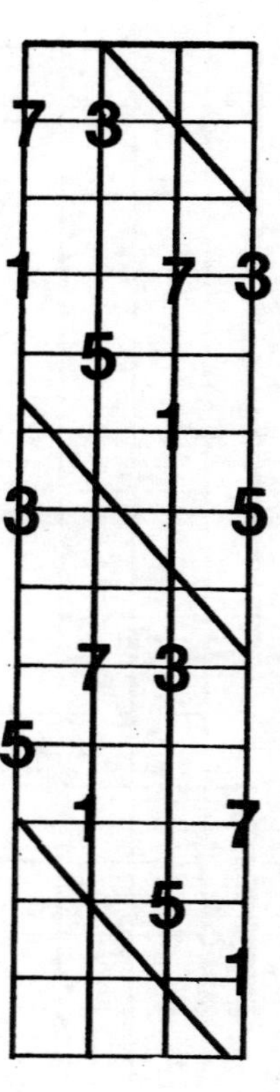

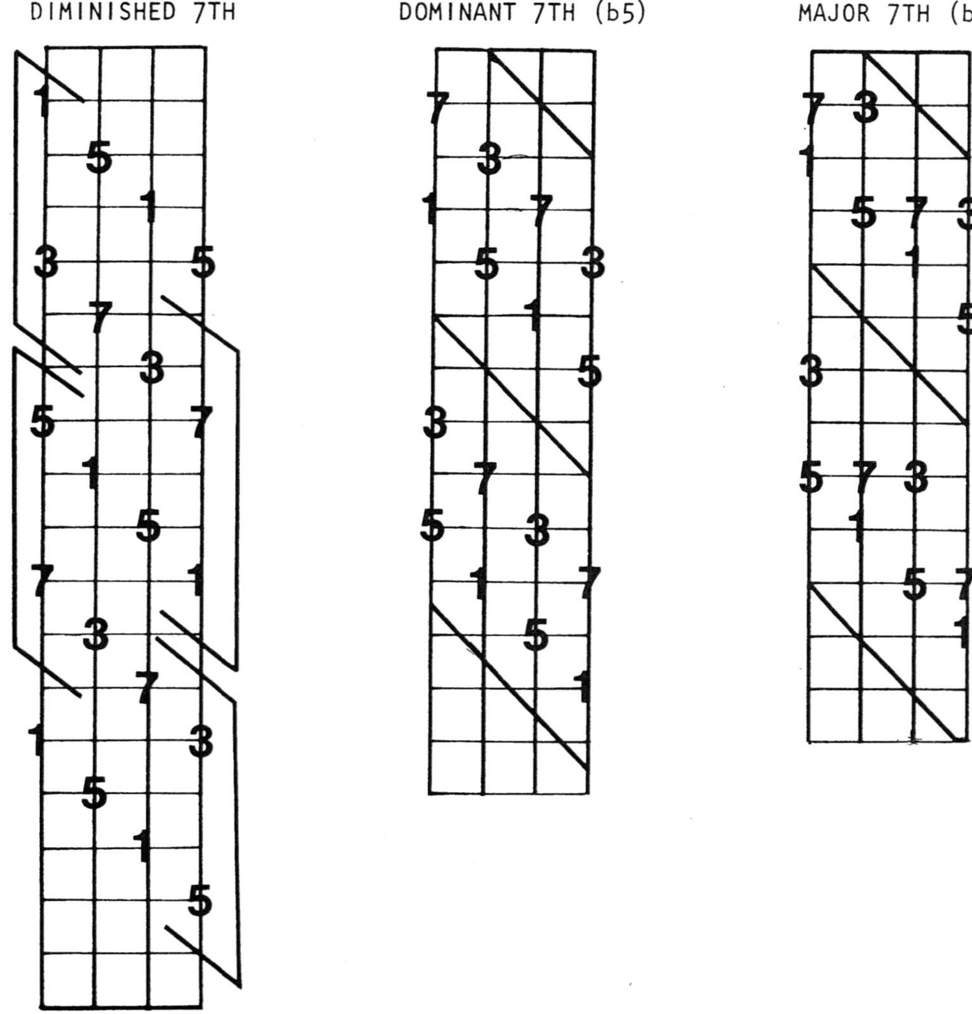

Exercise 2

Pick a particular chord, make a fingerboard chart for it and practice it one position at a time (both horizontal and diagonal).

Exercise 3

After that feels comfortable, try combining two adjacent positions. Play until the two positions become one functional unit. For fingering purposes, however, make sure you are always in one position or the other, e.g. G major 7.

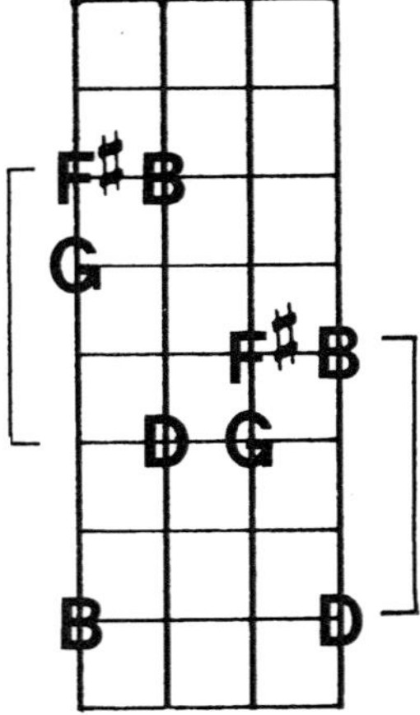

By doing this for each pair of positions, the whole fingerboard will become available to you on a given chord.

Exercise 4

Take one position of a chord and transpose that position to other chords,
e.g. here is the lowest C major 7th chord position transposed up whole steps.

Do this on lots of different starting notes until the configuration of each
position is clear to you.

Exercise 5

Use a two or four chord sequence repeated over and over (a vamp). Stay
in closely related horizontal or diagonal positions, e.g.

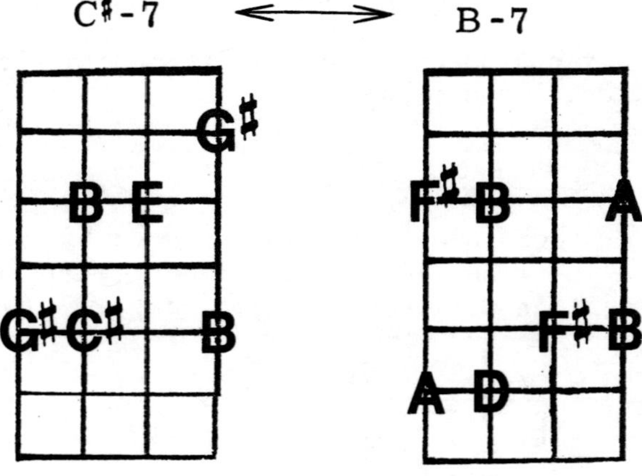

INVERSIONS

If you play the notes of an arpeggio where the lowest note is a note other than the root, you create different inversions of the chord. Here they are for C major 7th.

Exercise 6

Play horizontal or diagonal arpeggios one inversion at a time, e.g the lowest diagonal position for C major 7th.

Exercise 7

Play the inversions of two octave arpeggios, e.g. G7.

Exercise 8

Try playing the inversions in a non-linear fashion, e.g. C major 7th

Exercise 9

Try transposing one inversion to different starting notes:

a) Here are ascending and descending root position major 7th chords.

b) Here is the 2nd inversion of 4 different quality chords. This should be transposed to lots of different chords until the feeling of each inversion is clear to you.

Exercise 10

Play the arpeggios of the chord changes of a tune. Use one inversion (any one) per chord to create a basic walking line. Stay in one horizontal position, more or less, e.g.

CHORD PROGRESSIONS

Exercise 11

Take one kind of chord and start it on several different notes. For example, play the dominant 7th chords starting on C,F, and G. In the following sequence, they create the basic 12 bar blues progression.

Experiment with repeated notes, leaving out notes, changing the order of notes, different rhythms, etc. on this basic progression.

Exercise 12

Take one kind of chord and move it through the following chord progressions:

a) Up and down by half steps   b) Up and down by whole steps

c) Up and down by minor thirds   d) Through the cycle of 5ths

Notice that there are two different sequences using whole step movement and three different ones using minor third movements.

Play these as quarter note arpeggios first and then try changing the order of notes, repeating notes, changing the rhythms, etc. in order to give this exercise some life.

a) Here is one way to move minor 7th chords chromatically:

b) Here is one example of how to move major triads by whole steps:

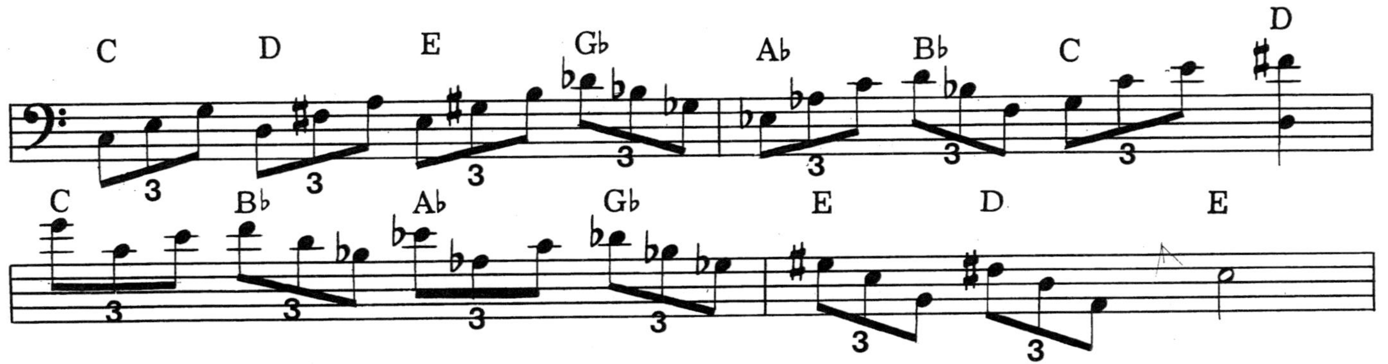

c) Here are dominant 7th chords moved by minor thirds:

d) Here are dominant 7th chords moved along the cycle of fifths:

Exercise 13

Play one inversion of each of the following chords in these chord progressions which utilize the cycle of fifths. Transpose the first three to
other keys as well. Try substituting a minor chord for the major 7th chord
in the 4th and 5th examples. Try starting the other ones up a half step.

(CONT.)

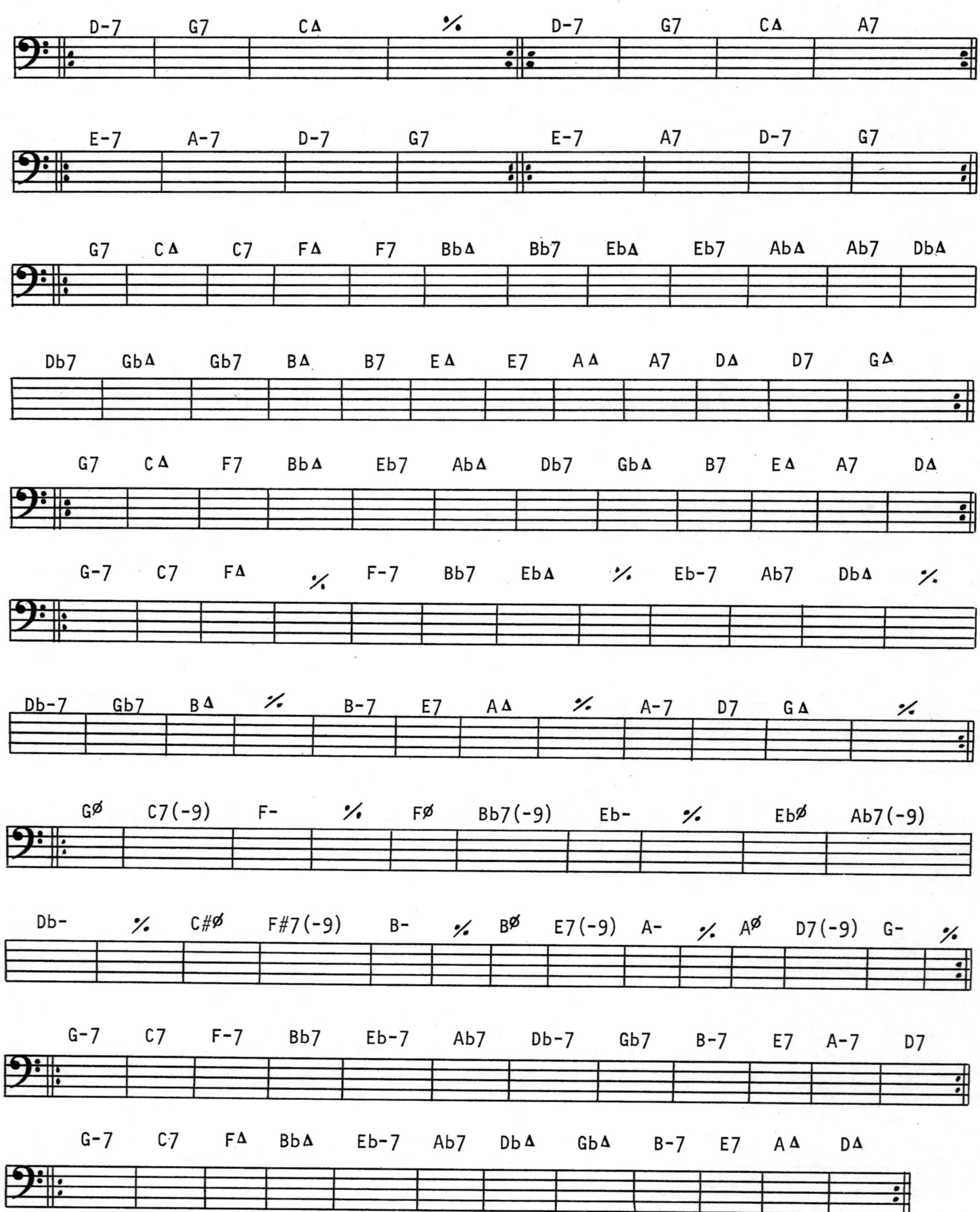

D-7 G7 C△ % D-7 G7 C△ A7
E-7 A-7 D-7 G7 E-7 A7 D-7 G7
G7 C△ C7 F△ F7 Bb△ Bb7 Eb△ Eb7 Ab△ Ab7 Db△
Db7 Gb△ Gb7 B△ B7 E△ E7 A△ A7 D△ D7 G△
G7 C△ F7 Bb△ Eb7 Ab△ Db7 Gb△ B7 E△ A7 D△
G-7 C7 F△ % F-7 Bb7 Eb△ % Eb-7 Ab7 Db△ %
Db-7 Gb7 B△ % B-7 E7 A△ % A-7 D7 G△ %
G∅ C7(-9) F- % F∅ Bb7(-9) Eb- % Eb∅ Ab7(-9)
Db- % C#∅ F#7(-9) B- % B∅ E7(-9) A- % A∅ D7(-9) G- %
G-7 C7 F-7 Bb7 Eb-7 Ab7 Db-7 Gb7 B-7 E7 A-7 D7
G-7 C7 F△ Bb△ Eb-7 Ab7 Db△ Gb△ B-7 E7 A△ D△

Exercise 14

Play triads in the following sequence. Notice that only one note changes per bar.

Exercise 15

Play the following sequence (the cycle of 3rds). This will continue to alternate major and minor thirds until, after all 12 of each have been played, you end up at the starting chord again. Little pieces of this, backwards or forwards, can be used to extend the sound of a chord.

SCALE CHORDS

Exercise 16

If you play every other note of a scale starting on each scale degree, you get the scale chords of that key. Notice that in a major key, the I and IV chords are major 7ths, the II, III, and VI chords are minor 7ths, the V chord is a dominant 7th, and the VII chord is half-diminished, e.g. F major.

Make up your own variations.

These are also the scale chords for the D minor scale, except that in the minor case, the A7 chord is often used instead of the Am7, in order to create a stronger dominant to tonic relationship, e.g.

Notice that in a minor key, the I and IV chords are minor 7ths, the III and VI chords are major 7ths, and the VII and often the V chords are dominant.

When a tune or a section of a tune contains nothing but scale chords of a particular key, it is said to be in that key, and the parent scale is used throughout. In fact, when a V7 to I major 7, IIm7 to V7 to I major 7, or even just a IIm7 V7 progression occurs, the I major key has been established (at least for the duration of those chords), since no other key would contain them as scale chords. (See chapter 9 for a more detailed discussion of this.) Thus a through understanding of scale chords is essential to understanding how to play on tunes.

Exercise 17

Take each pair of chords in Exercise 16 and play them using the closest horizontal or diagonal positions possible, e.g.

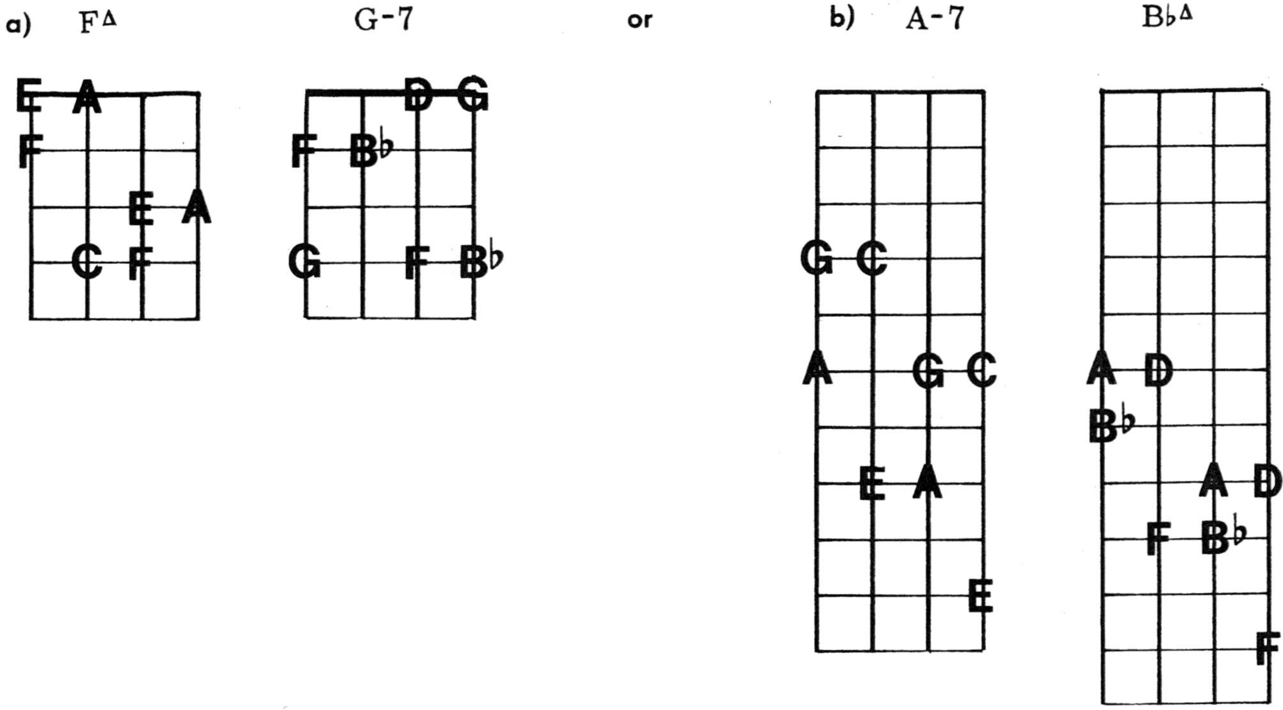

Try transfering this idea to other positions for each pair of chords.

Exercise 18

Try playing all the scale chords in one position, e.g. the lowest position of F major.

Exercise 19

Play the scale chords in the key of C in the following order which utilizes
the cycle of fifths. Many tunes make liberal use of pieces of this progression,
so take any 2,3, or 4 chord sequence from this progression and play it as a
vamp.

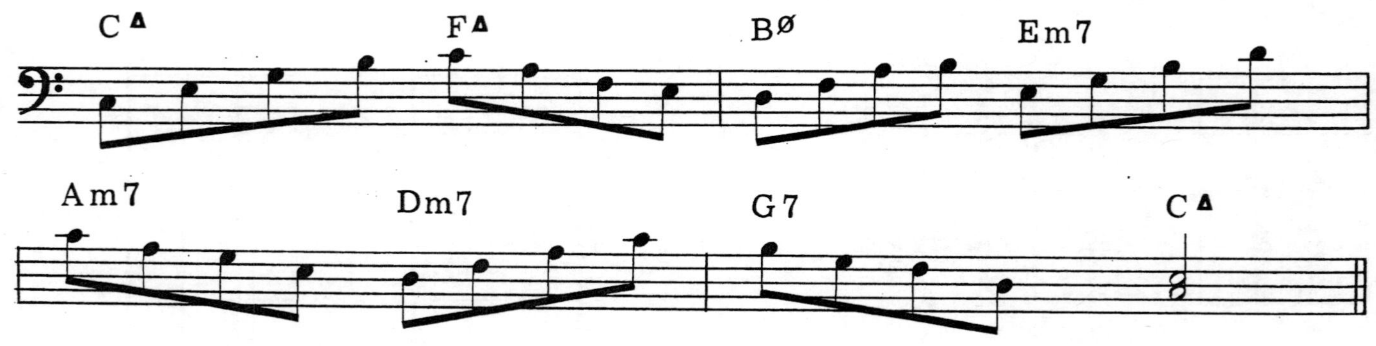

Exercise 20

Here are some variations on running the chords inherent in the C major
scale. There are, of course, many others.

a) Root position triads

b) Root position 7th chords

c) Other inversions

d) Using connecting scale tones

Exercise 21

Take the basic pattern from one of the examples in Exercise 20 and use it to build improvised phrases off of. In this next example, the notes marked with a circle above them are to be played as harmonics, which will make them sound an octave and a 5th above the written note. Let them ring.

ARPEGGIO VARIATIONS

Exercise 22

Play the following studies as written first, then make some music using the basic pattern of each. These basic patterns should also be transposed to other keys until transposing them is easy to do.

a) Using broken chords

b) Using repeated notes

(CONT.)

c) Using 2nds and 3rds

d) Using 4ths and 5ths

e) Using larger intervals

Exercise 23

Try adding an extra note to the arpeggio. See the chart at the beginning
of this chapter for the most commonly used ones, e.g.

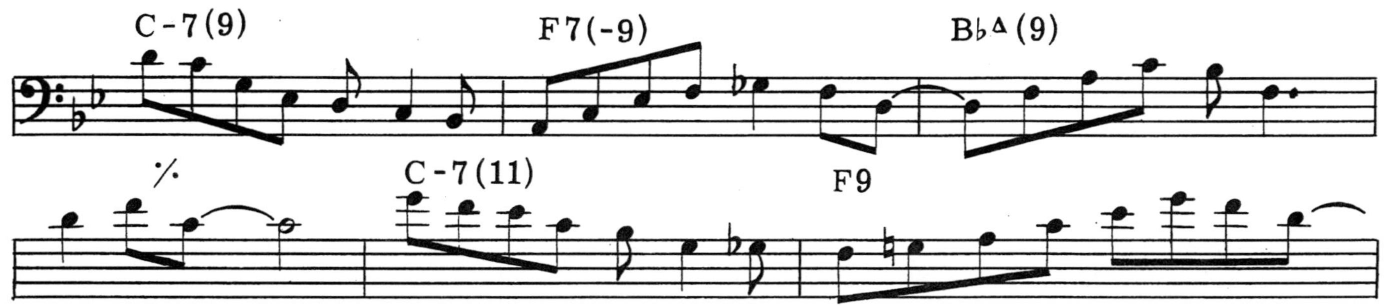

Exercise 24

Try adding scalar neighboring tones to the notes of an arpeggio, e.g.

Exercise 25

Think of the chord, but play scale fragments starting on chord tones, e.g.

Exercise 26

Try adding chromatic neighboring tones to the notes of an arpeggio, e.g.

Exercise 27

Try adding both chromatic and scalar neighboring tones as embellishments of chord notes, e.g.

Exercise 28

Take one way to play an arpeggio and use it on each chord of a two or four chord vamp. This example uses 4ths and 5ths (or b5ths) on each chord.

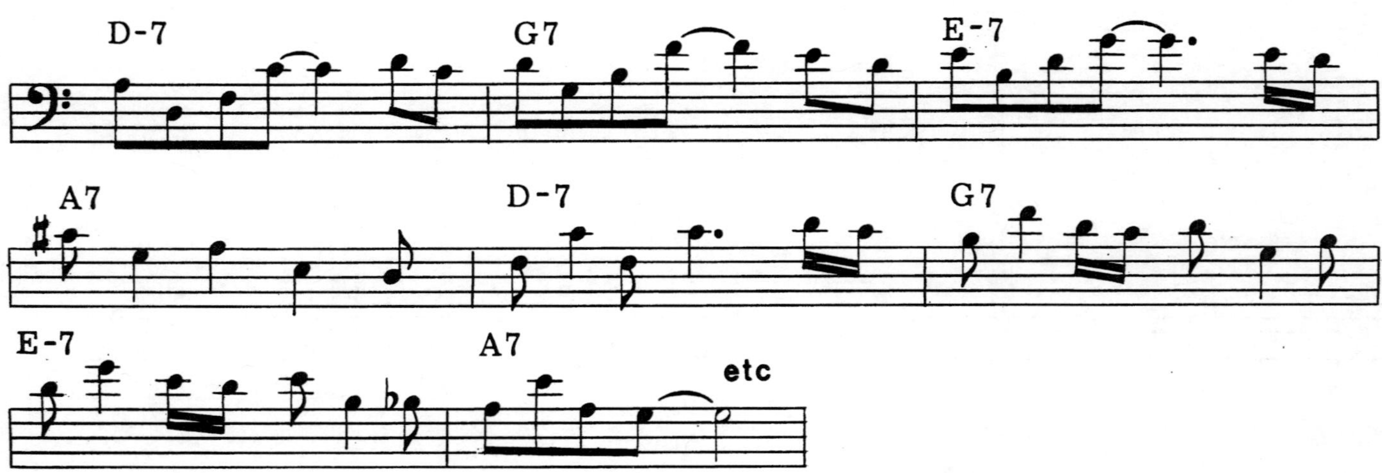

Exercise 29

Playing only chord notes, make up an improvised line on a tune, e.g.
"Blue Bossa."

TWO AND THREE OCTAVE ARPEGGIOS

Exercise 30

Here are several ways to play two octaves of several types of chords. The major 7th chord charts will also work for dominant 7th chords by just flatting the 7th. The minor 7th chord charts will work for half-diminished chords by flatting the 5th.

a) MAJOR 7th (Acoustic or Electric)   b) MINOR 7th (Acoustic or Electric)

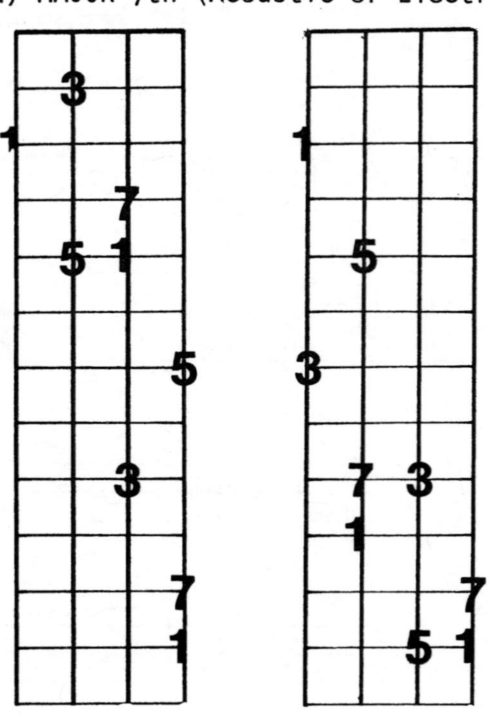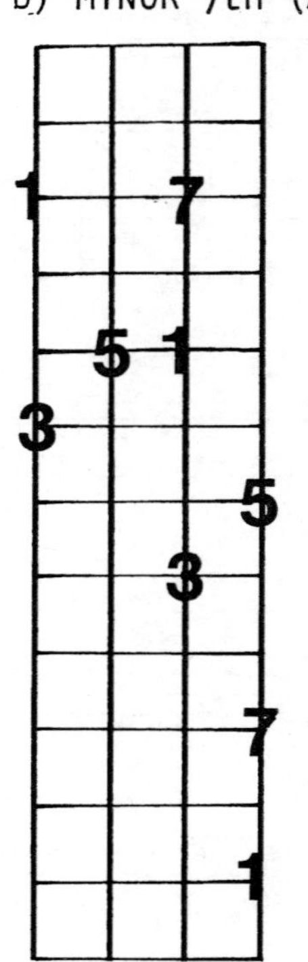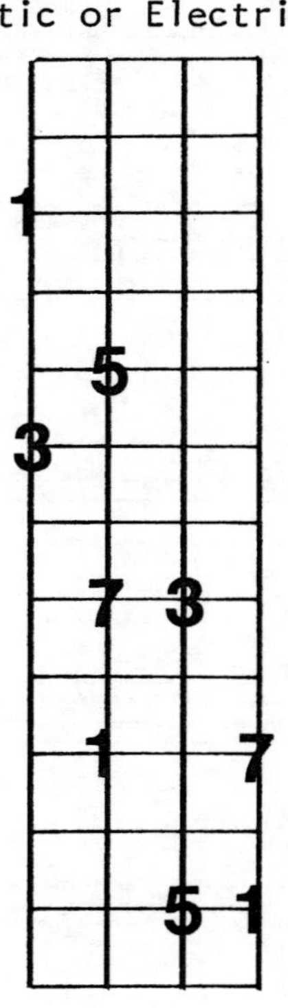

c) MINOR 7th (Acoustic)   d) DOMINANT 7th (Acoustic or Electric)

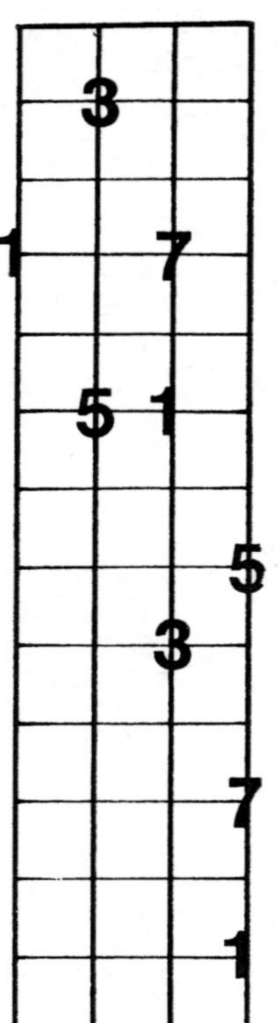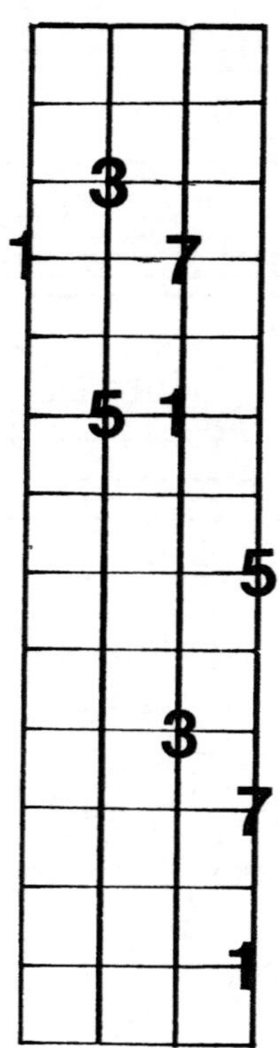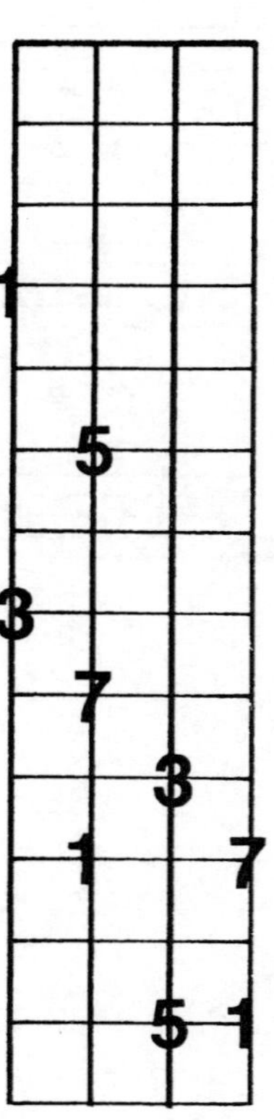

Exercise 31

Here are two octave arpeggios starting on the 5th of the chord. These will be useful for chords with roots from Bb up to E. They will work for dominant 7th chords and half-diminished chords, as in Exercise 30.

a) MAJOR 7th (Acoustic or Electric)   b) MINOR 7th (Acoustic)

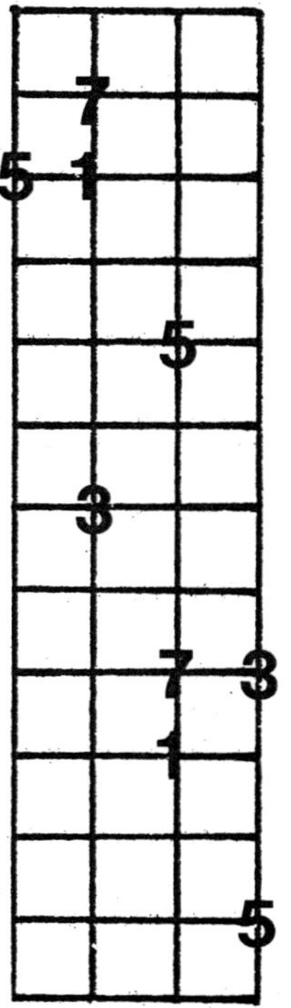
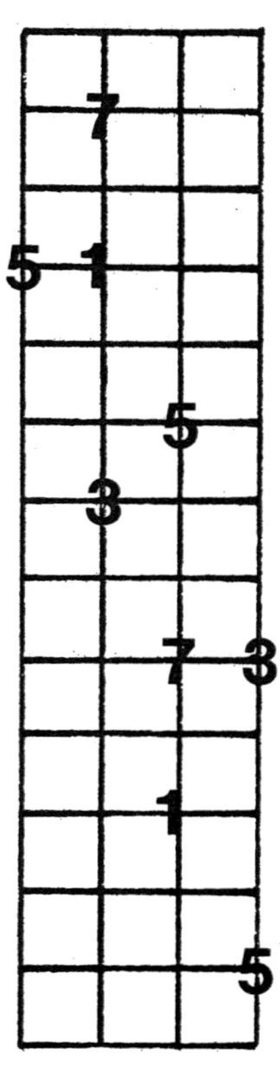

c) MINOR 7th (Electric)   d) DOMINANT 7th (+5) (Acoustic or Electric)

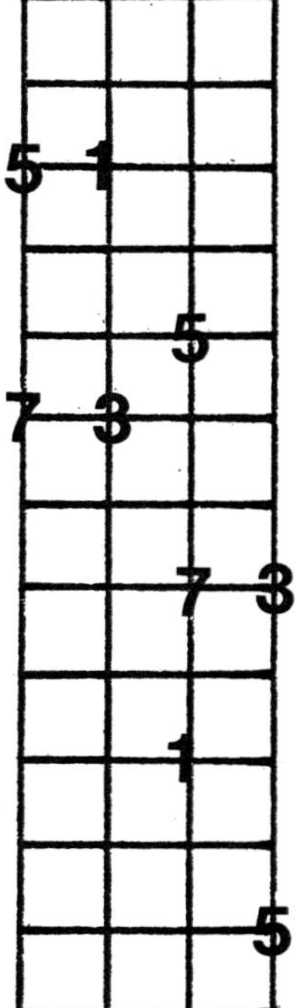
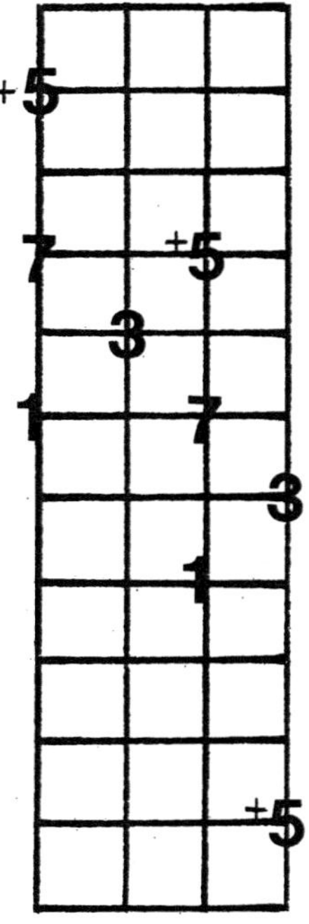

Exercise 32

Here are three different ways to play a three octave arpeggio of the
dominant 7th chord. Other quality chords can be similarly played. In addition,
those chords that contain the notes A,D, or G can be played using open strings
which will create more (often easier) ways to play it. Play these arpeggios
as is, then try leaving out notes, adding notes, or playing non-linear figures
off of them.

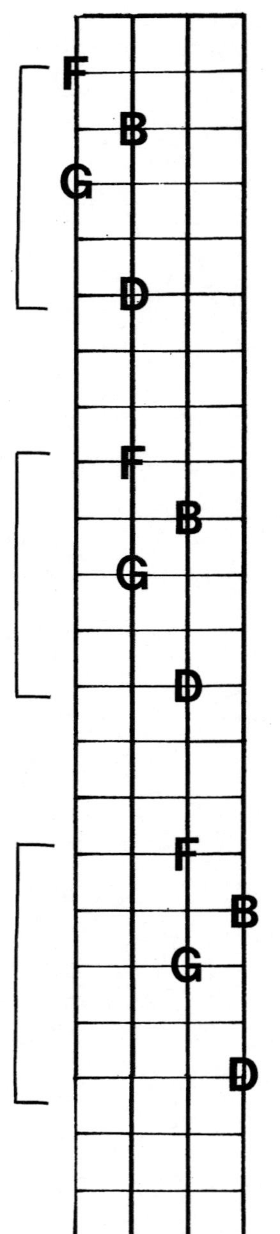

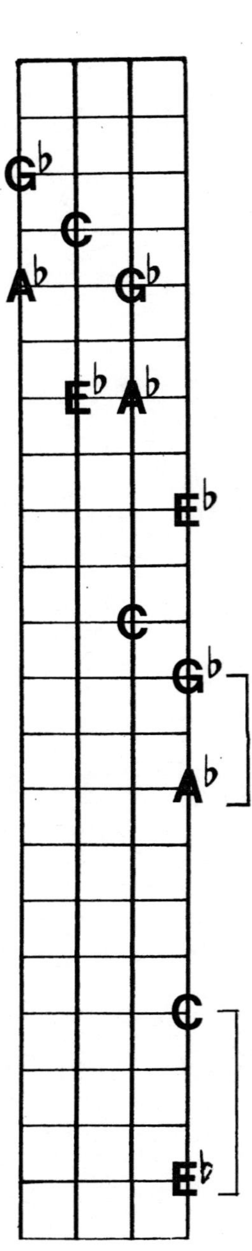

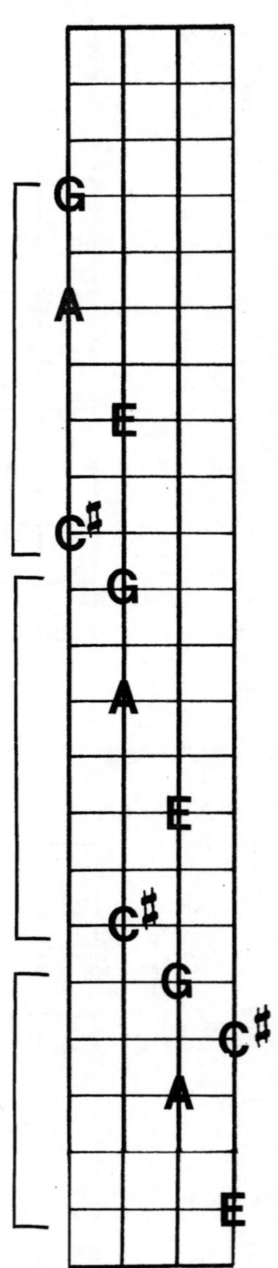

Chapter 5 — RHYTHM STUDIES

SUBDIVIDING THE BEAT

In 4/4 time, the quarter note gets one beat. This beat is often sub-
divided into two eighth notes, three eighth note triplets, or four sixteenth notes.

Exercise 1

Here are some examples of each subdivision and how they are counted.
Play these one bar at a time, then play a whole line without stopping.
Then make up variations of your own on each subdivision until you can
insert them into your lines at will. Try increasing the tempo once this
is comfortable slow.

a) Eighth Notes

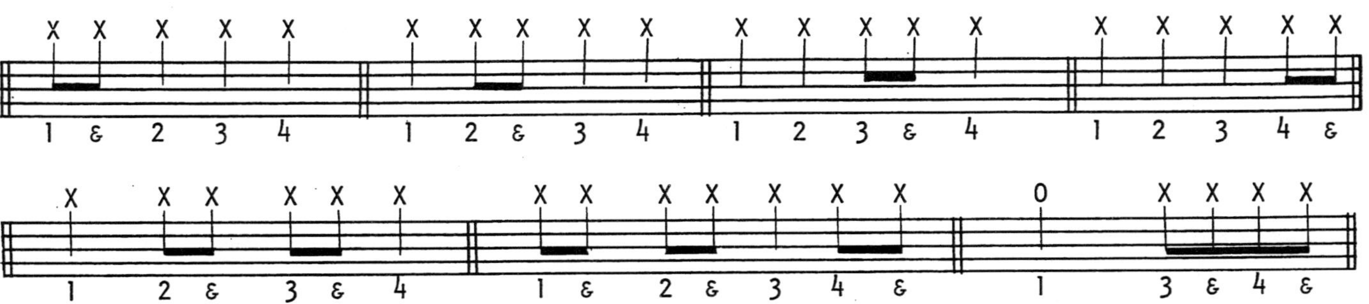

b) Eighth Note Triplets

c) Sixteenth Notes

Exercise 2

Play phrases that mix these different subdivisions. Play until you can feel each subdivision distinctly. Write out some more phrases like these for yourself.

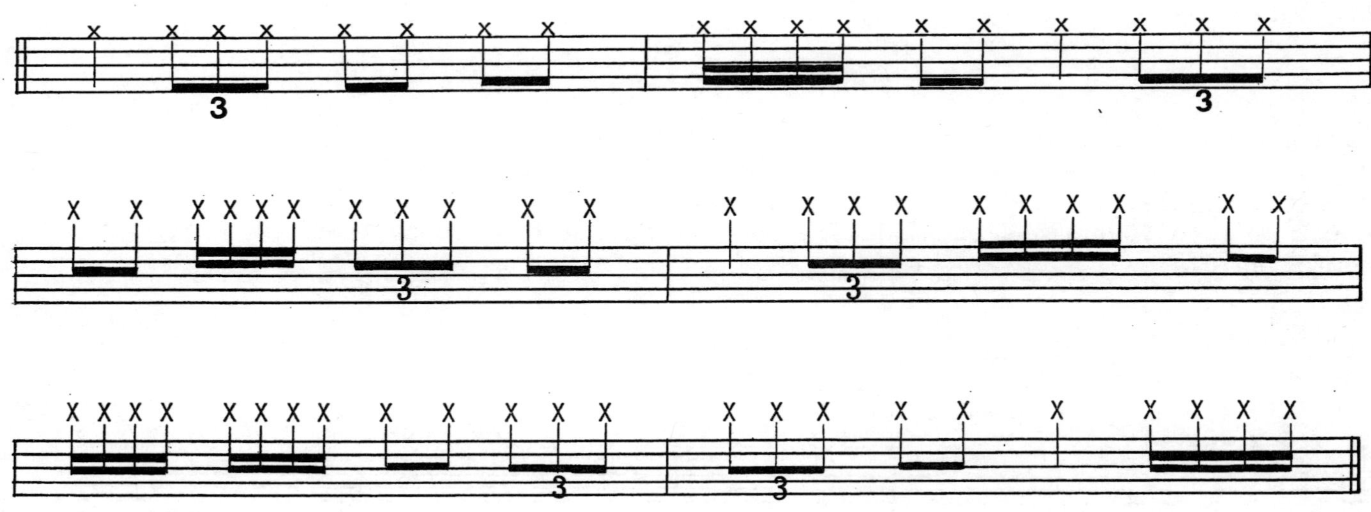

Exercise 3

Take a phrase from exercise 2 and use it to play a scale or arpeggio with, e.g.

Exercise 4

By combining different parts of these subdivisions, or by leaving some of them silent, different rhythmic figures can be created. Here are examples of different figures on each subdivision and how one of them might be used in an improvised line. Make up lines of your own on these figures, too.

(CONT.)

a) Eighth Notes

b) Triplets

In jazz music, X X or X. X figures are usually played as X X . This is a large part of what constitutes a "swinging" feeling.

(CONT.)

c) Sixteenth Notes

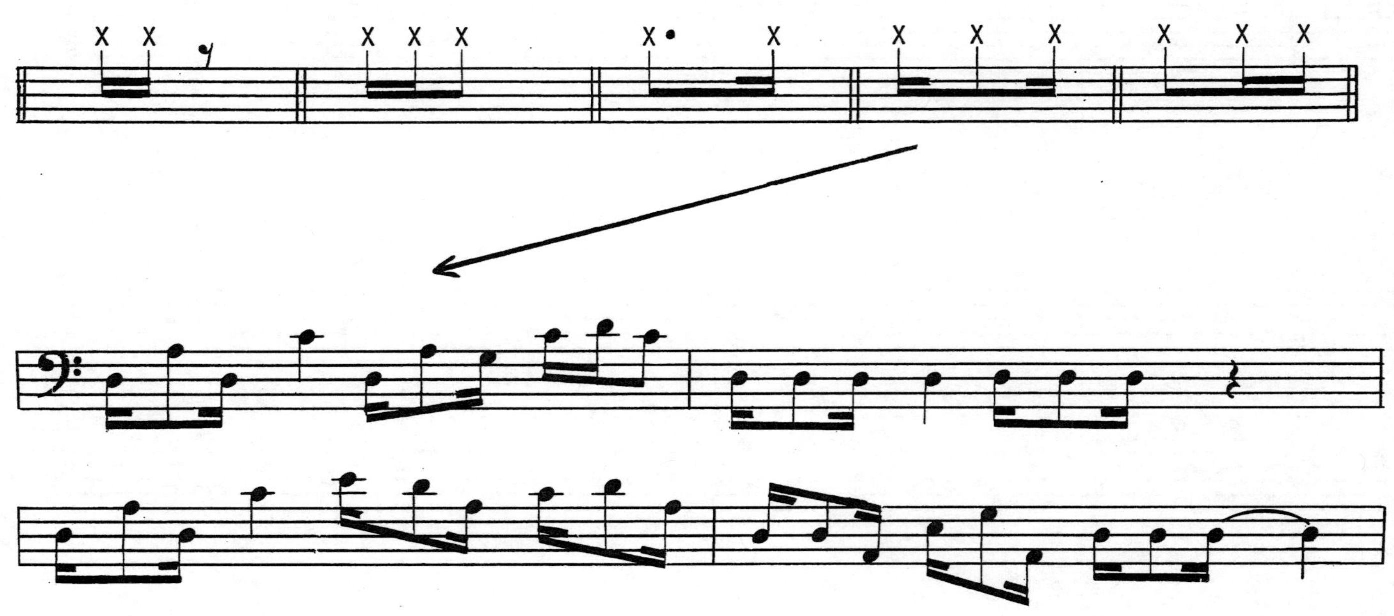

Exercise 5

Here are one bar figures that use rests, dotted notes, and tied notes. Try counting each subdivision (1 an uh, 2 an uh, etc.) and then try counting only when a note is played as is written underneath this example.

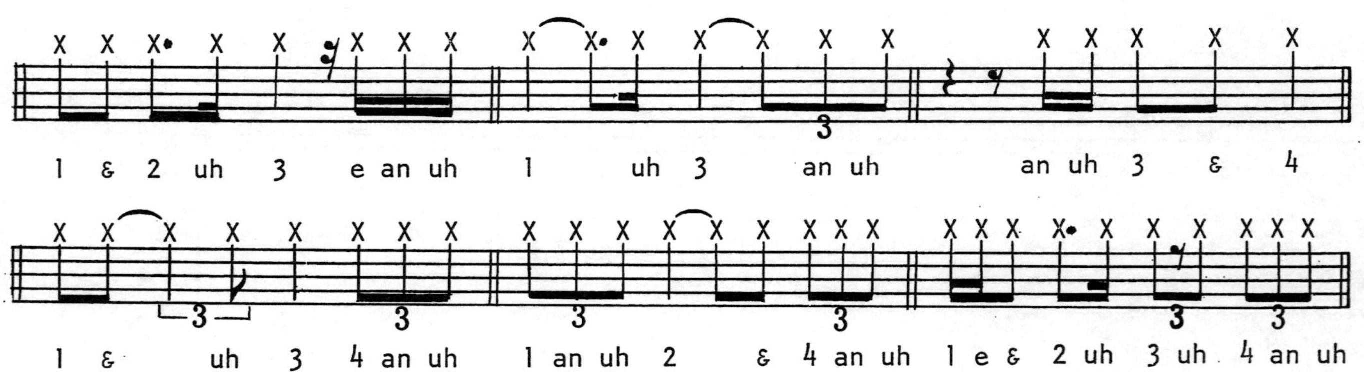

For more examples of rhythms written out, see Louis Bellson's book, "Reading Text in 4/4".

SYNCOPATION

Syncopations occur when you play a note between the beats instead of
playing it on the beat, or whenever you accent this normally weaker beat.
Syncopations are often felt as anticipations of the next main beat.

The key to learning syncopated rhythms is to feel the underlying pulses
go by, even if they aren't played. Tapping your foot on the beats is one way
to keep your place, but ultimately this should be internalized. For eighth
note phrases, everything will either be on the beat or between beats and can
be thought of as down, up, down, up, etc. After a while, you will be able to
feel where each of the syncopations lie in relation to beat 1 of the bar, and
then all you have to keep track of is the beginning of each bar. For 16th
note syncopations, thinking of the eighth note instead of the quarter note as
the basic pulse will turn it into an on or off the beat situation, just like
the syncopations shown next.

Exercise 6

Play the following syncopations one bar at a time over and over until it
is comfortable, then use it as the basic rhythm for some improvised music of
your own.

a) Anticipation of 1

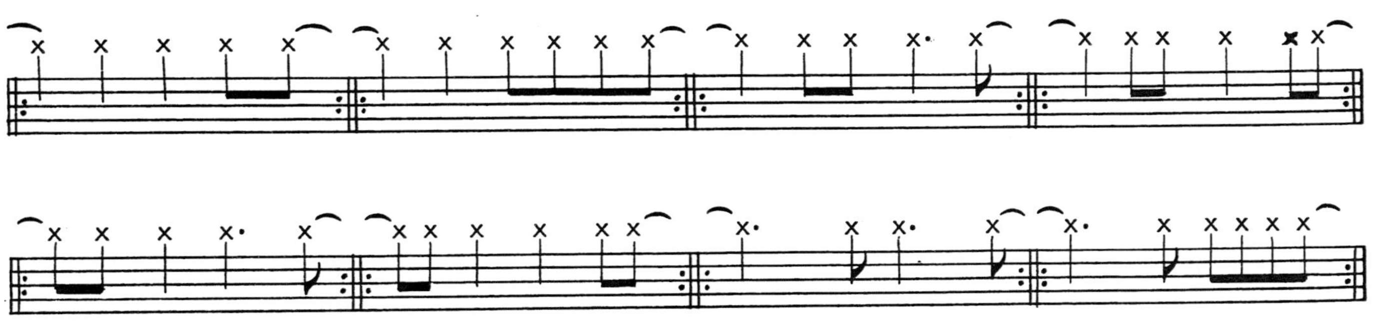

b) Anticipation of 2

c) Anticipation of 3

(CONT.)

d) Anticipation of 4

e) Multiple syncopations

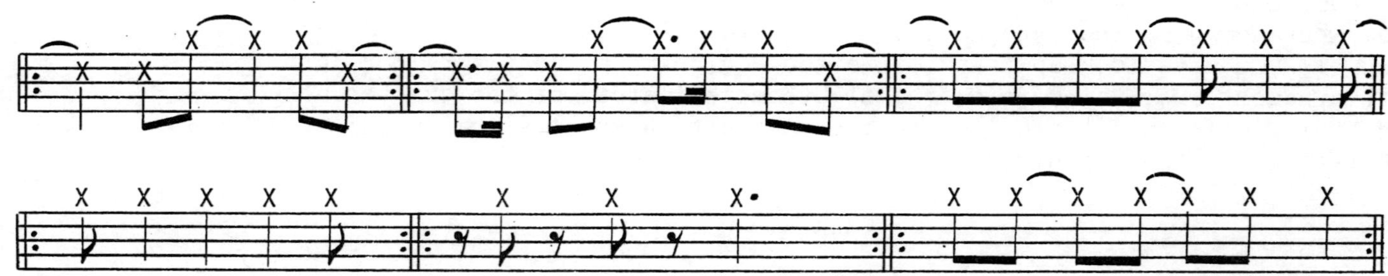

Exercise 7

Here are some syncopated figures using triplets. See exercise 26 for figures using 16th notes.

Exercise 8

Here is an exercise in syncopation. Play it using one note at first, then improvise in a key using the rhythmic structure given here.

PRACTICING RHYTHMS

Exercise 9

Set a metronome to play quarter notes, half notes, or whole notes. Clap or count out loud different rhythms against it. Try it with the metronome hitting on 2 and 4, e.g.

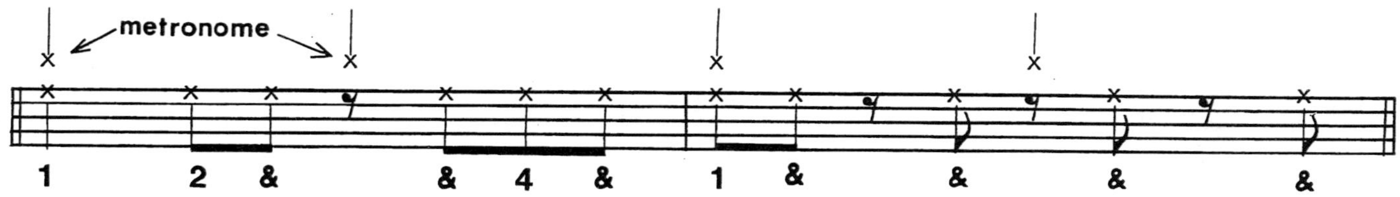

Exercise 10

Tap your foot on each of the beats of the bar. Play anything but keep the foot even and regular. Make sure that you know where the 1st beat of each bar is. Try tapping your foot on 1 and 3 only. Ultimately, the foot tapping should be internalized so that the basic pulse is just felt, e.g.

Practice Exercises 11-14 using the same rhythm for all of them or try playing several different rhythms on one exercise.

Exercise 11

Play a rhythm using one note at first, then add different notes until a one or two bar bass line is formed, e.g.

Exercise 12

Play a bass line keeping the same rhythm but changing the notes each time, e.g.

Exercise 13

Play a bass line keeping the same notes but changing the rhythm a little each time, e.g.

Exercise 14

Take a one or two bar rhythm and alternate it with an equal number of bars of an improvised rhythm, e.g.

Exercise 15

Listen to a record you like, transcribe a rhythm from it and improvise on it using the previous three exercises.

Exercise 16

Pick one eighth note per bar as a target note. Improvise around it, e.g. the eighth note after 2.

Try leaving the target note(s) as rests each time, e.g. beat 1

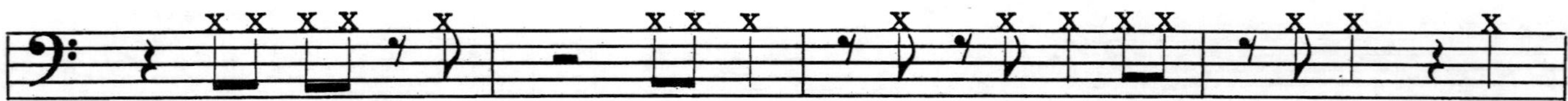

Exercise 17

Try playing phrases with little pieces of smaller subdivisions in them
until they are fast and accurate, e.g.

Exercise 18

Play a line with syncopations. Count 1 2 3 4 and also count the smaller
subdivisions when they occur in a beat, e.g.

Then try counting only when a note is played.

Exercise 19

Play an improvised line using two different subdivisions, e.g. 8ths and 16ths

Exercise 20

Play a line with a lot of 16th notes for a while, then try leaving out more
and more notes to create a syncopated funk line, e.g.

Exercise 21

Try using one or two specific rhythmic figures as the basic motif of an improvised line, e.g.

Exercise 22

Take a rhythm and use it to practice your scales and chords with, e.g.

Exercise 23

Try starting a rhythmic figure on different parts of the beat, i.e. rhythmic displacement, e.g.

Notice that the C,D, and F in the beginning of the 3rd bar all have a dotted 8th note time value. Instead of counting where they fall in relation to the basic pulse, try counting them 1 2 3, 1 2 3, 1 2 3, letting your foot keep the basic pulse. Once you've played it several times, it should feel natural and won't have to be counted at all.

Exercise 24

Divide the basic meter (i.e. the number of beats per measure) into smaller
sub-groups. Play anything, but keep one specific variation of this in mind.
This principle is very useful for playing odd time signatures. This next example
is in 11/8 and should be divided into groups of 8 and 3. The numbers underneath
some of the notes indicate how they are to be counted.

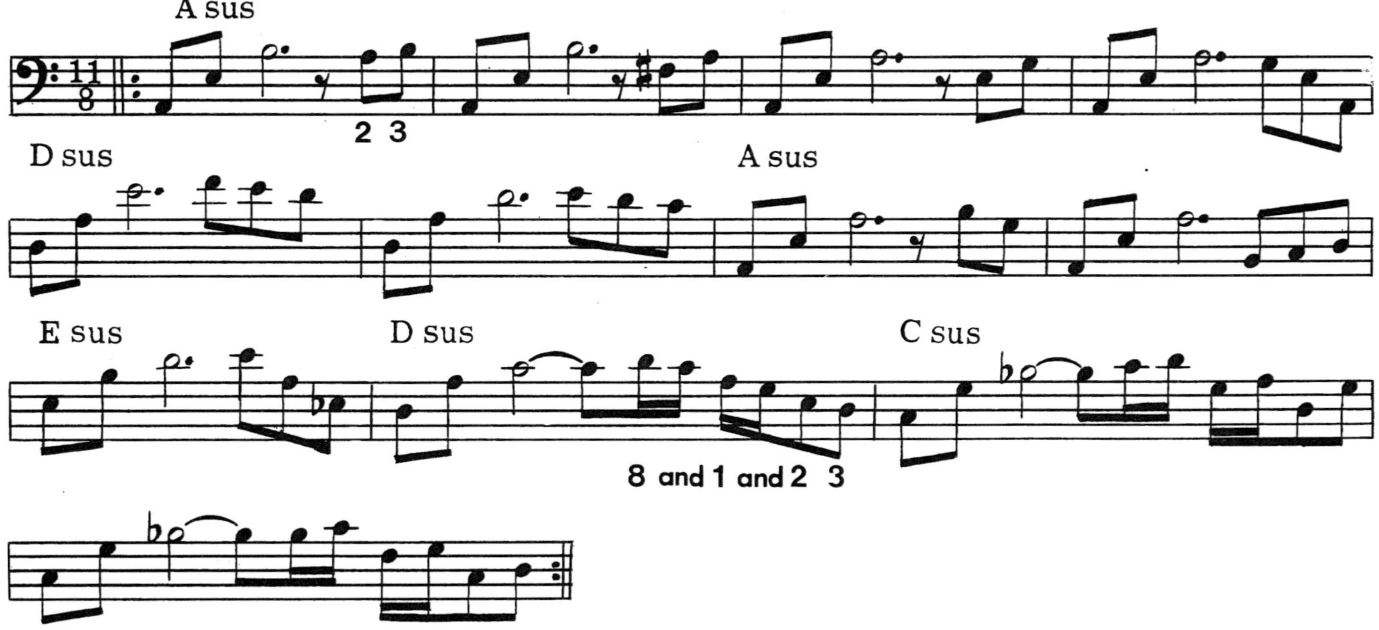

Exercise 25

For odd meters, especially at fast tempos, try counting every other beat, e.g.

Exercise 26

Play the following two bar syncopated phrases. The numbers underneath some
of the notes indicate the strongest notes that are played on the beat. After
each one is the same rhythm played twice as fast (i.e. double time). This
creates a one bar phrase with 16th note syncopations instead of 8th note ones.
Make up a bass line using each one.

Two Bar Syncopated Phrases   16th Note Version

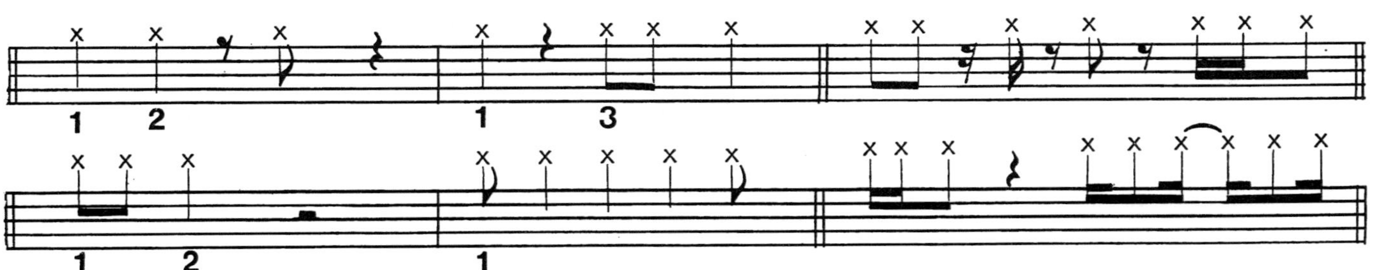

(CONT.)

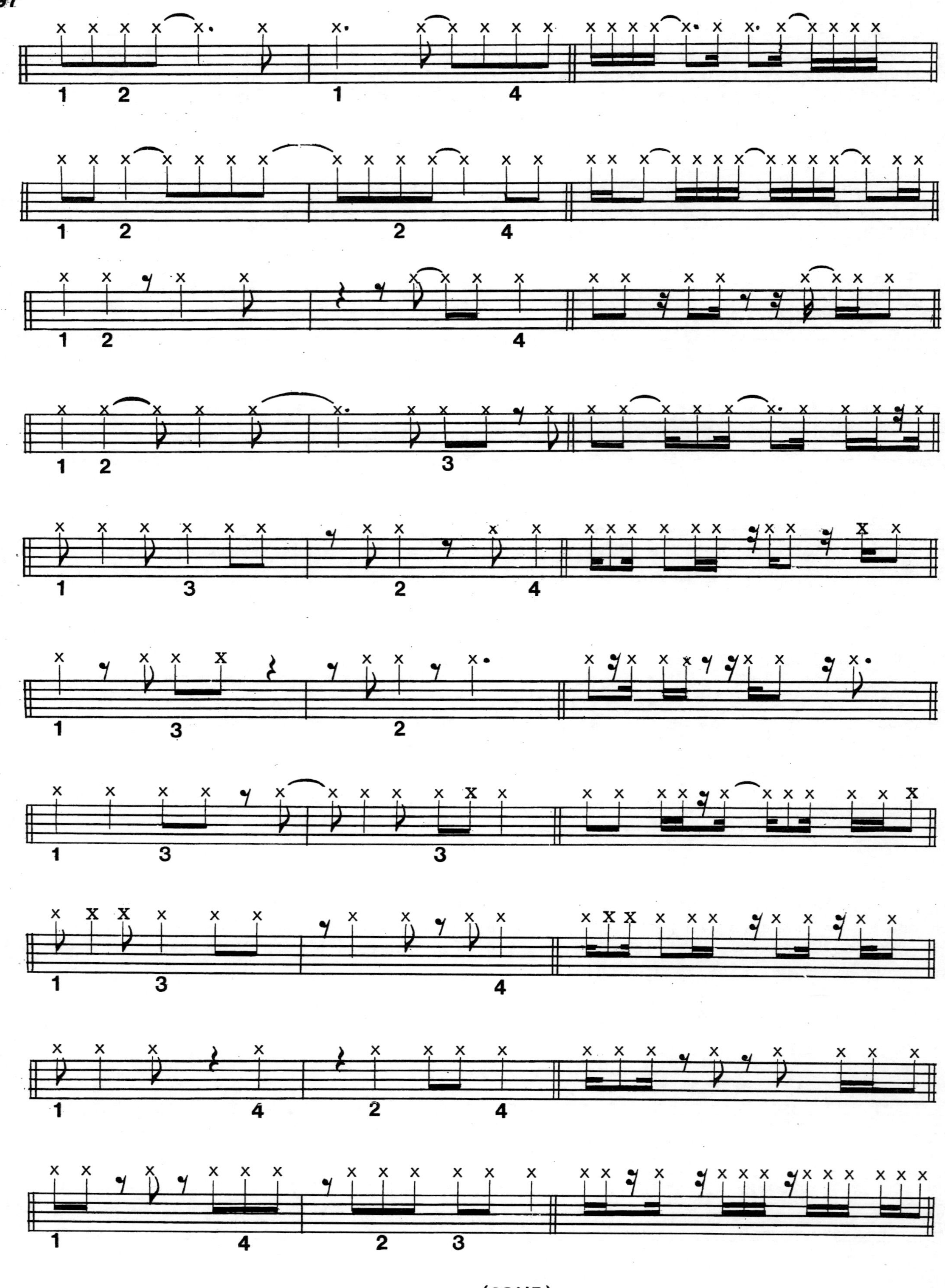

(CONT.)

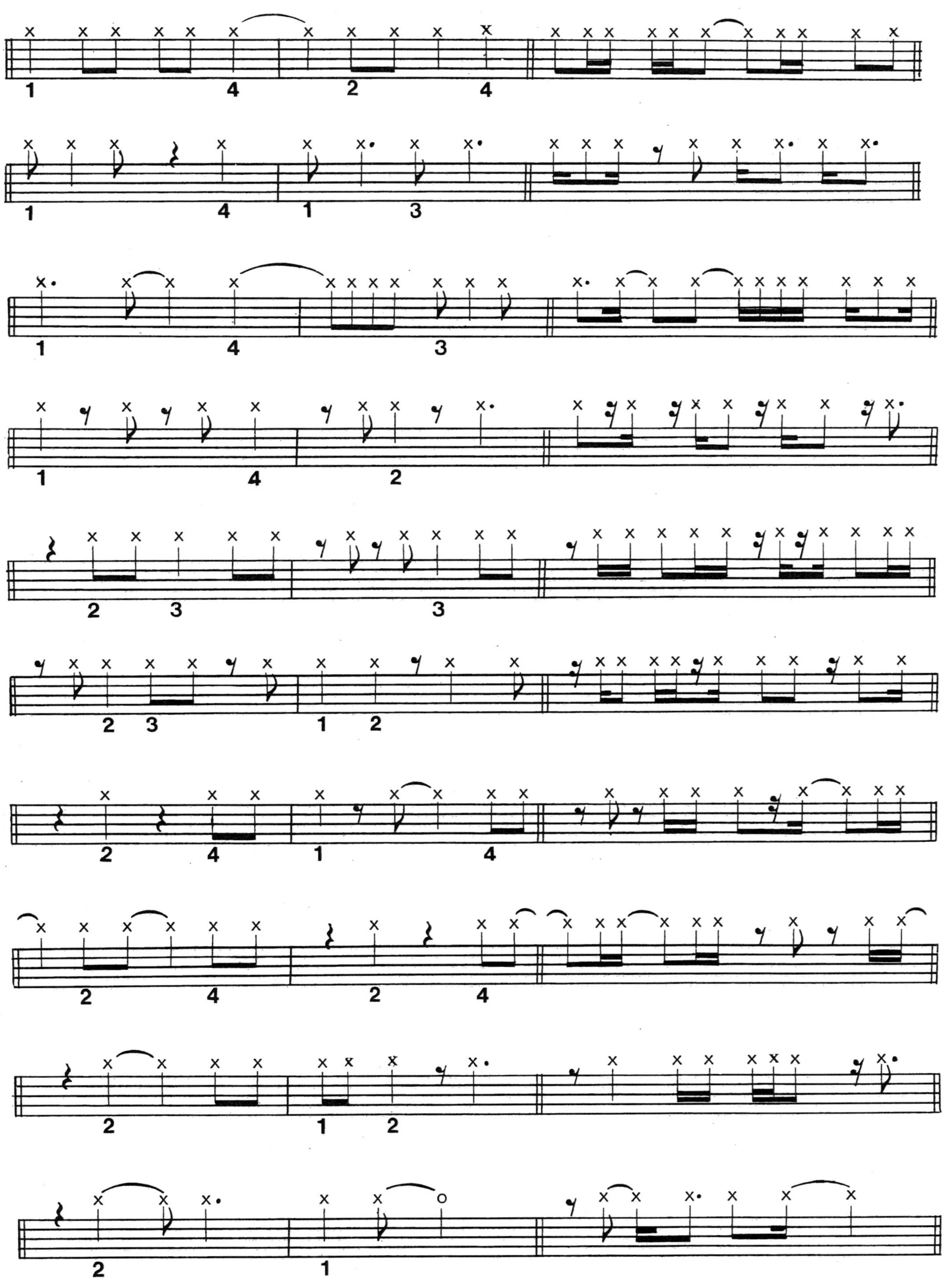

Exercise 27

Play the rhythms in Exercise 26 accenting different notes than the ones suggested above, but keep the feeling of rhythmic landmarks to head for, e.g. the 3rd rhythm in Exercise 26.

RHYTHMIC STYLES

Exercise 28

Here are some basic rhythmic figures for 5 different styles of music. Play
a 2 chord vamp, the blues, or a tune using mostly one of these figures.

Exercise 29

Here is the 1st section of "Softly as in a Morning Sunrise" played in
different rhythmic styles. Before reading these examples as written, try
taking each rhythmic variation (shown in brackets) and using it on the tune
until it is comfortable.

b) Walking

c) Latin Jazz

(CONT.)

d) Samba

e) Funk

Chapter 6 — INTERVAL STUDIES

INTERVALS OFF OF SCALES

Exercise 1

Play a C minor scale adding a scale note a second above or below each note. Try just thinking of the first note of each pair (the circled notes below) and let the other one follow automatically, in order to keep your place easier.

Exercise 2

Use seconds off of various scale degrees in the C minor scale to create an improvised line, e.g.

Exercise 3

Play the A major scale inserting a scale note a 3rd above or below each scale degree. Use either major or minor thirds, whichever keeps you in the scale., e.g.

Exercise 4

Make some music using scalar thirds as the basic motif, e.g.

Exercise 5

Try playing thirds off of the Ab major scale using different combinations of horizontal and vertical motion. For example, play the following phrase on the strings shown below,

Exercise 6

Play the D major scale using fourths off of each note, e.g.

Exercise 7

Here are several licks based on fourths in the key of D major. The first four can be played in one two-fret position. Once these are comfortable, transpose them.

Exercise 8

Play the E minor scale using fifths off of each note, e.g.

Exercise 9

Play the scale using alot of fifths. This example uses the open string (marked with a 0 underneath the notes) in addition to the fifths intervals.

Exercise 10

Play the Bb major scale in sixths, then improvise on it, e.g.

Exercise 11

Here is an example of the use of sevenths on the Bb major scale.

Exercise 12

Play octaves on the G minor scale, then improvise on it. This example
shows simple licks transposed up an octave, as well as straight octave intervals.

Exercise 13

Here is an example of what can be done with ninths in the key of E minor.

Exercise 14

Here are 10ths off of the Bb major scale.

Exercise 15

Staying in one 3-fret horizontal position, play off of the intervals in a scale. The notes marked with a circle over them in this example are to be played as harmonics and sound an octave higher than they are written.

PURE INTERVALS

Take each interval in the following exercises and play around with it, move it to different starting notes, make little tunes or bass lines using it, etc. until the sound of it and the feeling of how it is created physically is clear to you.

Exercise 16

Half steps

Exercise 17

Whole Steps

Exercise 18

Here is a rock-type bass line using minor thirds.

Here is a more advanced example of the use of minor thirds.

Exercise 19

All these intervals should be practiced chromatically, e.g. major thirds.

Exercise 20

All the intervals should also be transposed up and down by whole steps, e.g. 4ths.

Exercise 21

Here is the b5th interval transposed by minor thirds.

Exercise 22

Try playing the intervals as double-stops, i.e. both notes played at once, e.g. 5ths transposed by minor thirds.

Exercise 23

Try using the larger intervals as the basic motif on a tune. Here, for example, are minor sixths used on a standard chord progression. This example is in cut time, which means that the half note is the basic pulse.

Exercise 24

Here are major 6ths and minor 7ths above the root of a chord. The chord progression is part of the cycle of fifths. Extend this idea through the rest of the cycle.

Exercise 25

This example uses the major 7th above the root of the chord as the main theme.

Exercise 26

Here are octaves played both as double-stops and as single note lines.

Exercise 27

Play any kind of phrase ending with a specific interval. Build the next phrase off of that interval, e.g.

Chapter 7 — CREATING BASS LINES

HARMONIC LANDMARKS

The most basic function of the bass is to provide a harmonic bottom for the
music. This is done, in large part, through the use of landmark notes, usually
at the beginning of the bar, to signify what the harmonic motion is.

Exercise 1

Play the following exercises using only notes of the C major scale instead
of the X's. Try different scale notes instead of D. Play this with other rhythms
to create different style bass lines.

Exercise 2

Pick a tune and play the roots of the chords on beat 1 of each bar. Play
any other chord notes inbetween, e.g.

Exercise 3

Play Exercise 2 but use scalar runs to connect the landmark notes. See
Chapter 9 for a discussion of how to determine what scales to use.

Exercise 4

Here is a bass line that combines scalar, chordal, and chromatic ways to connect up the roots of a chord progression. There are an infinite variety of ways to do this, and bass players in every style of improvised music use this approach as the basis of creating a strong, yet interesting line. Play the example as written and then make up variations of your own.

Exercise 5

Here is a bass line on a blues progression that uses notes other than the root of the chord on beat 1.

In order for these non-root notes to sound logical, they must be set up by the notes in the previous bar. The next section of this chapter explains different ways to accomplish this.

LANDMARK SERIES

Exercise 6

Take the first chord of a tune and see if there are any notes that can be altered by a half step to become notes of the second chord, e.g.

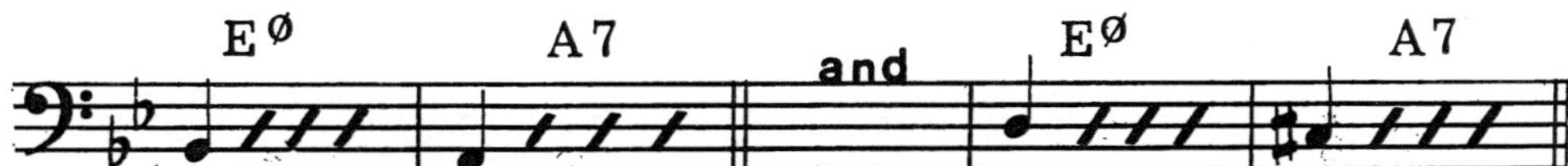

Do this for each pair of chords in the tune and use these moving voices as landmark notes on beat 1 of each bar, e.g.

Exercise 7

Try using the landmark note on beat 4 (more or less), so that it will resolve directly by a half step to beat 1 of the next bar, thus linking up each measure of the tune, e.g.

Exercise 8

Use either half step or whole step movements, whenever possible, to create a series of landmark notes through the changes of a tune. Use only chord notes. Here, for example, are the chords for "Stella by Starlight" with a landmark series written out. Make a tape of these chords; play just the landmarks as you play along with the tape the first time, then make up a bass line using these landmarks.

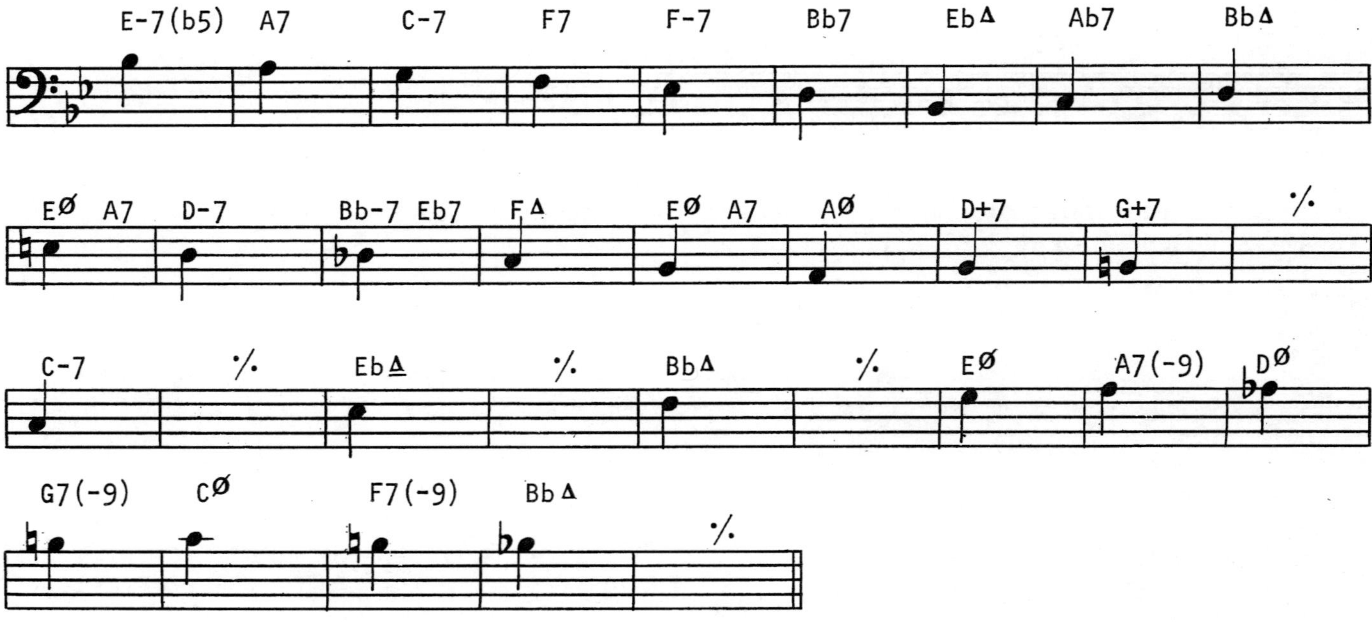

Here is one way to play a walking line using these landmark notes.

Exercise 9

Learn the melody to a tune and use the main melody notes as landmarks at the beginning of each bar, whenever possible, e.g. "Stella" with melody notes on beat 1 of every other bar.

Exercise 10

Dominant chords a flat fifth (tritone) away are often used as substitutes for each other. This is especially useful in II V I situations, where the tritone substitution creates a chromatic landmark series that is even stronger than the original progression. Pick a tune that uses II V I progressions and try this substitution, e.g.

Exercise 11

On Latin tunes, in addition to landmark series on beat 1, add a different series on beat 3 of each bar, so that two independent voices are created, e.g.

Exercise 12

Try using landmark notes every other bar to create a feeling of longer phrases. Play anything at the beginning of the inbetween bars, e.g.

Exercise 13

If one note is a chord tone in four consecutive chords, try using it as a pedal tone at the beginning of each bar, e.g.

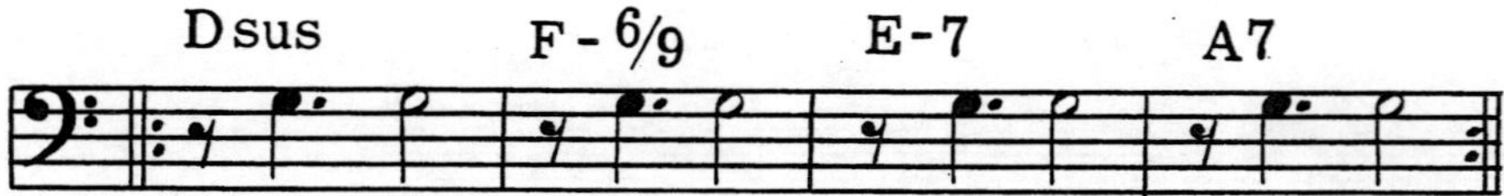

Exercise 14

Instead of preplanning these series of landmarks notes, just be aware of them and extend them as they occur spontaneously while you are playing.

MORE IDEAS FOR CREATING BASS LINES

Try practicing the following exercises through the changes of a tune, the blues, a two or four chord vamp, or in a modal-type of setting. Some of the examples are given in both quarter notes (walking bass) and with more complex rhythms, which are useful for creating Latin or funk lines.

Exercise 15

Take each four chord section of a tune and figure out how the chords relate to each other by finding all the possible scale-like series of notes that can be created using only chord tones, e.g.

	G	Bb7	A-7	D7 (altered)
1.	G	Ab	A	Ab or Bb
2.	G	Ab	G	F#
3.	G	F	E	Eb or D
4.	B	Bb	A	Ab or Bb
5.	B	Bb	C	D
6.	B	D	C	Bb
7.	D	D	C	C
8.	F#	F	E	Eb or D
9.	F#	F	G	F# or G#
10.	F#	Ab	G	F#

Try using a D pedal along with any of these.

The usefulness of this approach lies more in the internal structure of your lines as opposed to a landmark series on beat 1. Here, for example, is one way to use the first series shown above:

Exercise 16

Take one or two bars of a tune at a time and figure out a bass line that you like on the chords. Write it down and then play it leading into the next section of the tune, etc. until you finish the tune. Composing bass lines in this way is good training for improvising which has been called "spontaneous composition."

a) Try singing a line to yourself and then approximating it on the bass.

b) Listen to 8 bars of the tune on a record. Try to make your line have the same feeling &/or notes as the original.

(CONT.)

c) Use the basic idea of virtually any exercise in this book as the source of your line, e.g. try playing one inversion of each chord per bar, e.g.

(same changes)

Exercise 17

Take a short lick and use it or variations on it as a recurring theme in a bass line. These licks are all based on a Bb7 chord.

Here is how the first lick shown above might be used in a bass line.

Exercise 18

For tunes with long modal (one chord) sections, try playing the tonic on beat 1 every 2 or 4 bars. Play anything you hear inbetween, e.g.

Exercise 19

Play a line so that each bar sounds remote from the next one, creating a question and answer type of line, e.g.

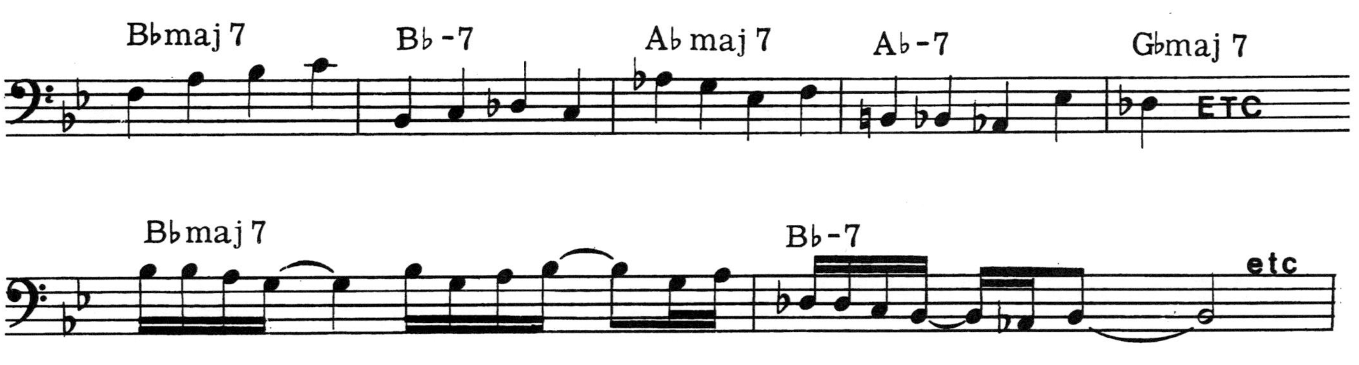

Exercise 20

Do Exercise 19, but use a lead-in note on beat 4, give or take an 8th note, e.g.

Exercise 21

Try putting a large interval between the first and second notes in each bar.

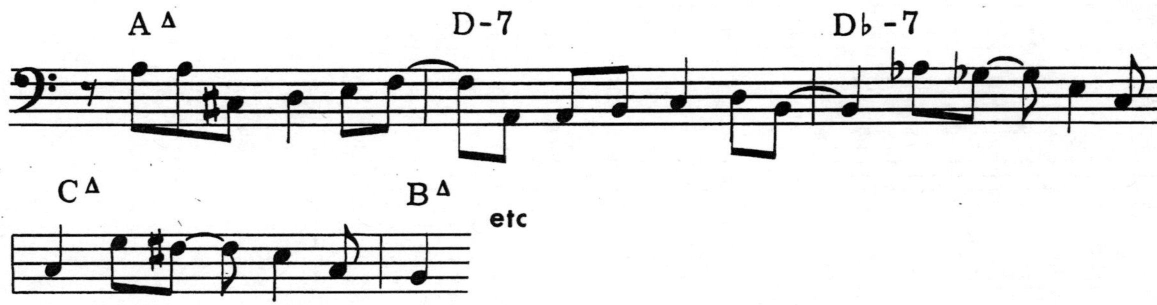

The next three exercises are specifically for walking bass.

Exercise 22

Try playing one type of interval between beats 1 and 2 and between beats 3 and 4, e.g. thirds.

Exercise 23

Try playing one type of interval between beats 4 and 1 and between beats 2 and 3, e.g. half steps. This use of chromatic leading tones, for example, is typical of many bass lines.

Exercise 24

Try Exercise 22 or 23, but use any interval, not just one kind. Keep
the feeling of pairs of intervals as long as possible, e.g.

Exercise 25

Try taking two different rudiments and mixing them together to create a
bass line, e.g.

a) Scales and chords

b) Thirds and fifths off of a scale. This example uses the Db diminished scale.

Exercise 26

Play bass lines on simple tunes or vamps thinking of nothing but the
pulse, the rhythmic feeling you are producing, or accurate phrasing. Tape
yourself playing this exercise until you are happy with the improvement.

Exercise 27

Try accenting one or two notes per bar, e.g.

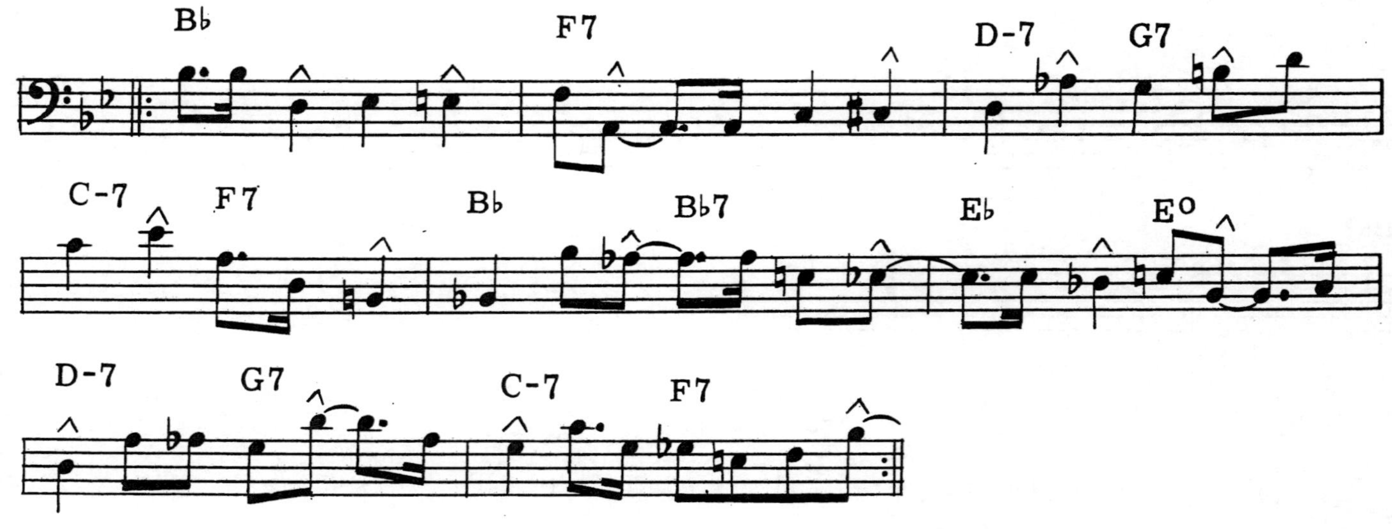

Exercise 28

Use the main notes or contours of the melody to a tune to create a bass line, e.g. "All The Things You Are."

Exercise 29

Play lines that use the full range of your instrument, e.g.

Exercise 30

Here are some more examples of how to use large interval leaps in walking bass lines. (Written by Bob Magnusson, jazz recording artist and teacher at the L.A. Bass Institute of Technology.)

Chapter 8 — CHORD VOICINGS

FOUR NOTE HORIZONTAL VOICINGS

By leaving out certain notes of the chord when playing in a horizontal
position, we get different voicings for the chord. The charts shown here give
all the four note voicings for one horizontal position of the dominant 7th chord.
The same idea can be used for the other dominant 7th chord positions and for
other quality chords as well. Also, two or three note voicings can be
created by leaving out one or two notes on any of the voicings shown below.

Exercise 1

Take a voicing, play it with a particular root, then transpose it. Do this
on a vamp, the blues, a tune, or wherever you hear it moving to. Play around
with the order of notes, the rhythms, etc.

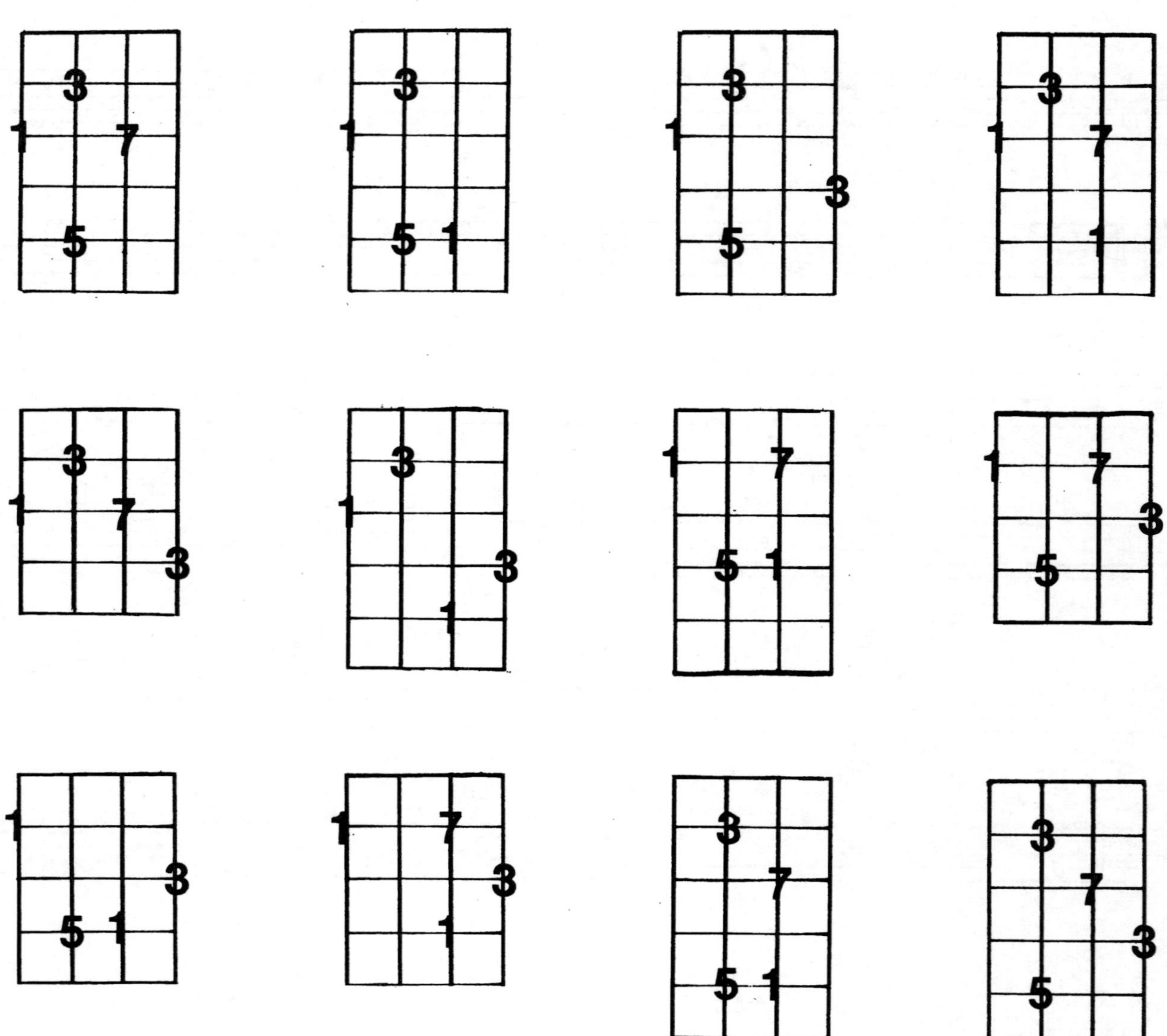

(CONT.)

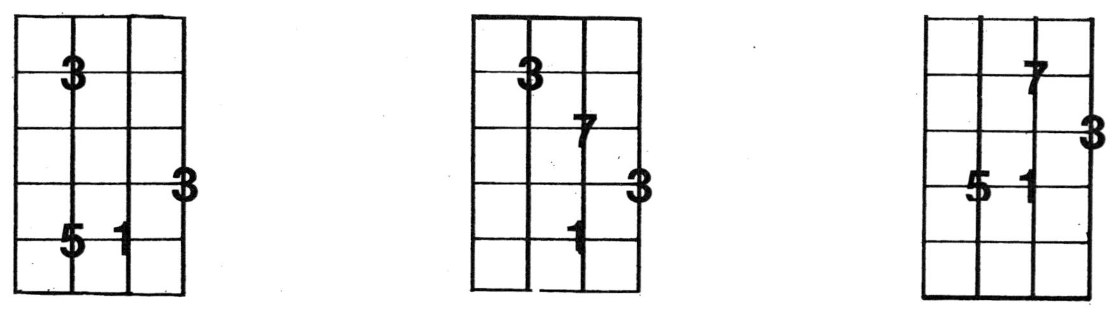

Exercise 2

Use each one as the framework for a specific lick, then transpose it, e.g. the fifth voicing on F7 and Bb7.

Exercise 3

Use each voicing as a home base to improvise off of, e.g. the fifth voicing on an F blues.

Exercise 4

Try playing these voicings as double stops instead of single note lines. Here, for example, is the eighth voicing.

Exercise 5

Try adding the ninth or other note. to these voicings, especially in the upper part of the chord, e.g.

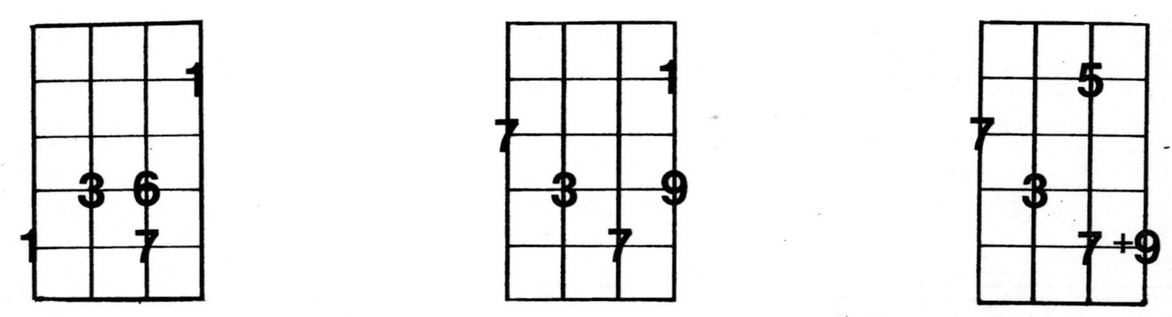

Exercise 6

Take voicings from two different positions and use them to create a question and answer type of line, e.g. two voicings on Gb7.

FOUR NOTE VERTICAL VOICINGS

On this and the next page are some four note chord voicings using larger than 3-fret positions.

Exercise 7

Take one voicing and play it with a particular root, then transpose it. Do this on a vamp, the blues, or a tune. Improvise on each voicing once it is comfortable, e.g. the 2nd voicing shown below.

Exercise 8

Try these voicings in the middle of the fingerboard to connect the upper and lower registers, e.g. the 1st voicing shown below in Bb.

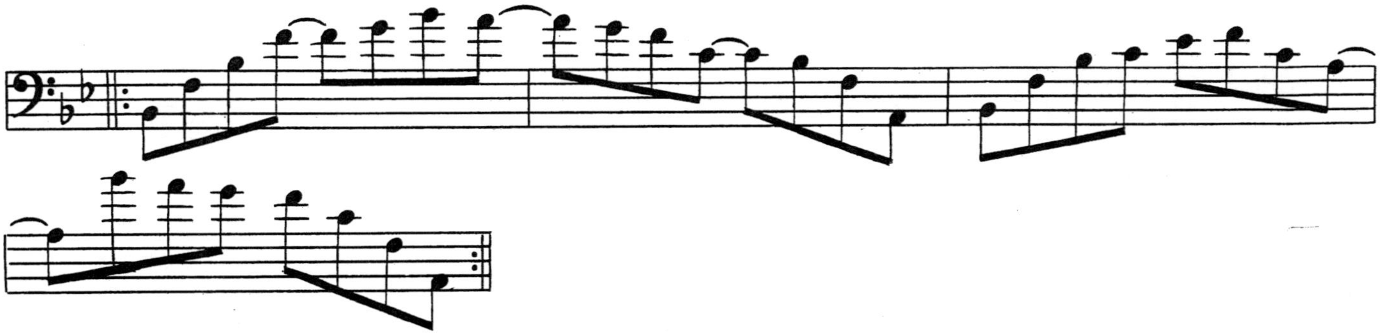

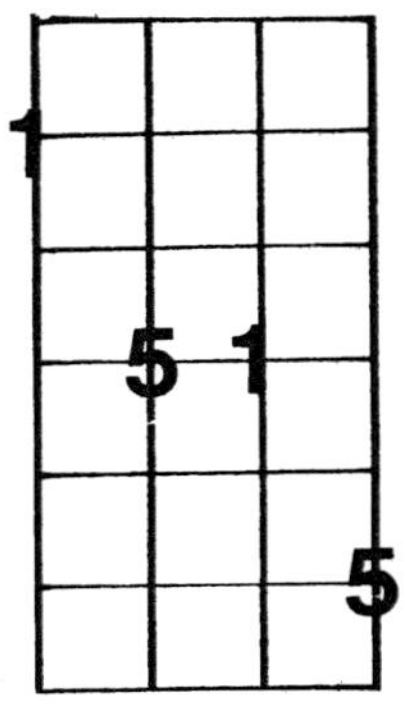

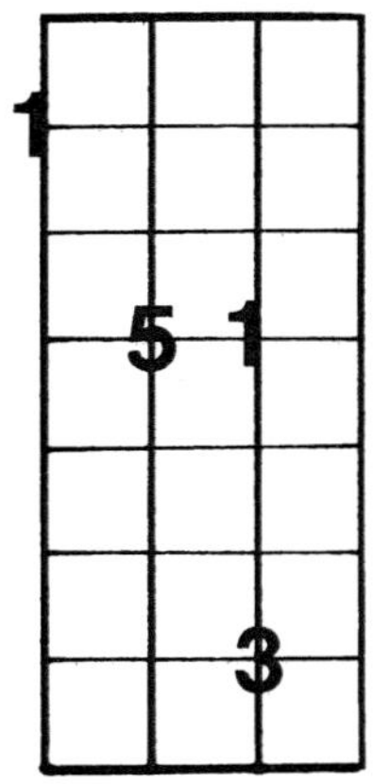

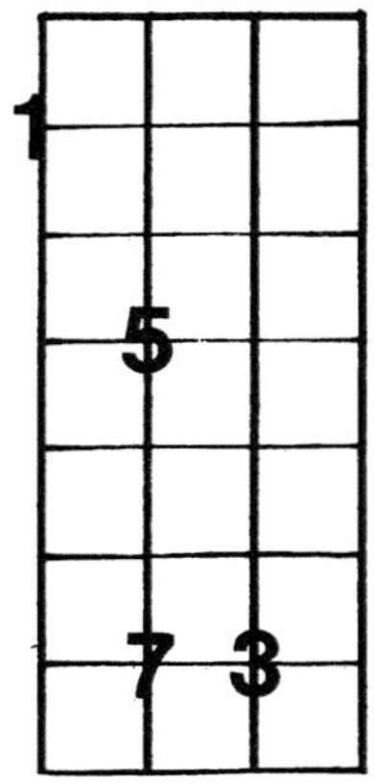

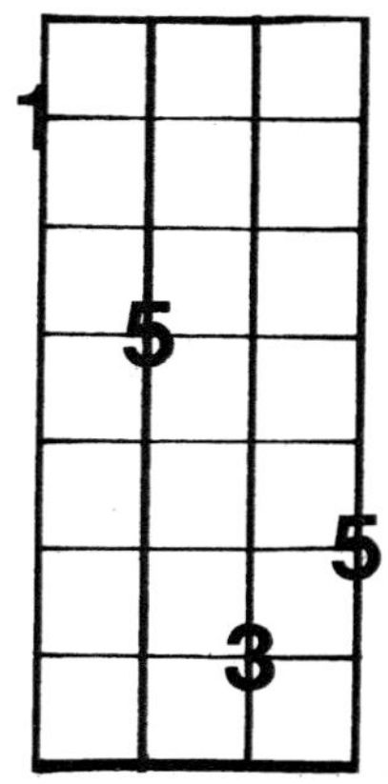

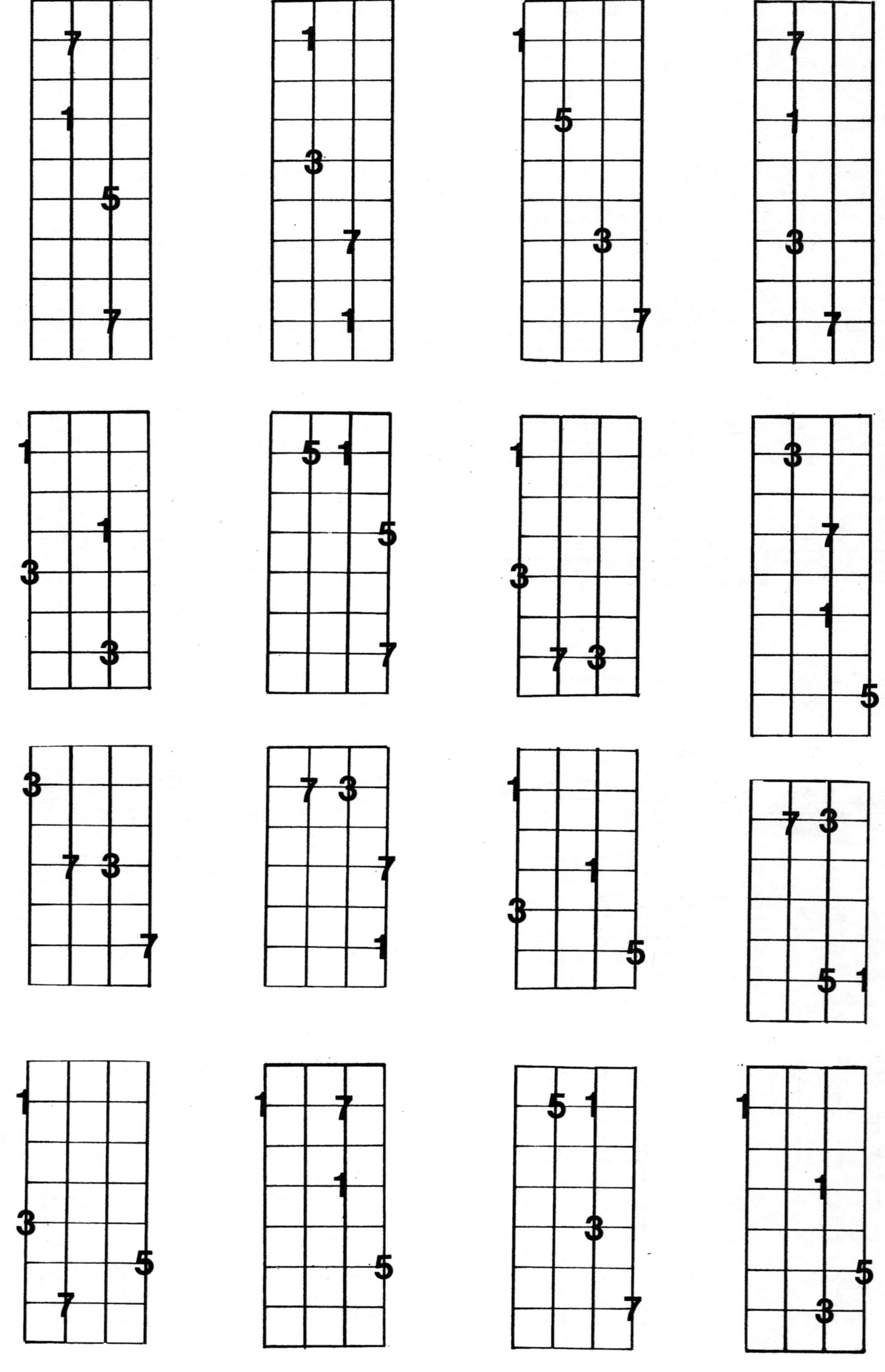

THUMB POSITION VOICINGS (Acoustic Bass)

These can all be strummed so that the notes sound simultaneously. The circle with the cross on top means that the thumb holds that string down. When more than one note is shown per string, try one at a time.

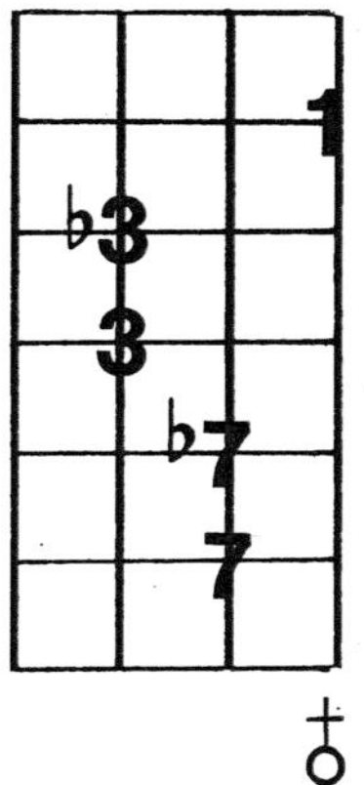 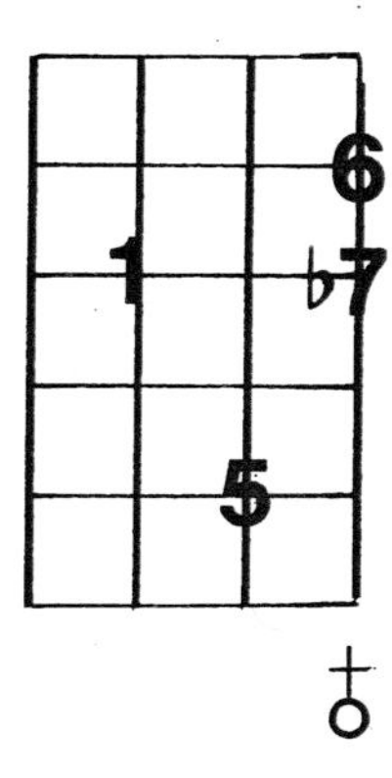 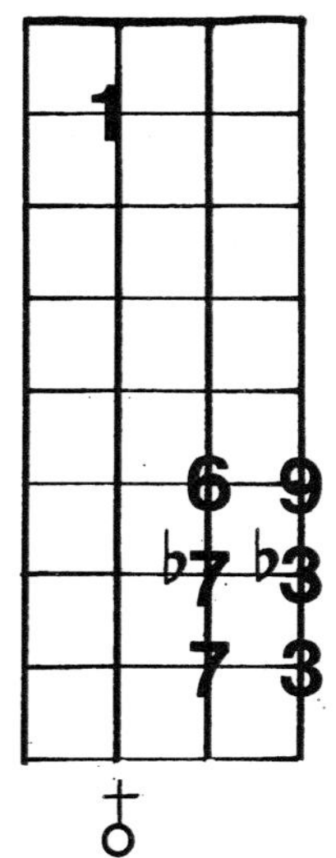 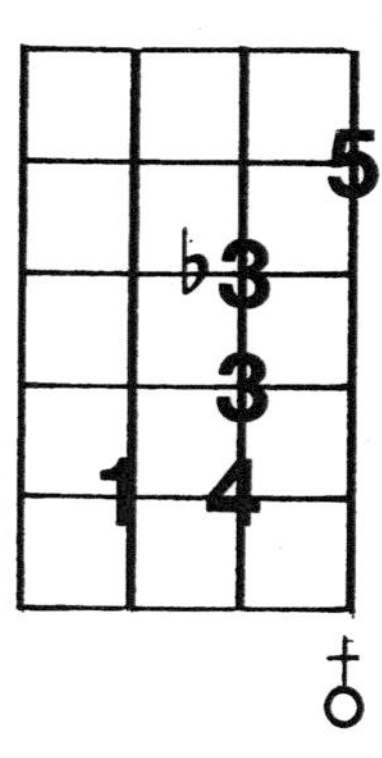

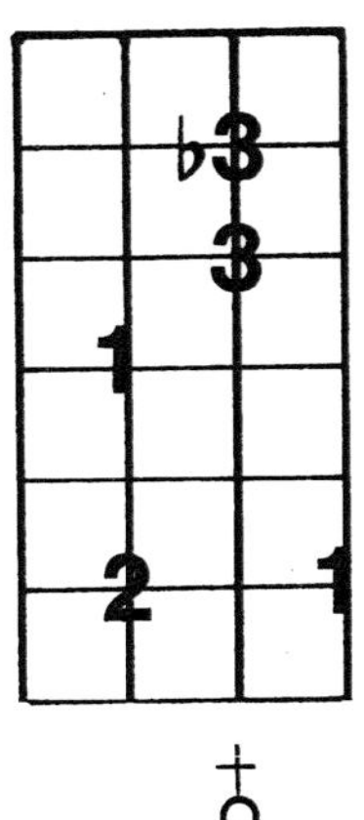 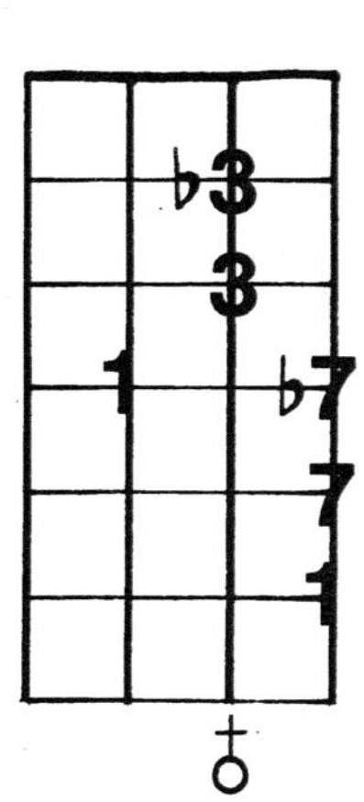 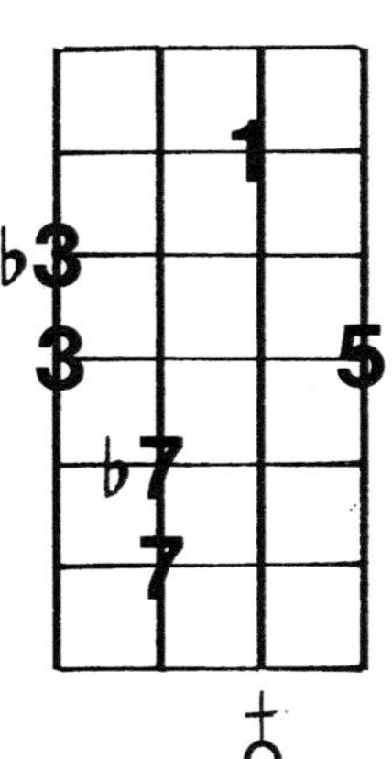 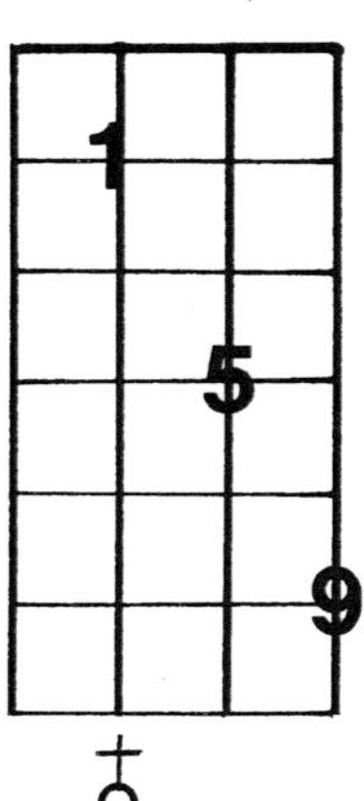

Chapter 9 — ANALYZING TUNES

CHORD FUNCTIONS

Chords in tunes, generally speaking, will have one of three functions:

1) Tonic Chords - resting place, resolution

2) Dominant Chords - suspension, tension; calls for resolution to the tonic

3) Subdominant Chords - halfway between tonic and dominant functions; used either to temporarily break up a section of tonic chords, or as the dominant of the dominant, e.g. II as the dominant of V.

Exercise 1

Play the chords in each of the three groups below. Notice that the ones in each group have similar sounds when compared to chords in another group. Also notice that there is only one note difference between the 1st chord in a group and the other one(s). This example is in the key of C major.

a) Tonic Chords   I△ = C△   III-7 = E-7   VI-7 = A-7

b) Dominant Chords   V7 = G7   VII-7(b5) = B-7(b5)

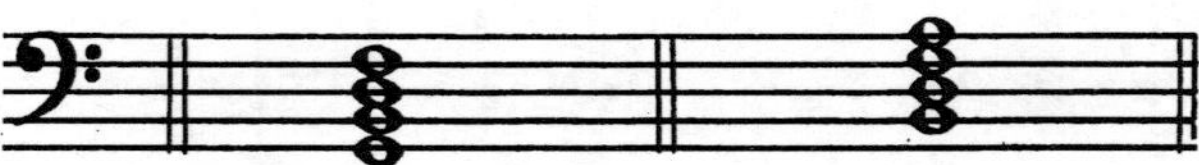

c) Subdominant Chords   IV △ = F△   II-7 = D-7

Exercise 2

Play the scale chords of a minor scale. They will have basically the same functions as their major counterparts. The chord built on the 5th degree is often changed from a minor 7th to a dominant 7th chord in order to create a stronger V to I resolution. This temporarily changes the accompanying scale to harmonic or melodic minor. Similarly, the chord built on the 7th degree has two forms. In the natural minor case, it is a dominant 7th chord built on the b7th which usually resolves to III major instead of I minor. By using the harmonic minor instead of natural minor, the chord on the 7th degree is a #VII° chord, which is used as a substitute for V7. Here they are for the key of A minor:

a) Tonic Chords   I-7 = A-7   III△ = C△   VI△ = F△

b) Dominant Chords   V7 = E7   VII° = G#°

c) Subdominant Chords   IIø = Bø   IV-7 = D-7

REDUCING CHORD PROGRESSIONS TO SCALES

Tunes should be analyzed in terms of what changes of key occur (modulations) and what the function of each chord is in each key.

Exercise 3

Pick a tune (e.g. "All The Things You Are") and use the following steps to analyze it:

a) Take the first 2 chords and put them together to make a scale. There will often be several scales that will work, e.g.

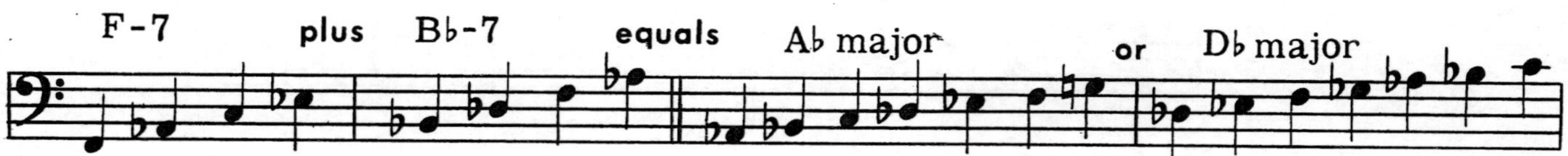

b) Then see if one of those keys contains the first three chords in the tune as scale chords, etc. Continue this process to include as many chords as possible in the same key. It will usually be the same key as the key signature of the tune. For example, Ab major (or F minor) is the only key that includes all the chords in the first 5 bars of "All The Things You Are.'

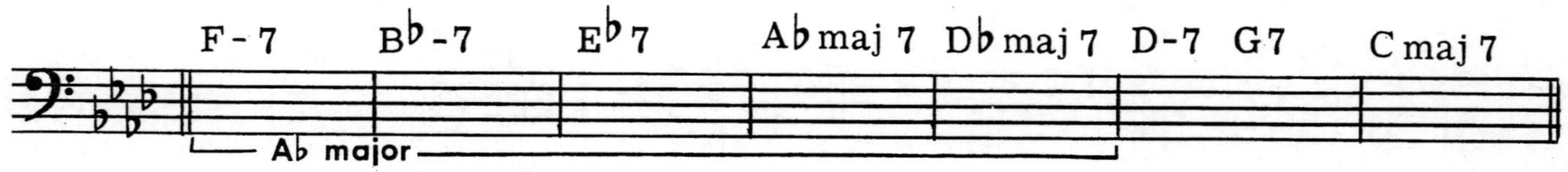

c) When you come to a chord that isn't a scale chord of the first key and that lasts for two beats or more, a modulation is occuring. Sometimes the new key will only last a bar or two before returning to the previous key. Determine what the new key is in the same way you did for the original key, e.g.

(CONT.)

If a minor chord exists followed by a dominant chord a 5th below it, they are functioning as the II-7 and V7 chords of a key, e.g.

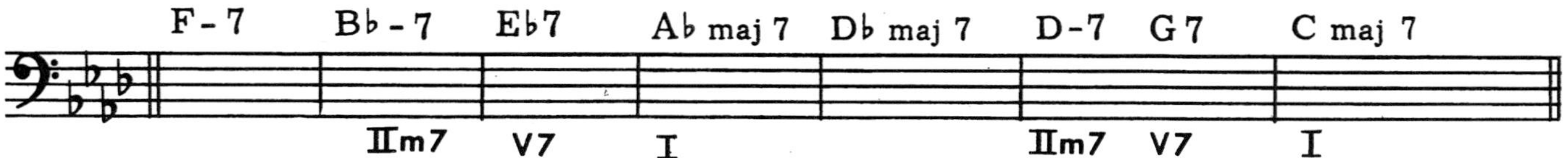

This II V progression is part of the cycle of fifths and strongly wants to continue to the I chord, the next chord on the cycle. Even if the II V progression never resolves to the I chord, the I key has occurred, since it is the only key that contains both chords. Thus identifying II V progressions when they occur is essential to analyzing tunes.

d) If there is a question of whether a major key or its relative minor is the real key, look for a V7 chord or a II-7 V7 progression leading you to one or the other. If it is leading to a minor key, the II chord will often be half-diminished, since that is the scale chord built on the second degree of the minor scale, e.g. the 1st 5 bars are in Ab, not F minor.

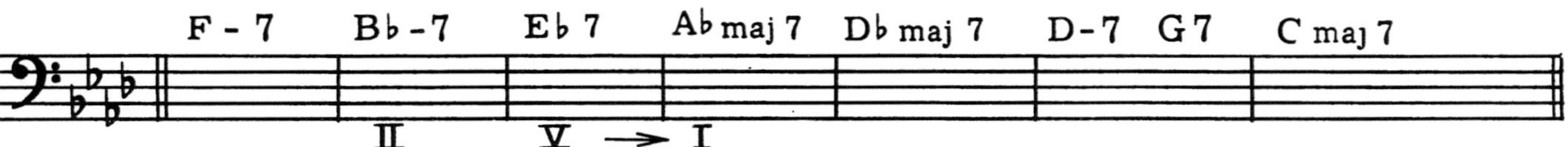

e) Repeat this process for the entire tune until you have reduced the chord progression to a series of keys. Memorize this series and how long each one lasts.

f) Analyze the function of each chord within each key, e.g.

Modulations are often done to closely related keys of thé original key. This is done through the use of secondary dominants, i.e. dominant chords which lead to keys suggested by the scale chords of the original key. Here are the secondary dominants in the key of C along with the note in the dominant chord that is outside of the C major scale. So if you hear one of these notes being played in a C major passage, it is a good bet that it belongs to the corresponding secondary dominant chord.

Secondary Dominant	New Key Based on Scale Chord	Note not in the Original Key
A7	D minor	C# (b2 of C)
B7	E minor	D# (b3 of C)
C7	F major	Bb (b7 of C)
D7	G major	F# (b5 of C)
E7	A minor	G# (+5 of C)

Exercise 4

Here is all of "All The Things You Are" with the chord progression and the series of keys that the progression reduces to. Keeping the melody in your head, play the tune as a series of scales. This is especially valuable for soloing. When more than two chords do not fit into any key (e.g. bars 29-32), divide that section into four chord or four bar phrases, if possible, and memorize them seperately. This will lend some coherence to your thinking.

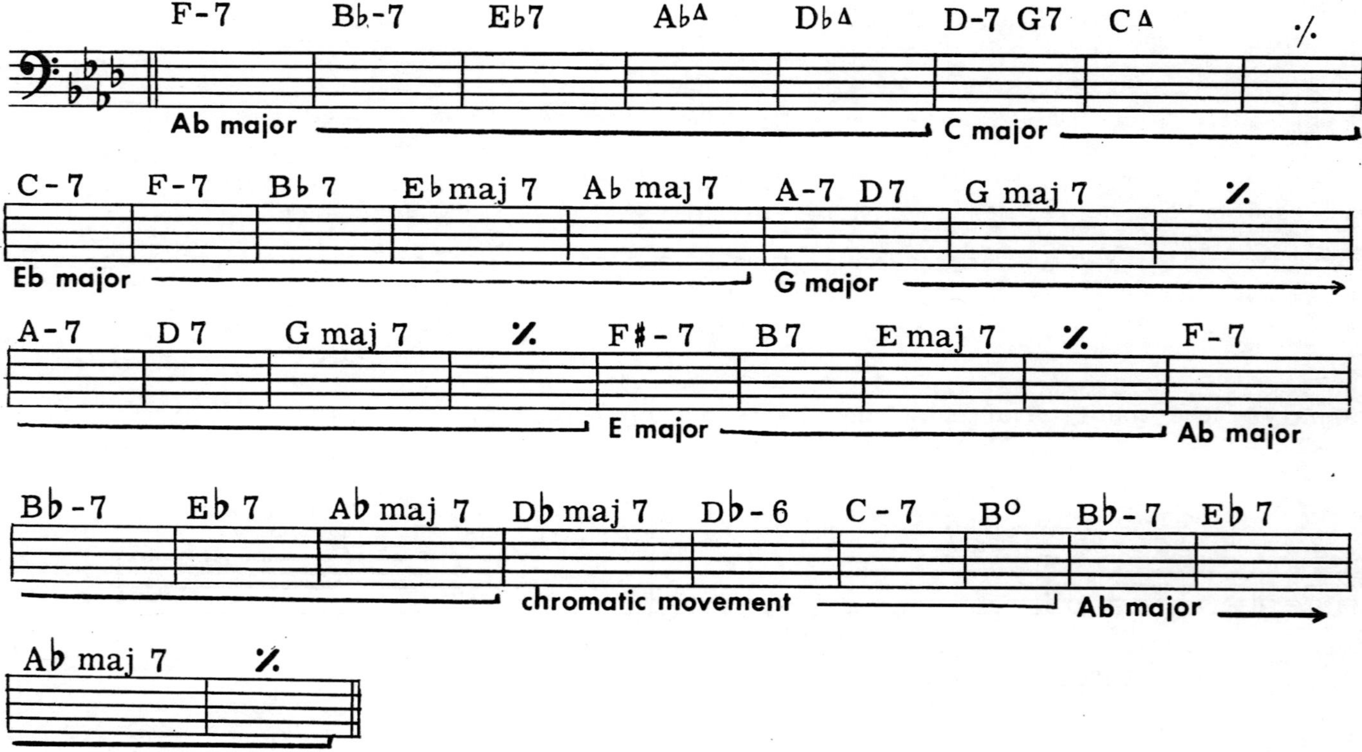

KEY CENTERS AND CHORD SUBSTITUTIONS

Often, chords in tunes will not fit into one scale, but are functionally related as if they were in the same key. This looser conception of a key is sometimes called a key center or tonality. The next example can be viewed as having one primary key center (F) that all the chords function within.

Exercise 5

from "Easy Living"

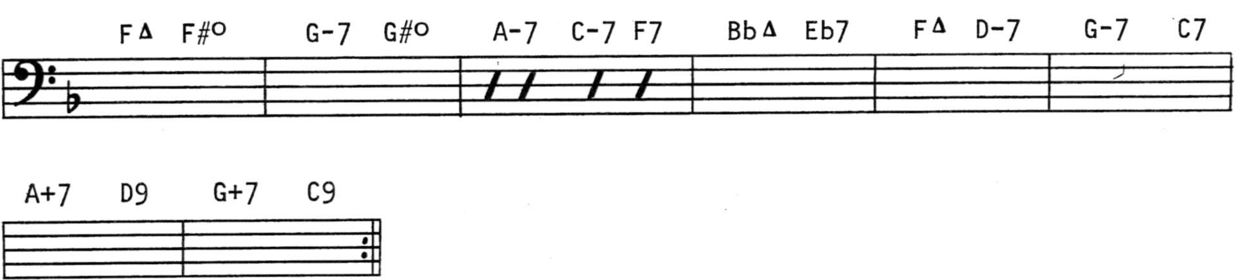

The F major 7th chord states the tonic sound right away in bar 1. This moves to the II-7 chord in bar 2, thus creating a very common progression - tonic to subdominant. The diminished chords in bars 1 and 2 work well because they create a chromatic bass line and also because they function as the dominant of the following chord (F#o is D7-9 without the root and G#o is E7-9 without the root). Bar 3 states the tonic sound again and then sets up a modulation to the key based on the IV chord, Bb major, in bar 4. The Eb7 is justified by being the next chord on the cycle of fifths and also because of its close relationship to Bb-7, the minor version of the subdominant of F. This major to minor progression is very strong and is used in many different situations.

The 5th and 6th bars are an example of the most common four chord progression, I VI II V. This is called a turnaround and works so well because I to VI, while remaining in the tonic sphere of influence, has some harmonic motion. From there on, the cycle of fifths takes over, ending on the V7 chord which usually leads back to the tonic. Often the III chord will substitute for the tonic giving you a III VI II V progression (as in bars 7 and 8), creating a cycle of fifths movement all the way through.

Exercise 6

from "Early Autumn"

Bb△	A7(-9)	Ab△	G7(-9)	Gb△	F7(-9)	Bb△	C-7 F7

In this tune, the major chords are set up by dominant chords a half step above them instead of a 5th above. For example, instead of Eb7, A7 is used as the dominant of Ab (bar 2). Both A7(-9) and Eb7(-9) are derived from the E° chord and are often used as substitutes for each other. This b5th (tritone) substitution is used on other quality chords too, especially in a II V situation, e.g. instead of D-7 G7 to C, you will often see D-7 Db7 or D-7 Db major 7th or even D-7 Db-7 (used mostly when going to C-7), etc. By using this tritone substitution, a descending chromatic root progression is created, which is even stronger than the original cycle of fifths bass movement.

Here is a list of substitute turnarounds created by using different combinations of cycle of fifths and chromatic movement. Experiment with using different quality chords and try substituting III for I in any of them.

1	b3	2	b2	1	b3	b6	b2	1	b6	2	b2
1	6	b6	5	1	b3	b6	5	1	6	b7	7
1	b2	2	5	1	b7	b6	5	1	b2	2	b2
1	6	b6	b2	1	b3	2	5	1	4	#4	5

Exercise 7

from "Jordu"

G7 C7	F7 Bb7	Eb7 Ab7	Db7	F7 Bb7	Eb7 Ab7	Db7 Gb7	B7

This is an example of the use of the cycle of fifths. This progression is an extention of the basic dominant to tonic movement, and as such is strong enough to justify moving to keys far away from the initial tonality.

Exercise 8

from "The Duke"

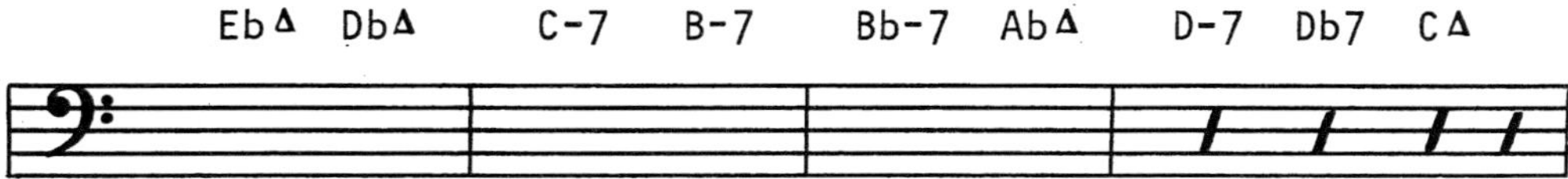

The root progression here combines half step and whole step movements into
a scalar-like series that is very effective in producing the illusion of
related chords even as it moves to distant keys. Notice the Db7 is used as a
substitute for G7 in the 4th bar. The 1st two bars have to be played as four
seperate chords &/or scales.

Exercise 9

Here are several different ways to play the 12 bar blues. The chords written
on the staff lines are substitutes. Try adding another substitute each chorus
until you are using all of them instead of the chords above them.

(CONT.)

Minor Blues

Exercise 10

Here is the chord progression known as "rhythm changes", based on "I Got Rhythm", with some substitute chords underneath.

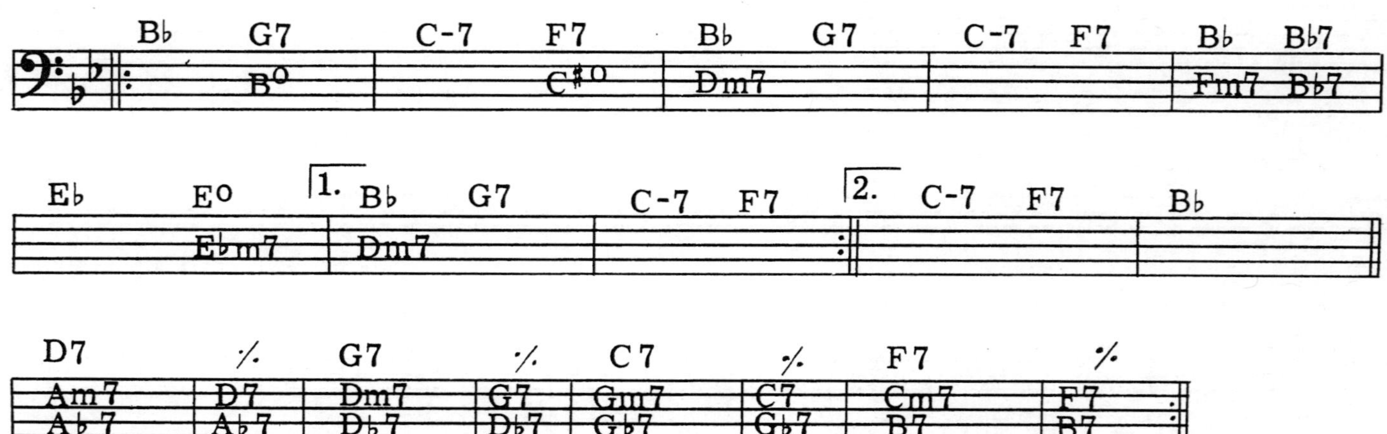

Exercise 11

Here are some substitute chords for the V7 chord in a II-7 V7 progression. Notice that you can play half-diminished chords off of each note of the G7 chord (except G), and major 7(b5) chords off of each note of the Db7 chord (the tritone substitute for G7), in the following example.

D-7	G7	C		and		D-7	G7	C
	BØ						Db Δ (b5)	
	DØ						F Δ (b5)	
	FØ						Ab Δ (b5)	
							B Δ (b5)	

a) Try using one of these substitutions on different II V progressions.

b) Try using one whenever II V occurs in a tune.

c) Try transposing it up a step to create substitute chords for the V7 and VI 7 chords in a II V III VI vamp, e.g.

The Db Δ (b5) and the Ab Δ (b5) chords won't survive this transposition as well as the others because the other chords can be seen as some kind of G7 chord without the root.

d) In addition to transposing the same substitute chord up a step, try mixing these substitutions, e.g.

e) For soloing, try playing two different substitutes during one bar.

f) For longer sections of a dominant chord, try playing either series above in its entirety.

g) Also, try the following sequence of parallel substitutes for a G7 chord. They are all diminished triads with the major 7th on top:

PRACTICING TUNES

Exercise 12

Take a particular exercise from Chapters 2 through 8 and use it throughout the changes of a tune. This can be done keeping strictly to the exercise or just using it as a point of reference as you play through the tune.

Exercise 13

Do Exercise 12 but instead of using the whole tune, take a four chord or four bar section of the tune and play it as a vamp until it feels comfortable.

Exercise 14

Play the changes to a tune (or have someone else do it) on piano or guitar along with a metronome. Tape this and play along with the tape; or play along with records or the radio.

Exercise 15

Mentally hear a bass line as the changes to a 4 or 8 bar section of a tune is being played. Play the section again trying to play a bass line with the same feeling, contours, or specific lines as the one you sang to yourself.

Exercise 16

Try alternating soloing and playing bass lines through the changes to a tune.

Exercise 17

Here are several ways to approach the tonalities of a tune. Try them one at a time.

a) Chordal - Think only of the notes of each chord as it occurs.

b) Scalar-sounding Chordal - Think of the chords, but connect the chord tones with other notes from the scale.

c) Scalar - Think only of the scales that the chord progression reduces to. Play different patterns off of the scales.

d) Chordal-sounding Scalar - Think only of the keys of the tune, but play patterns built mostly off of thirds.

e) Polychordal - Play an extention chord on top of each original chord in the tune (see Chapter 10).

f) Modal - Establish one note as the tonic for a section of a tune. Play anything resolving back to that tonic note.

Chapter 10 — CHORD EXTENTIONS

CHORDS AND THEIR COMPLIMENTARY SCALES

Besides playing the notes of the chord, it is possible to add other notes to it and still maintain the basic chord sound. This involves finding a scale that compliments the chord in its particular context. For example, a C-7 chord will often take a C natural minor scale when it is the tonic chord of a section of a tune. When it is functioning as the II-7 chord in the key of Bb, however, it will take the C Dorian mode (i.e. the Bb major scale starting on C), e.g.

Cm7   Fm7   Ab7   G7   or   Bb   Gm7   Cm7   F7

Natural Minor / Dorian

Here is a chart of some chords and their most common complimentary scales.

CHORD	COMPLIMENTARY SCALES
C maj 7	C Major; C Lydian
C maj 7 (b5)	C Lydian; D Mixolydian (#4)
C maj 7 (+5)	A Melodic or A Harmonic minor
C min. 7	C Natural minor; C Dorian
C min. (maj.7)	C Melodic minor; C Harmonic minor
C min. 6	C Dorian; C Melodic minor
C min. 7 (b5)	C Locrian; Eb Melodic minor (= C natural minor b5 scale)
C diminished 7	C Diminished scale; Db,E,G,or Bb Harmonic minor scales
C suspended 7	C Mixolydian; C Natural minor; C Dorian; any F minor scale; C,D,F,G,A, or Bb Minor Pentatonic scale.
C7 or C9	C Mixolydian; C Blues scale
C9 (b5 or +5)	C Whole Tone scale
C9 (#11)	G Melodic minor (=C Mixolydian #4)
C9 (b13) *	F Melodic minor (=C Mixolydian b6)
C7 (b9,b13) *	F Harmonic minor
C7 (b9,altered 5th)	C Altered scale (=Db Melodic minor)
C7 (+9,altered 5th)	C Altered scale
C7 (b9,regular 5th)	Db Diminished scale
C7 (+9,regular 5th)	Db Diminished scale

* Note: (b13) chords are the same as (+5) chords, except that the unaltered 5th is included in the scale.

CHORDS OFF OF CHORDS

Exercise 1

Pick a chord and an accompanying scale. Choose a ninth, 11th, and 13th to go above the 7th chord, using only scale notes. This extended chord will contain all the notes of the scale (assuming it is a 7 note scale), only stacked in thirds instead of step-wise, e.g.

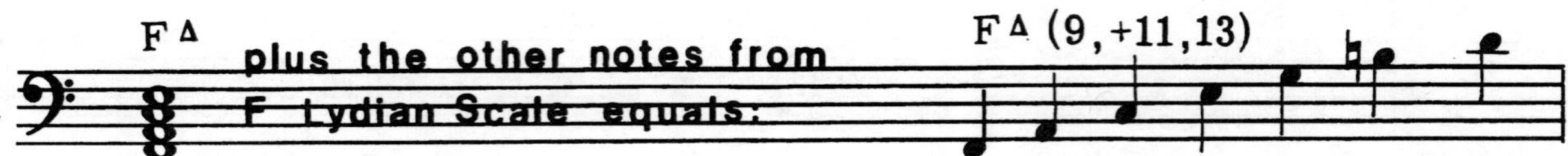

Other 7th chords can be extracted from this extended chord by starting on the 3rd, 5th, 7th, and 9th in the following manner:

Exercise 2

Play a lick based on the original chord, then add a lick from one or more of the extention chords, e.g. C major 7th and its Lydian extentions.

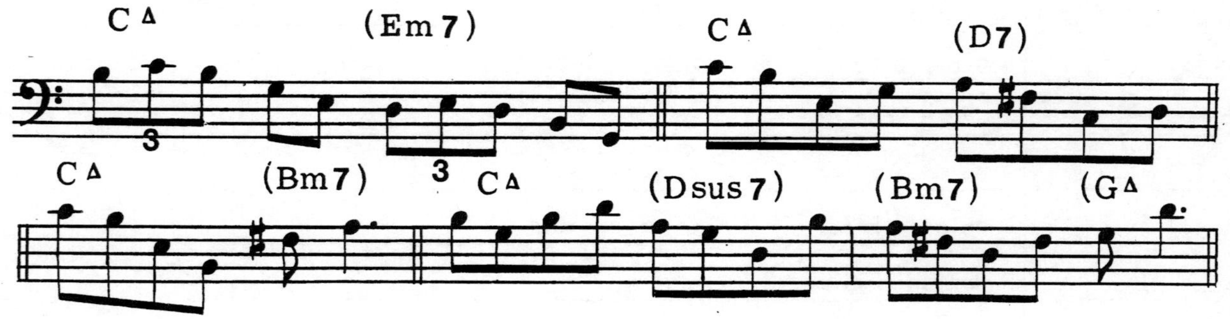

Next is a chart for some chords and their extentions, given a complimentary scale. Alternative chords are given when more than one chord can be built on a scale degree. They are grouped so that a series of chords is created, each chord being an extention of the previous chord, whenever possible.

(CONT.)

CHORDS	SCALE CHOICE	RESULTING UPPER EXTENTIONS			
C maj.7	C Lydian	E-7	G△	B-7	Dsus or D7
C min.7	C Dorian	Eb△	G-7	Bb△	D-7
C-7(b5)	Eb Melodic Minor	1) Eb-6 2) Eb△	Gb△(b5) Gb△(+5)	Bb+7 Bb7	D+7 D-7(b5)
C9(+ or -5)	C Whole Tone	E7(+ or -5)	G#7(+ or -5)	Bb7(+ or -5)	D7(+ or -5)
C9(#11)	G Melodic Minor	1) E-7(b5) 2) E-7(b5)	G-6 G△	Bb (b5) Bb (+5)	D+7 D7
C9	C Mixolydian	1) E-7(b5) 2) E-7(b5)	G-7 G-6	Bb△ Bb△(b5)	D-7 Dsus
C7(-9)	Db Diminished	1) Eo 2) Eb7 3) Ebo 4) Eb-7	Go Gb7 Gbo Gb-7	Bbo A7 Ao A-7	Dbo Co
	F Harmonic Minor	1) Eo 2) Eo 3) E+	Go G-7(b5) 	Bbo Bb-7 Bb-7(b5)	Dbo Db△ Db△
C Altered (-9,+9,-5, &/or +5)	C Altered Scale	1) E△(b5) E△(+5) 2) Eb-7	 Gb7	Ab7 Bb-7(b5)	C-7(b5) Db-6/9 Db△

Try extending these sequences to the 11th and 13th as well, giving you chords built off of each scale degree. This can be a valuable tool for improvising in a modal situation.

Exercise 3

Play licks off of several related extention chords as a substitute for playing on a chord, e.g.

POLYTONALITY OFF OF UPPER EXTENTIONS

When basic chords plus an extention chord are played or conceived of simultaneously, they are called polytonalities. Here are the chords of Bill Evan's tune, "Time Remembered," with Bill's voicings analyzed into basic chords on the bottom plus upper extentions.

Exercise 4

Go through the above tune in the following ways:

a) Play an arpeggiated line containing the basic chord and its extention. Try playing only part of one of them, e.g.

b) Alternate licks off of the two chords, 2 beats or a whole bar apiece, e.g.

c) Use just the triads of the upper chord to create a stronger sense of polytonality, e.g.

(CONT.)

d) Extention chords are often used as substitutes for the basic chord, especially when soloing, so try just playing the upper chord while someone else plays the bottom chords for you.

e) Play keeping the scale that the two chords create in mind, e.g. C Lydian in bar 2, E Dorian in bar 4, etc. Using this scale, play scale fragments, scalar patterns, etc. off of the notes of the basic chord, e.g.

Exercise 5

On altered dominant chords, try playing an upper extention triad plus the 3rd and 7th of the basic dominant chord. This is especially useful for soloing or following the voicings of pianists who use these sounds alot. Try the following arpeggios while someone plays a C7 chord for you. Also try using the Bb below the E instead of above it, and try different inversions of the upper triad.

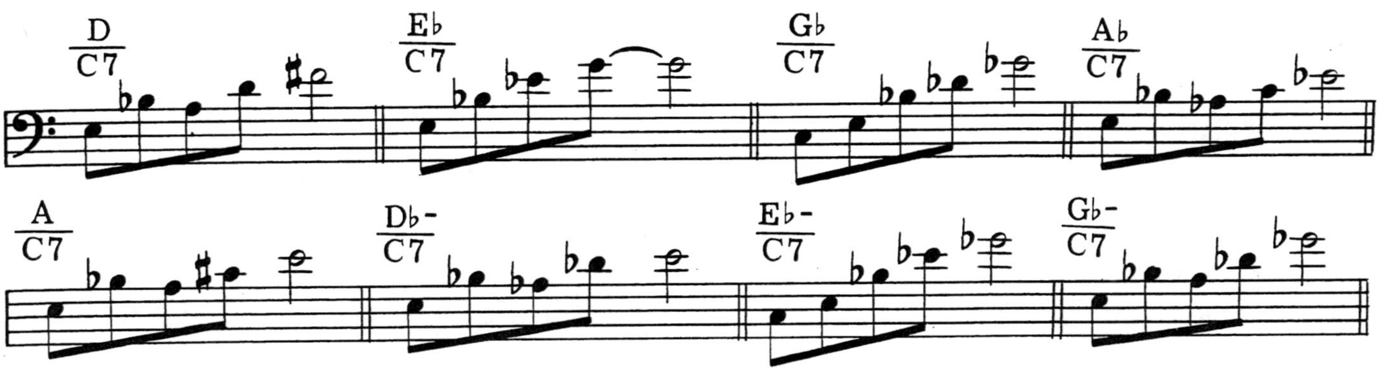

This procedure can be used to reharmonize any dominant chord by hitting a chord note and then making it part of one of the triads shown above. For example, here are several ways to play G7 to C.

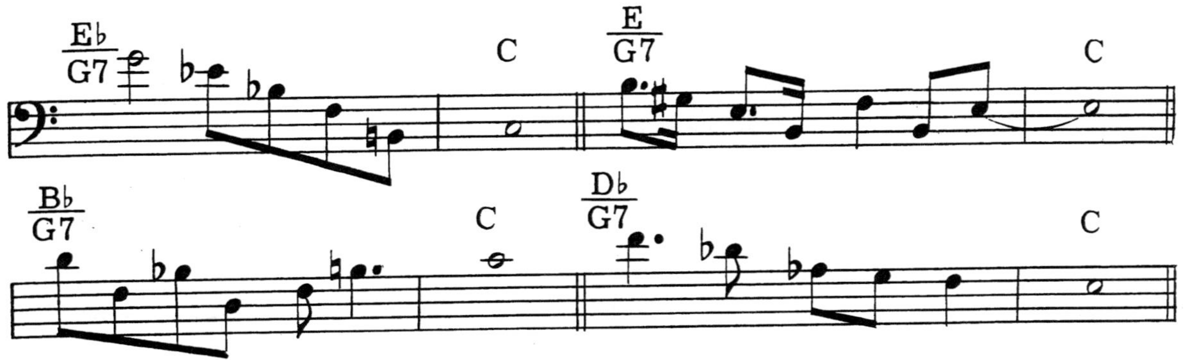

POLYTONALITY USING NON-CHORD BASS NOTES

Exercise 6

Chords can also be extended by putting non-chord bass notes underneath the original chord, producing a more or less polytonal sound. The following chart gives you 14 different chords with non-chord bass notes and their translation into functionally equivalent chords built off of those bass notes. Try playing the bottom note as a single note or as 15[1] underneath the chord.

CHORD	USING 6th IN BASS	USING 4th IN BASS	USING 2nd IN BASS	USING OTHER NOTES
Cm7	$\frac{Cm7}{Ab}$ = Ab maj.7,9	$\frac{Cm7}{F}$ = F sus.7	$\frac{Cm7}{Db}$ = Db maj.7 (9,+11,13)	
Cm7(b5)	$\frac{C\o}{Ab}$ = Ab9	$\frac{C\o}{F}$ = F sus (-9)	$\frac{C\o}{D}$ = D7(-9,+5)	
C°	$\frac{C°}{Ab}$ = Ab7(-9)	$\frac{C°}{F}$ = F7(-9)	$\frac{C°}{D}$ = D7(-9)	$\frac{C°}{B}$ = B7(-9)
Cm6		$\frac{Cm6}{F}$ = F9	$\frac{Cm6}{D}$ = D sus (-9)	$\frac{Cm6}{B}$ = B7(-9,+5)
Cm(maj.7)	$\frac{C\triangle}{A}$ = Am7,9 (b5)	$\frac{C\triangle}{F}$ = F9(#11)	$\frac{C\triangle}{D}$ = D sus(-9,13)	
C maj.7	$\frac{Cmaj7}{A}$ = Am7,9	$\frac{Cmaj7}{F}$ = F maj.7 (9,#11)	$\frac{Cmaj7}{D}$ = D sus.7 (9,13)	
C △ (b5)	$\frac{C \triangle (b5)}{A}$ = Am6/9		$\frac{C \triangle (b5)}{D}$ = D9,13	$\frac{C \triangle (b5)}{Ab}$ = Ab7 (+5,+9)
C △ (+5)	$\frac{C \triangle (+5)}{A}$ = A-9(△)		$\frac{C \triangle (+5)}{D}$ = D9 (#11,13)	
C+7		$\frac{C+7}{Gb}$ = Gb9,#11	$\frac{C+7}{D}$ = D9 (#11,-13)	$\frac{C+7}{Eb}$ = Eb sus.7 (-9,13)
C sus.7	$\frac{Csus}{Ab}$ = Ab maj.7 (9,13)		$\frac{C sus.}{Db}$ = Db maj.7 (#11,13)	$\frac{C sus.}{Eb}$ = Eb 6/9
C9		$\frac{C9}{Gb}$ = Gb7 (-9,#11,b13)		
C7 (-9)	$\frac{C7(-9)}{A}$ = A7 (-9,+9)	$\frac{C7(-9)}{Gb}$ = Gb7 (-9,#11)		$\frac{C7(-9)}{Eb}$ = Eb7(-9,13)
C7 (+9)	$\frac{C7(+9)}{Ab}$ = Ab (9,+5)	$\frac{C7(+9)}{Gb}$ = Gb7 (-9,#11,13)		
C7 (b5)	$\frac{C7(b5)}{Ab}$ = Ab9(+5)		$\frac{C7(b5)}{D}$ = D9(+5)	

By taking the extended chords that these polytonalities produce and grouping them according to what quality chord is created, we get the following chart. These can all be used, singly or together, as substitutes for the basic chord type shown at the left of each column.

BASIC CHORD   POLYTONAL EQUIVALENTS

C Major Chords	$\dfrac{\text{E-7}}{\text{C}}$	$\dfrac{\text{Esus7}}{\text{C}}$	$\dfrac{\text{G}\triangle}{\text{C}}$	$\dfrac{\text{Asus7}}{\text{C}}$	$\dfrac{\text{B-7}}{\text{C}}$	$\dfrac{\text{Bsus7}}{\text{C}}$
C Minor Chords	$\dfrac{\text{Eb}\triangle}{\text{C}}$	$\dfrac{\text{Eb}\triangle\text{(+5)}}{\text{C}}$	$\dfrac{\text{Eb}\triangle\text{(b5)}}{\text{C}}$	$\dfrac{\text{G-7}}{\text{C}}$	$\dfrac{\text{Bb}\triangle}{\text{C}}$	
C Sus. Chords	$\dfrac{\text{G}\emptyset}{\text{C}}$	$\dfrac{\text{G-7}}{\text{C}}$	$\dfrac{\text{A+7}}{\text{C}}$	$\dfrac{\text{Bb}\triangle}{\text{C}}$	$\dfrac{\text{Bb}\triangle}{\text{C}}$	
C9 Chords	$\dfrac{\text{E}\emptyset}{\text{C}}$	$\dfrac{\text{E7(b5)}}{\text{C}}$	$\dfrac{\text{Gb+7}}{\text{C}}$	$\dfrac{\text{G}\triangle}{\text{C}}$	$\dfrac{\text{Bb7 (+ or - 5)}}{\text{C}}$	$\dfrac{\text{Bb}\triangle\text{(+ or - 5)}}{\text{C}}$
C7(-9) Chords	$\dfrac{\text{Eb7(-9)}}{\text{C}}$	$\dfrac{\text{E}^{\text{O}}}{\text{C}}$	$\dfrac{\text{Gb7(+ or -9)}}{\text{C}}$	$\dfrac{\text{A7(-9)}}{\text{C}}$	$\dfrac{\text{Bb-7(b5)}}{\text{C}}$	
C Altered Chords	$\dfrac{\text{E}\triangle\text{(b5)}}{\text{C}}$	$\dfrac{\text{Gb7(+9)}}{\text{C}}$	$\dfrac{\text{Gb9}}{\text{C}}$	$\dfrac{\text{Bb-7(b5)}}{\text{C}}$		

Exercise 7

In addition to the above polytonalities, putting chord tones other than the root underneath the chord can often sound polytonal too. Try playing these whenever the chord on top occurs in a tune.

$\dfrac{\text{Bb9}}{\text{C}}$ $\dfrac{\text{Db}\triangle}{\text{C}}$ $\dfrac{\text{Gsus}}{\text{C}}$ $\dfrac{\text{D7}}{\text{C}}$ etc

Chapter 11 — SOLOING

CONCEPTS FOR SOLOING

Exercise 1

Almost all the ideas and exercises in this book can be used to practice soloing as well as bass lines. So first, go back and review some of these exercises, using them as solo ideas. "Freedom is having alot of choices", as someone once said. E.g. Take a tune, reduce the chord progression to scales and solo thinking only of those scales (Chapter 9, Exercise 4). For example, "Recordame."

Exercise 2

Practice soloing over the changes of a tune using each four chord or four bar section of the tune as a vamp. Practice just the arpeggios first until the relationship between each chord is clear to you, then add scalar and chromatic passages to connect chord notes.

Exercise 3

When soloing, try using seperate, distinct phrases instead of the more
continuous quality that many bass lines have, e.g.

Exercise 4

Try keeping the melody to the tune in your head as you solo. Use little
pieces of it, embellish it, or follow its general contour, e.g. "Autumn Leaves".

Exercise 5

Aim for main, expressive notes and connect them with smooth sounding runs, e.g.

Exercise 6

Focus only on ending each phrase with an interesting interval and with a
definite and accurate rhythm, e.g.

Exercise 7

Harmonize your own lines by hitting a main note and then making that part of an arpeggio, e.g.

Exercise 8

For difficult progressions, or whenever there are two chords per bar, try soloing on every other chord and implying the next one by playing just a note or two on it, e.g.

Exercise 9

Play a phrase, then play the next phrase keeping either the beginning or the ending the same, e.g.

Exercise 10

Use transposed licks (rhythm and/or melody) to give continuity to your solo lines. Both rhythms and notes can be altered somewhat from chord to chord without losing the unifying effect of the patterns, e.g.

JAZZ LICKS

Exercise 11

Next are several pages of licks taken primarily from jazz tunes, which are fun to insert into your solos. Try using them in the following ways:

a) Take one at a time and play it whenever the appropriate situation (usually II V) arises in a tune.

b) Transpose the II V licks down or up a step to create a III VI II V chord progression. Try using two different patterns instead of transposing the same one.

c) Take a particular lick and transpose it to different starting notes so that it becomes a part of your playing vocabulary. They are especially useful to begin or end your phrases with.

d) By doubling the time value of each note, these licks can be used as walking bass lines.

e) By changing any A to Ab in these licks, they can be used for D∅ G7 instead of D-7 G7.

f) Play the same notes (more or less) but use a different rhythmic style.

Using the II minor arpeggio at the beginning of the phrase.

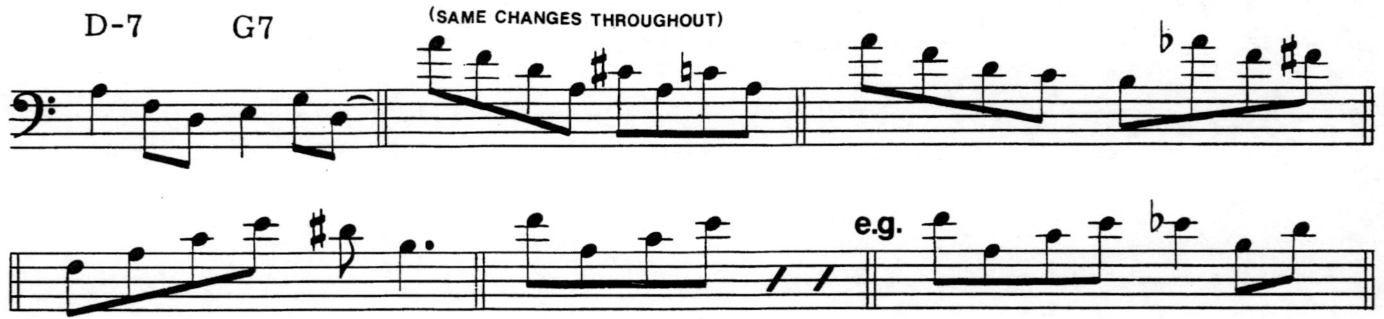

Using neighboring notes of a chord note, then a big interval to another chord note.

Using a contour in which the last note is a neighbor of the 1st note.

Using primarily one arpeggio.

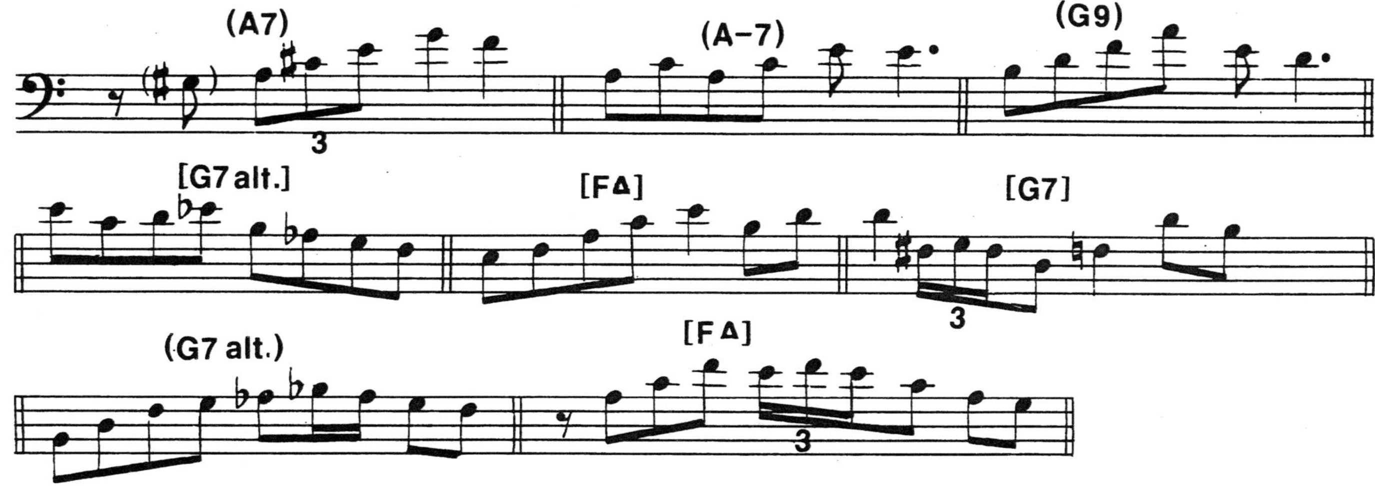

Using primarily two arpeggios.

Combining arpeggios and scale fragments.

Using phrases starting with a quarter rest.

Using scale fragments (more or less).

Using repeated note or notes.

Using parallel intervals.

Using phrases based on thirds.

Using chromatic approaches to important notes.

Using phrases which end on a large interval.

Using transposed licks.

* start on any note

of G mixolydian

Using C to B movement.

Using A to Ab movement.

Using F to E movement.

e.g.

Using a 56^1 resolution.

Using 13^{45} licks.

Using other scalar patterns.

start on any note of D dorian.

Miscellaneous licks.

Using scales other than C.

(C dorian)   (C harmonic minor)   (Synthetic scale)

G# Diminished Scale

Whole Tone Scale

* try viewing this as an Ab°7 chord with added whole steps below each note.

THE THUMB POSITION (Acoustic Bass)

(This section was contributed by Lennie Lasher, bassist with the San Francisco Symphony and jazz recording artist.)

The exercises that follow are for the purpose of helping the player become more comfortable with the upper range of the acoustic bass, which is used quite frequently in contemporary bass playing, especially for solos. Start slowly to build up a callous on your thumb. After the exercises in this section are comfortable, go back and transpose any of the exercises in earlier chapters up an octave, using thumb position fingerings.

Exercise 12

This exercise gives you different patterns using the thumb to hold down the octave G on the G string. Repeat each bar until it is comfortable, then play all eight bars and repeat that. The fingerings are given above the note and the name of the string used is underneath the staff. When playing this exercise arco (with a bow), slur all six notes in one bow direction.

ↀ = thumb. The fingering is the same for each bar in this example.

Play the above patterns starting on other notes besides G, both above and below it and on other strings too, e.g.

Exercise 13

Repeat each bar, slowly at first, until the intonation of each note sounds correct, then play all eight bars straight through and repeat that.

This exercise should also be played in all keys and on other strings too, e.g.

Exercise 14

Here are some scales in thumb position. They should be transposed to all keys. The bottom fingerings are for a small bass &/or a large hand. The top fingerings are alternate ones for a large bass &/or a small hand in the lower thumb positions.

a) Major scales going across the strings

b) Natural minor scales going across the strings

c) Major scales going up one string. Do this on the other strings too. Start this slowly, making sure you shift smoothly and accurately. * = shift.

Exercise 15

Here are some other scales in thumb position. Find another fingering for each of these scales besides the one given here.

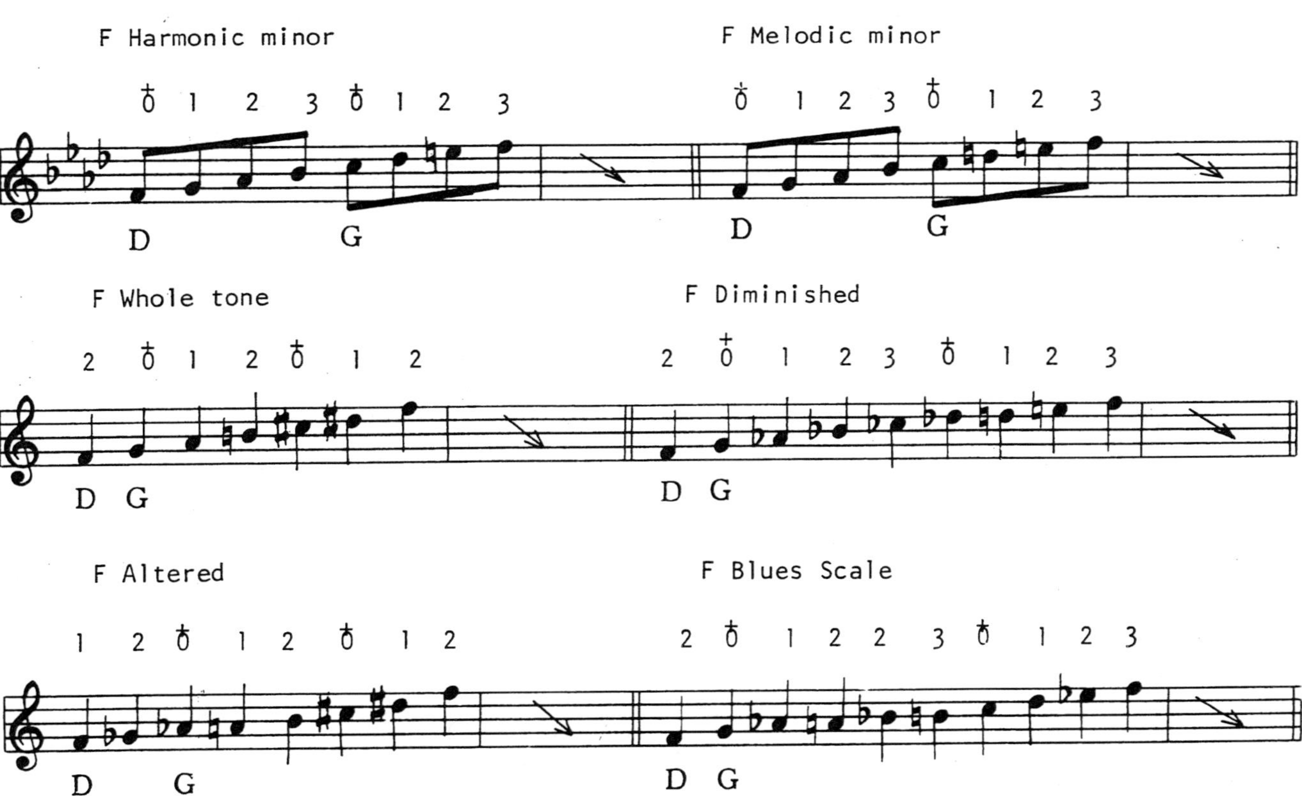

(CONT.)

Exercise 16

Here are some scalar patterns on one string.

a) Shifting on the 1st finger

b) Shifting on the thumb. This only works on ascending scales. Shift on the
   1st finger when descending.

c) Compare the speed at which the following passage can be played using thumb
   and non-thumb positions.

Exercise 17

This exercise gives you various arpeggios in thumb position. * = shift.

a) Across the strings

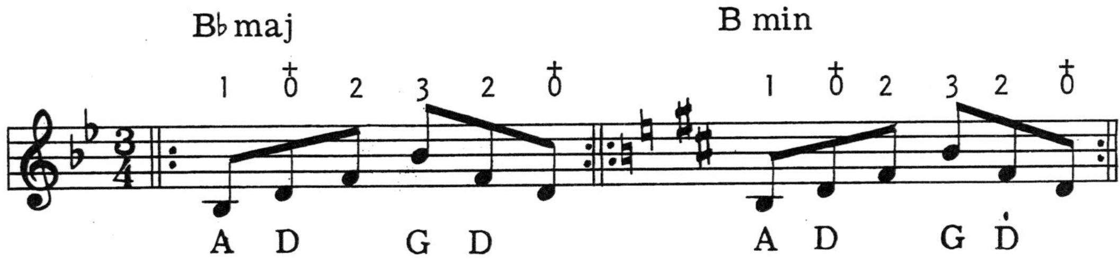

b) On one string

c) Here is the A-7 (9,11) chord using the "crawling thumb". If the 1st finger is used, the pattern stays the same. The 2nd finger is used when you have a small hand and a large bass.

d) Here is c) transposed up a minor third.

Exercise 18

This next one uses two moving fingers and two stationary ones. If this is played arco, slur all four beats in the bar. The moving fingers should stop the string at the same time. Do this until it is relaxed and accurate.

a) Keep the thumb and 3rd finger down on the string at all times. Move only the 1st and 2nd fingers.

b) Keep the thumb and 2nd finger down. Move only the 1st and 3rd fingers.

Exercise 19

Here is the Bb major scale played in thirds. Both this and the previous exercise are hard to play accurately. Do them slowly first.

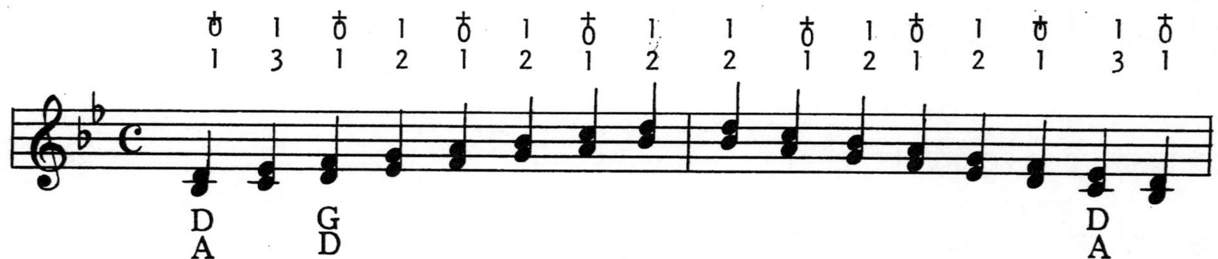

Exercise 20

Here is the unison break on Chick Corea's tune "Spain" played in the thumb position. X = shift the thumb down a half-step. For players with a small hand and a large bass, the (3 2) can be substituted for the 2 1 throughout this passage. Also notice that the thumb is used at various point to bridge two strings when notes a perfect fourth away are played.

(CONT.)

Exercise 21

This exercise is to develop the ability to shift to and from thumb position.
✶ = shift to thumb postion or back.

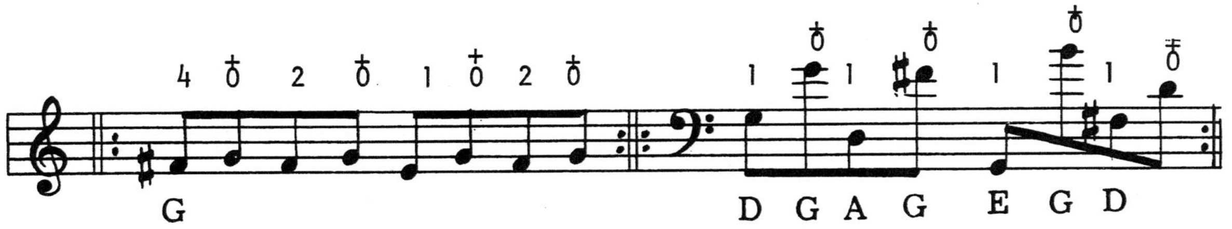

The last example above and the ones that follow should be played slowly at first so that the shifting is smooth and the intonation is accurate.

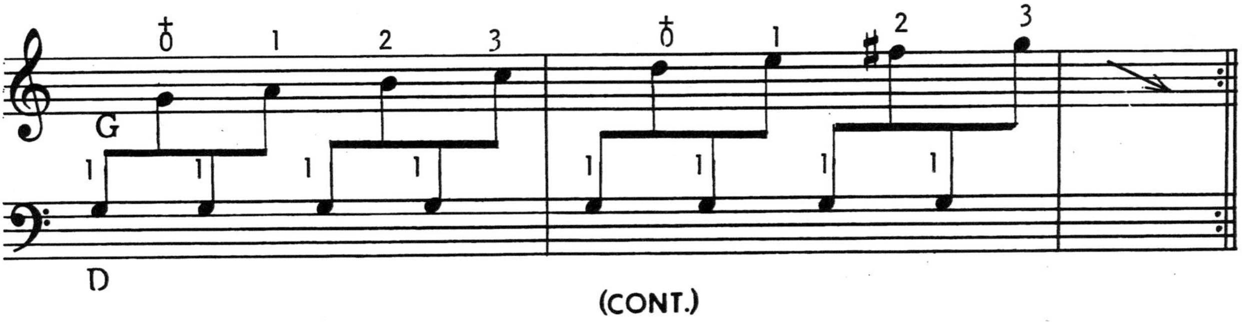

(CONT.)

Also, try shifting from the 2nd and 4th fingers on the low G, and try using different low notes on the A and E strings.

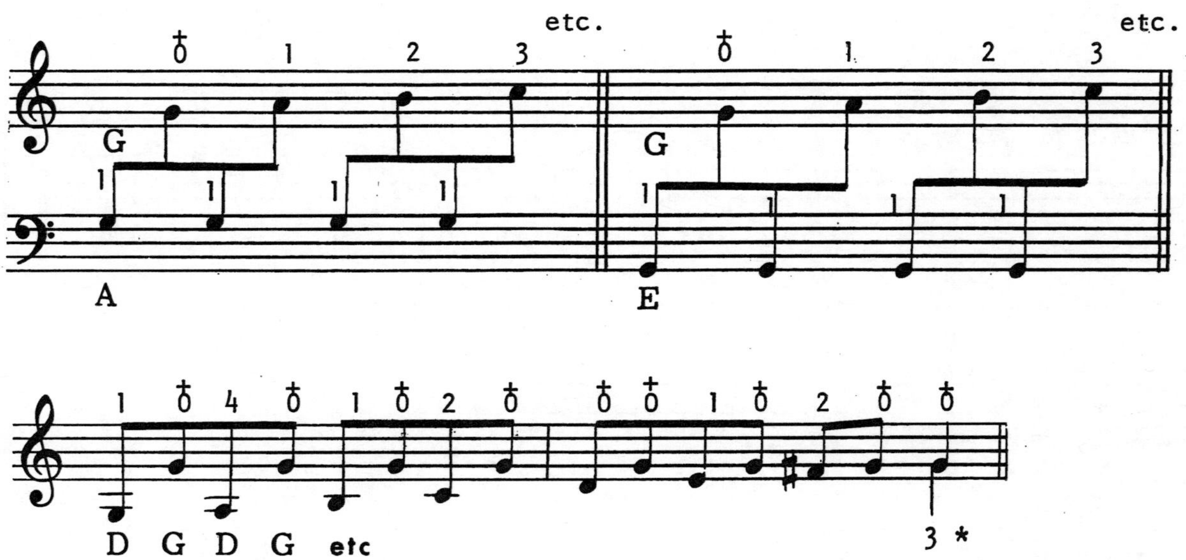

* This last note is played in unison on both the D and G strings.

Exercise 22

Artificial harmonics are played by holding the string down with the thumb and lightly touching it a 4th or a 5th above with the 3rd finger. Touching the string a 5th above the thumb gives you a note an octave and a 5th above the thumb's note, while touching it a fourth above creates a note 2 octaves higher than the stopped string. The top line is written to show the higher note's actual pitch, while the lower lines (as is generally the case with music for bass) actually sound an octave lower than written. Try this on other strings too, like the last two bars below.

Chapter 12 — DEVELOPING MUSICIANSHIP

BUILDING TECHNIQUE

Exercise 1

Here are four different ways to spend your practice time, each with its own validity:

a) Inside - Take a particular exercise and do it, slow and relaxed at first, without trying to improvise on it. It is the mental grasp of the rudiments that is important here, not just technical facility. Watch the physical aspects of playing, i.e. correct hand positions and hand movements, good breathing, good right hand tone production, etc. Practice this way for reading written material, too.

b) Inside ⟶ Out - Take a particular exercise and play it as is at first, then make some music with it as the basic motif. This can be done modally off of one tonic, on a two or four chord vamp, on the blues, or on a tune.

c) Outside ⟶ In - Play freely without reference to any structure except those that spontaneously occur. When you come to something that particularly interests you (2 or 3 notes, even), focus on it, solidify it, keep that kind of sound in the air, move it around the fingerboard, play variations, alternate it with other things, create little tunes based on it, sing along with it, and in general carry on in any manner that you so desire.

d) Outside - Just play. This can be either totally free (try to hear the notes in your head before you play them), or within some large form such as repeating similar contours every four bars or modal explorations off of one tonic. There are many aspects of music that can be explored from this perspective: emotional, physical and spiritual.

Exercise 2

Feel, focus on the basic pulse consistently. Play anything but don't let your concentration on this waver.

Exercise 3

Focus on the time feeling you are creating. Tape your practicing or tape yourself playing along with records to see if you are projecting the time feeling you wanted.

Exercise 4

Try playing an idea, especially difficult ones, over and over until the tone is firm, the fingering is smooth and the feeling is strong and relaxed. Then transpose it.

Exercise 5

Do exercise 4 but change the ending of the phrase each time, e.g.

Exercise 6

Do exercise 5 but transpose the phrase instead of starting it on the same note, e.g.

Exercise 7

Practice connecting the whole fingerboard with your phrases.

a) Try using just one or two notes with approach notes to them. Then try more complex harmonies, e.g.

b) Playing open strings whenever possible makes large interval leaps much easier, e.g.

Exercise 8

Practice transposing phrases up an octave. Over a period of time this will develop into a sense that there is just one octave to think about, everything else being a transposition of that octave, in the same way that a piano keyboard repeats its one octave pattern over and over.

EAR TRAINING

Exercise 9

Hear something mentally first, then try to sing &/or play it. Start with nursery rhymes or other simple melodies.

Exercise 10

Try taking each interval within an octave and associating it with the first two notes of a common melody to help you remember what the interval sounds like.

Exercise 11

Try singing a bass line along with a record. Tape this and transcribe your ideas.

Exercise 12

Sing along with anything you are practicing. This is good to do with a piano too, because the pitch will be standard. Try alternating played and sung phrases.

Exercise 13

Sing a phrase, then play it. If at first you don't succeed.......

Exercise 14

Bow a long tone or play an open string. Sing scales, chords, intervals or melodies with that note as the tonic.

Exercise 15

Make a tape of random intervals and practice identifying them. Try this with the notes sounded simultaneously or successively. Do this for chords and other patterns too.

Exercise 16

Practice sight-singing written material. Check your intonation with a piano.

Exercise 17

Sing or whistle an interval. Imagine it on the bass. Then add more notes in the same way, one at a time. If you get lost, start with the first interval again.

Exercise 18

Transcribe the bass line, the melody, or a solo off of a record. Then try identifying the chords (start with the tonics &/or the top note of the piano voicing). If a modulation is present, you might find the following relationship between tonalities useful. C is used as the original key.

G C F	Bb Eb Ab	Db Gb B	E A D
Original & Closely Related Keys	Minorish Sounding in Relation to C	Chromatic Sounding in Relation to C	Majorish Sounding in Relation to C

CONCEPTS FOR IMPROVISING

1. Try to always play lines, not just notes. This involves lengthening the thoughts behind your phrases. Try thinking in two bar phrases instead of one, for a start. In general, any concept that you use while playing will tend to lend coherence to your lines. Hopefully, this book will be of use in this regard.

2. Always try to make your phrases relate to each other. This can be done through the use of transposed patterns, similar contours, related rhythms, or continuity of feeling. The goal here is a sense of form, balance and symmetry in your lines.

3. Be aware of the highest &/or lowest important notes in your phrases. Be aware of the expansion and contraction of those limits, e.g.

4. Use the principle of tension and release. This can be done in several ways.

a) Try using landmark notes as releases. Create different amounts of tension between them.
b) Alternate specific licks (release) with more improvised phrases, both melodically and rhythmically.
c) Try playing off of the soloist's or other rhythm section player's ideas inbetween times of holding up the bottom.
d) Try using different dynamics (loud-soft) and tone qualities to create varying amounts of tension.
e) Try alternating simpler and more complex lines, to keep the texture interesting.

5. Always try to hear something mentally before you play a phrase. Strive to hear all the notes and rhythms exactly, but anything at all helps: a main note to aim for, a type of rhythmic feeling, a specific rhythm of the next phrase, the beginning or the ending of the next phrase, the contour of it (ascending and descending aspects), etc. Singing to yourself while you play is very helpful here.

6. As Paul Jackson once said, "The real challenge in music - after you've learned all the other bullshit and gone through the countless number of years and dues of just learning how to play your instrument - is how well did you listen? How well a musician listens is how well he can play with someone else."

Appendix I — TRADITIONAL LATIN BASS LINES

These bass lines are reprinted from "Latin Sounds for the Drum Set" by
Frank "Chico" Guerrero (Try Publishing Co., Hollywood, Ca.)

(CONT.)

Appendix II – TRANSCRIBED BASS LINES & SOLOS

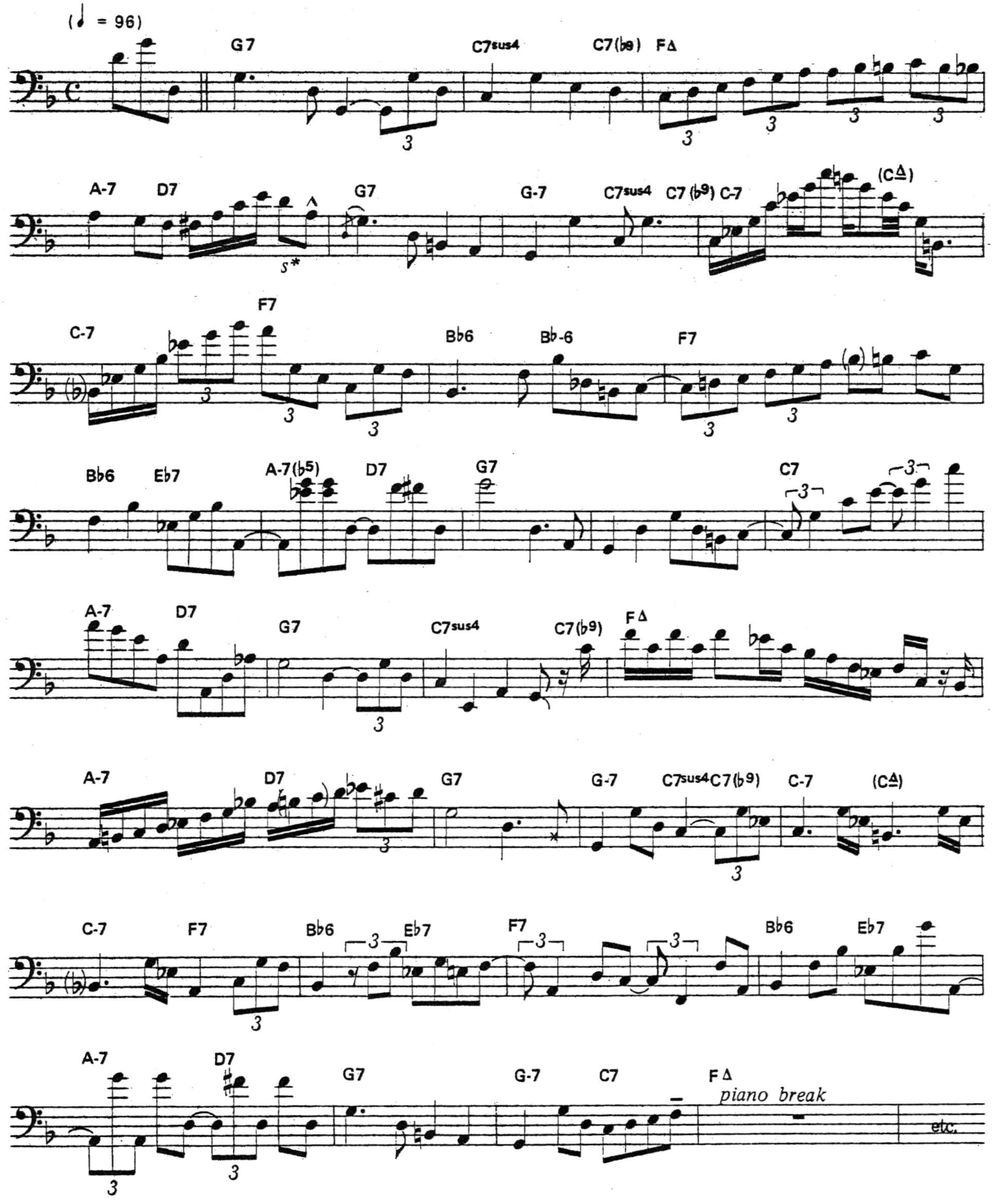

RON CARTER'S Bass Line on   "Eye of the Hurricane"   by Herbie Hancock

(intro)

F Blues

(CONT.)

Transcribed by Bob Bauer from Herbie's 1st "V.S.O.P." album

© 1980 Fourth Way Music. Used By Permission.

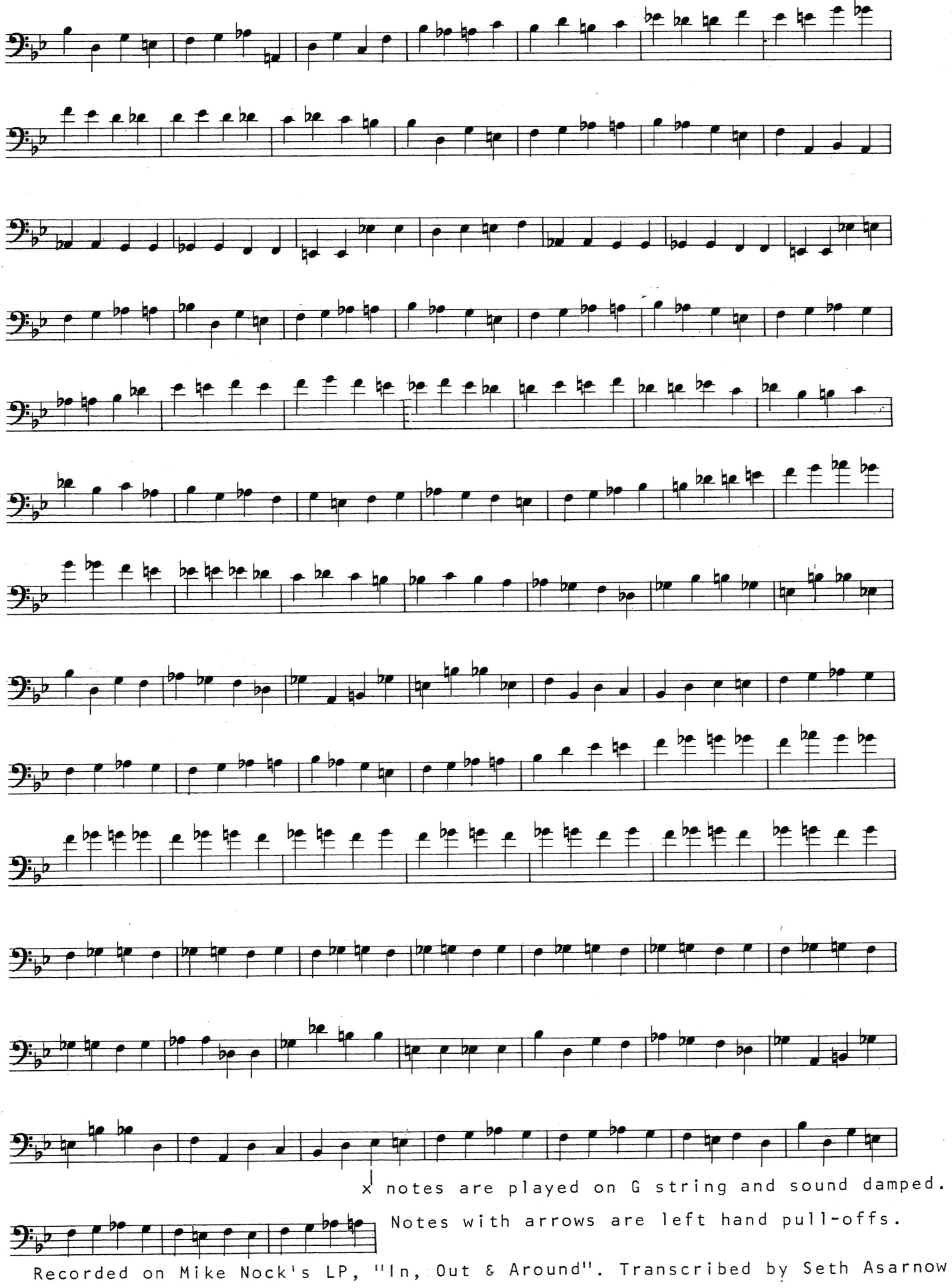

x notes are played on G string and sound damped.
Notes with arrows are left hand pull-offs.
Recorded on Mike Nock's LP, "In, Out & Around". Transcribed by Seth Asarnow.

PAUL CHAMBERS' Solo on   "Bass Blues"   by John Coltrane

Ab Blues

Solo -

(CONT.)

STANLEY CLARKE'S Bass Line on "What Game Shall We Play Today" by Chick Corea

(CONT.)

Joe's solo
Chick's solo
etc.

<u>RICHARD DAVIS'</u> Bass Line and Solo on   "Shiny Stockings"   by Frank Foster

(RICHARD'S SOLO)

DAVID FRIESEN'S Melody on   "Autumn Ballet"   by David Friesen

Guitar plays A once after brief solo - then plays off figure B
Guitar then states A twice then go to % , the D.C. al Fine.

© Color Pool Music   Used by permission
Recorded on David's Inner City LP., "Through the Looking Glass"

DAVID FRIESEN'S Melody on   "Children's Song"   by David Friesen

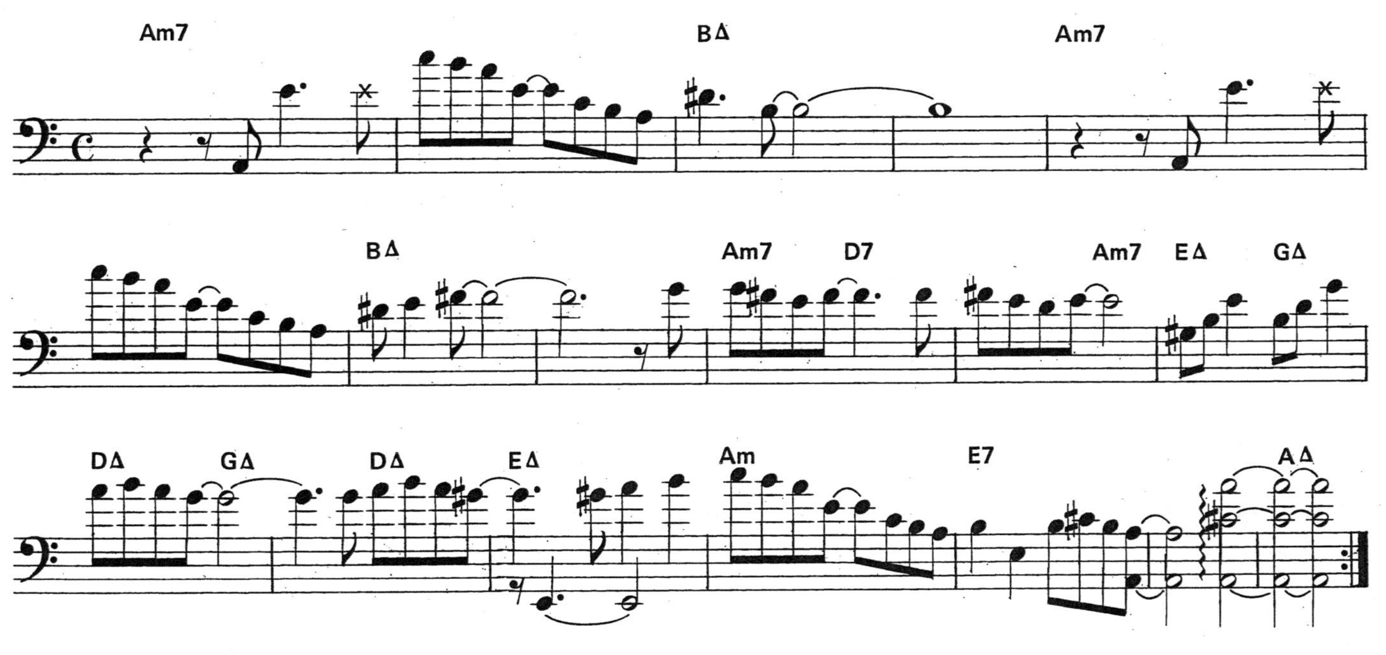

© Color Pool Music   Used by permission
Not yet recorded

DAVID FRIESEN'S Melody on   "Flight of the Angels"   by David Friesen

Solos on E-11 in 7/4 time. After solos, D.C. repeat to fine.

© Color Pool Music   Used by permission.
Recorded on Muse LP, "Flight of the Angels" and Inner City LP "Waterfall Rainbow"

JIMMY GARRISON'S Bass Line on   "Lonnie's Lament"   by John Coltrane

(CONT.)

All ♩♩ figures in this transcription are to be played as ♩♪ 3

Transcribed by Bob Bauer from John's Impulse LP., "Crescent"

JIMMY GARRISON'S Bass Line on "Crescent" by John Coltrane

(CONT.)

All ♩♩ figures in this transcription are to be played as ♩♩ —3—

Transcribed by Bob Bauer from John's Impulse LP, "Crescent"

© 1979 Thalian Music   Used by permission

Transcribed by Bob Bauer from Chick's LP, "Friends"

EDDIE GOMEZ' Melody on "Caprice" by Eddie Gomez

193
EDDIE GOMEZ' Bass Line on "Comrade Conrad" by Bill Evans
Bill's Solo → Bb-7   Eb+7   AbΔ   DbΔ   G∅   C+7
F-7   DbΔ   C+7   F-7   /Eb
3
D∅   G+7   C-7   F-7   Bb+7
EbΔ   AbΔ   D∅   G+7
C-7   AbΔ   G+7   C-7
3
/Bb   A∅   D+7   G-7   C-7
F+7   BbΔ   EbΔ   A∅   D+7   G-7
EbΔ   D+7   G-7   /F   E∅   A+7
D-7   G-7   C+7   FΔ
BbΔ   E∅   A+7   D-7

Bb△
A+7
D-7
/C
B∅
E+7
A-7
D-7
G+7
C△
F△
B∅
E+7
A-7
3
F△
E+7
A-7
/G
F#∅
B+7
E-7
A-7
D+7
G△
C△
F#∅
B+7
E-7
C△
B+7
E-7
/D
C#∅
F#+7
B-7

EDDIE GOMEZ' Solo on "Twelve Tone Tune" by Bill Evans

(CONT.)

CHARLES MINGUS' BASS LINE on "II B S"
by Charles Mingus
freely
swing
(♩ = 210)
3
6
6
3
3
play
10x
G min.
blues
Gm
Gm
G7
Cm
Gm
D7
Gm
stop
time

piano
solo
2
4
4
4

PAUL JACKSON'S Bass Line on   "Steppin' In It"   by Herbie Hancock

PAUL JACKSON'S Bass Line on   "Suntouch"   by Herbie Hancock
Intro
F#-9/B   F#-9/B   G+7   F#-9/B   A-11
F#-9/B   1 E-7/D   F#-9/B
2 E-9   Eb-9/Ab
1 Db-9   2 F#-9/B   3 Db-9/Gb   4 E-11
F#-9/B   E-9   (1st & 3rd times)   (2nd & 4th times)
F#-9/B   1 D-9
Solo
2 E-9/B   3 D-9   4 E-9   Eb-9/Ab
Db-9   D. S. al   A-9/D

JAMES JAMERSON'S Bass Line on "Home Cookin" by

Melvin Moy Henry Cosby
& Eddie Willis

©1968 by Jobete Co. Inc. International Copyright Secured
All Rights Reserved   Used by Permission
Transcribed by Jeff Neighbor from Soul LP, "Jr. Walker & The All-Stars
Greatest Hits"

ALPHONSO JOHNSON'S Bass Line on   "Lusitanos"   by Wayne Shorter

ALPHONSO JOHNSON'S Bass Line on   "Gibralter"   by Josef Zawinul

Recorded on Weather Report's LP, "Black Market"

SCOTT LaFARO'S Bass Line and Solo on "Gloria's Step" by Scott LaFaro

Head

Scott's solo on following pages →

(CONT.)

SCOTT LaFARO'S Bass Line on "Alice in Wonderland" by Fain & Hilliard

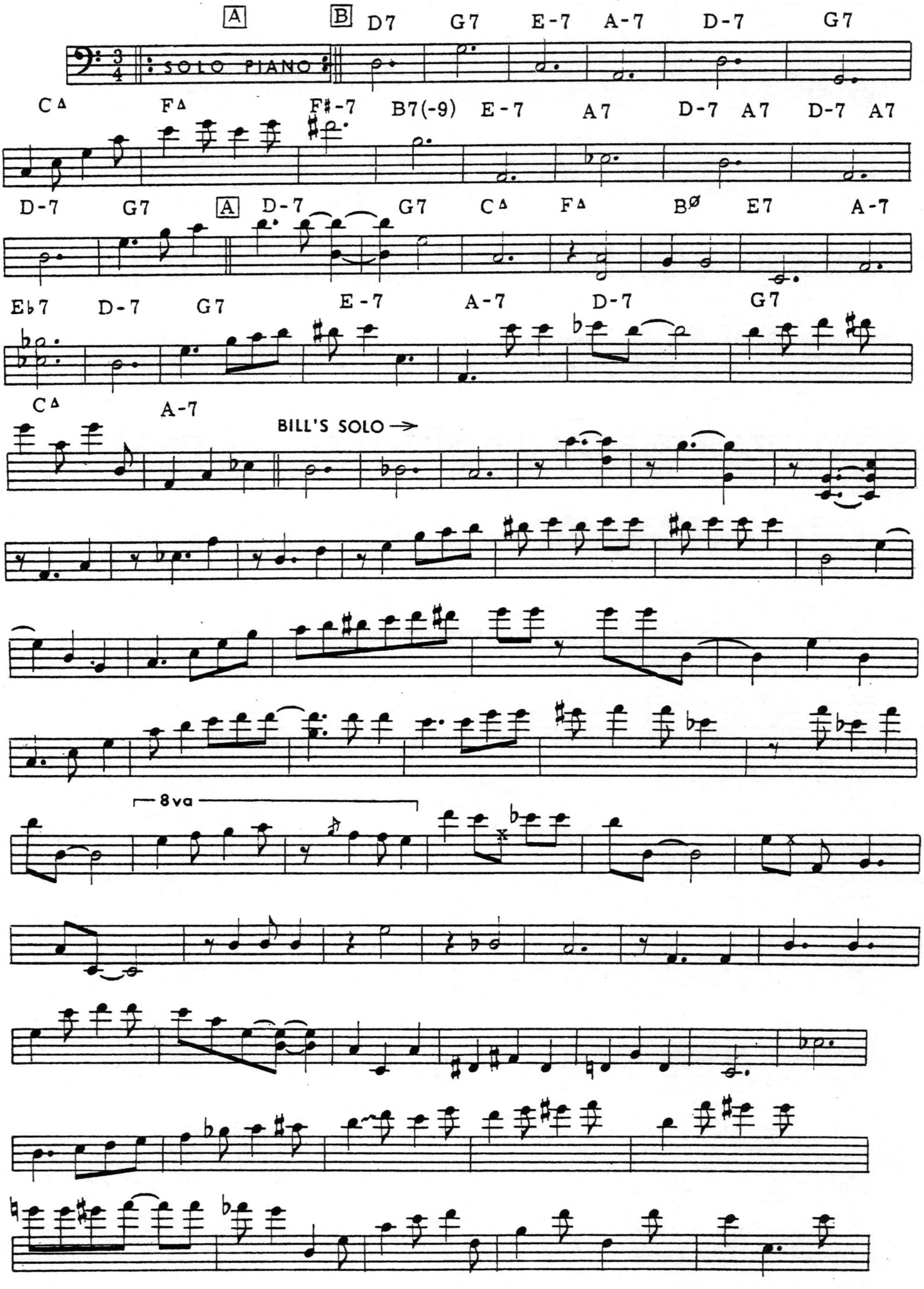

(CONT.)

© 1951 Walt Disney Music Co. This arrangement © 1979 Walt Disney Music Co.
Used by permission.
Transcribed by Bob Bauer from Bill Evans'' LP, ''The Village Vanguard Sessions''

LENNIE LASHER'S Solo on "Pocrasni"

by Lennie Lasher

(CONT.)

211
GEORGE MRAZ' Bass Line on   "Relaxin' at Camarillo"   by Charlie Parker
(C Blues)
Head
Tommy's solo
(CONT.)

George's solo
etc

JACO PASTORIUS' Melody on "Continuum"   by Jaco Pastorius

© Happala Music   Used by permission
Recorded on Jaco's Epic LP, "Jaco Pastorius" . Transcribed by Bob Bauer.

JACO PASTORIUS' Bass Line on "Cannonball" by Josef Zawinul

JACO PASTORIUS' Bass Line on "Birdland"
by Josef Zawinul
A
1-6.
7.
B
G7
23
C
D
G B- E- G   CΔ C#ø
B-7   E7   A-7   D7 sus   G B- E- A-7   C#ø D-
CΔ   A-   E G B- E   G   C#9(-5) C9(-5)
B-7   E7   A-   D7 sus   G B- E   G   C#9(-5) C9(-5)
B7   E7   A-   D7 sus   F G7   20   7x
3   Repeat last 4 times of A   Repeat B   Repeat D   Repeat, Fade on E

ROBERT "POPS" POPWELL'S Bass Line on "Free as the Wind" by Joe Sample

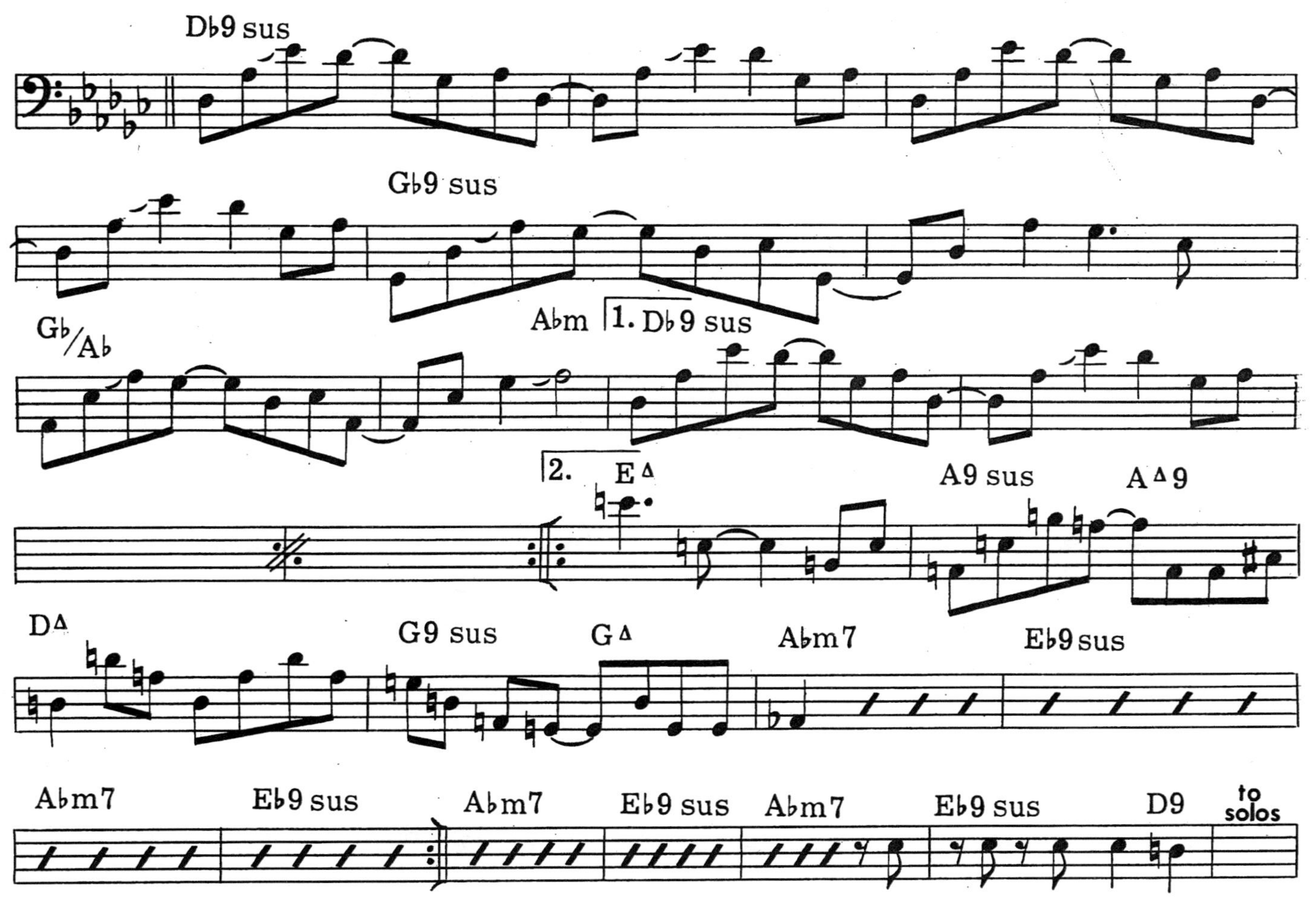

© Four Knights Music. Bass line composed by Joe Sample. Used by permission. Recorded on the Crusaders'' LP, "Free as the Wind"

MARCUS MILLER'S Bass Line on   "Roxanna"   by Michal Urbaniak

"Roksana"

Transcribed by Bob Bauer from Ursula Dudziak's LP, "Future Talk"

ROB WASSERMAN'S Solo Bass Melody on "Bass Space"   Rob Wasserman

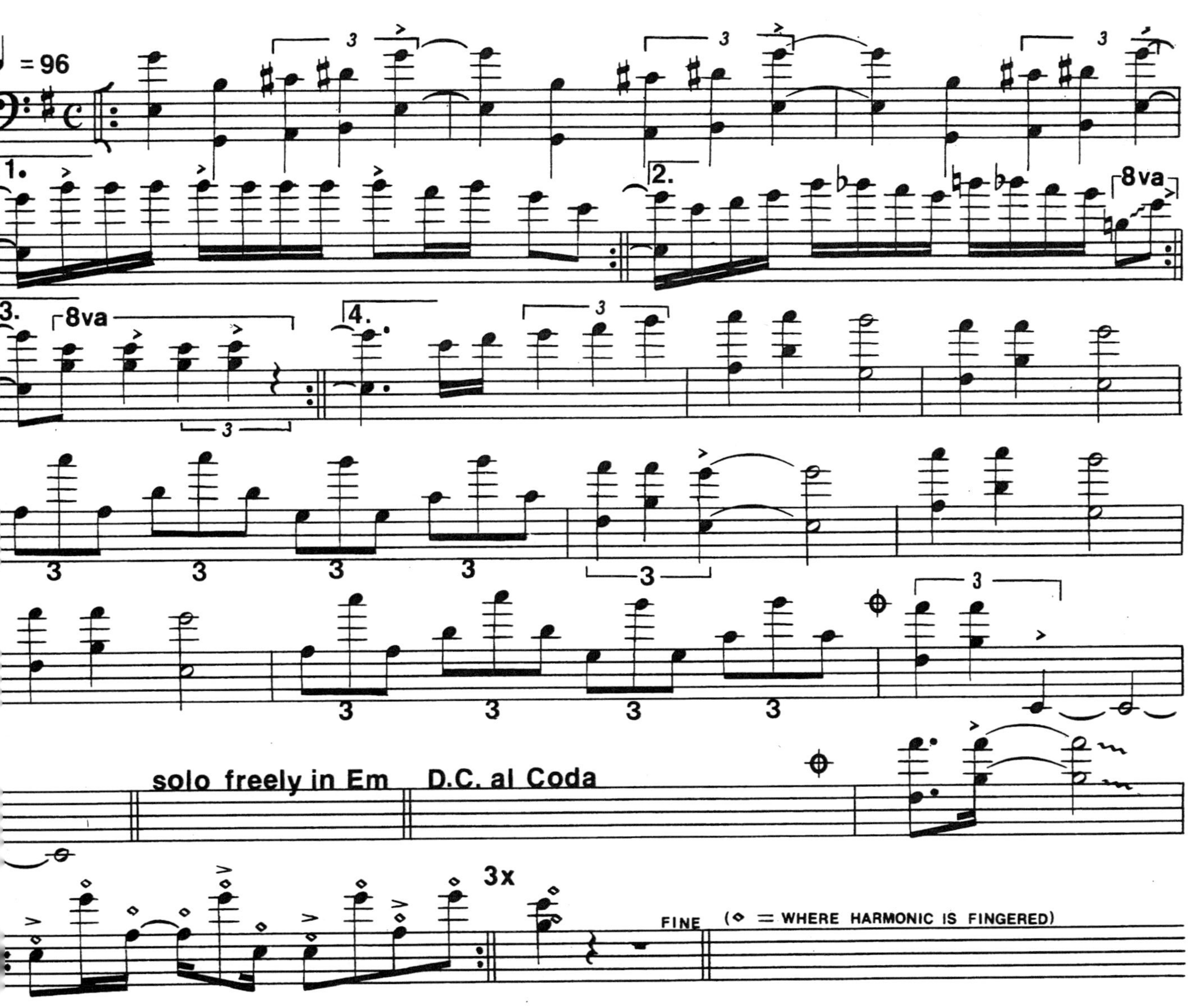

© 1980 by Rob Wasserman, bassist with the David Grisman Quintet, to be
included on Rob's upcoming solo bass album.